TORONTO
DURING THE FRENCH RÉGIME

ÉTIENNE BRÛLÉ
At the mouth of the Humber, 1615.

TORONTO DURING THE FRENCH RÉGIME

A HISTORY OF THE TORONTO REGION
FROM BRÛLÉ TO SIMCOE, 1615 - 1793

By

PERCY J. ROBINSON, M.A.

Illustrated by
C. W. JEFFERYS, R.C.A., LL.D.

UNIVERSITY OF TORONTO PRESS

First published 1933 by The Ryerson Press, Toronto
and University of Chicago Press, Chicago

Second edition
© University of Toronto Press, 1965
Reprinted in 2018
ISBN 978-1-4875-7324-9 (paper)

Printed in the U.S.A.

To
MY WIFE

PUBLISHER'S NOTE

The University of Toronto Press is happy to present this new printing of a classic in the history of Toronto, long unavailable. The author had made many marginal notes in a precious personal copy of the first edition, and these were examined when the present edition was planned. The notes reveal the author's continued fascination with the subject and his careful attention in his reading of early Canadian history to every new bit of information about early Toronto. He continued to write about it, and, in addition to correcting a few typographical errors and adding several notes (indicated in the text proper by asterisks), the present edition offers as an additional appendix section several important summaries of his later research. The first is from an article which appeared in the *Toronto Evening Telegram*, August 27, 1938; it corrects the account given in the book of the Toronto Purchase. The second selection printed here is an excerpt from an article "Montreal to Niagara in the Seventeenth Century," *Transactions* of the Royal Society of Canada, 1944, Section II; the passage deals with the name "Toronto." The third selection, "More about Toronto," originally appeared in *Ontario History*, 1953, and is the author's final word about the city. He died at Toronto on June 19, 1953.

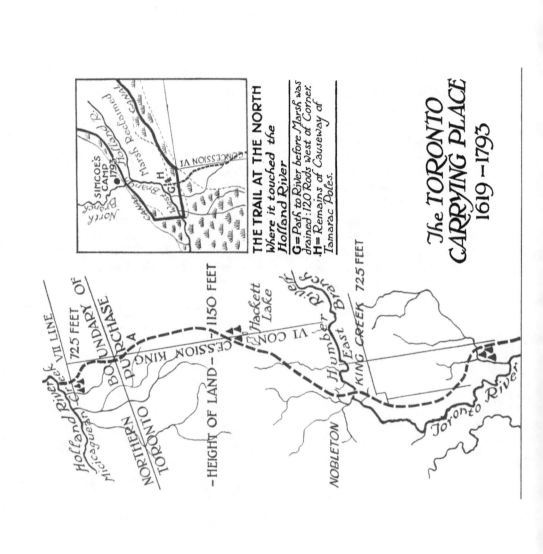

The TORONTO
CARRYING PLACE
1619–1793

THE TRAIL AT THE NORTH
*Where it touched the
Holland River*

G=*Path to River before Marsh was
drained:120 Rods west of Corner.*
H=*Remains of Causeway of
Tamarac Poles.*

SIMCOE'S CAMP 1793

North Branch

Holland River

Marsh Reclaimed

CONCESSION VI

HOLLAND CANAL

CANAL

West Branch

Holland River

Holland River

Michiguan Creek

VII LINE

725 FEET OF

BOUNDARY

PURCHASE

CESSION KING

HEIGHT OF LAND—1150 FEET

NORTHERN

TORONTO

Hackett Lake

VI CON.

Humber River

East Branch

NOBLETON

KING CREEK 725 FEET

Toronto River

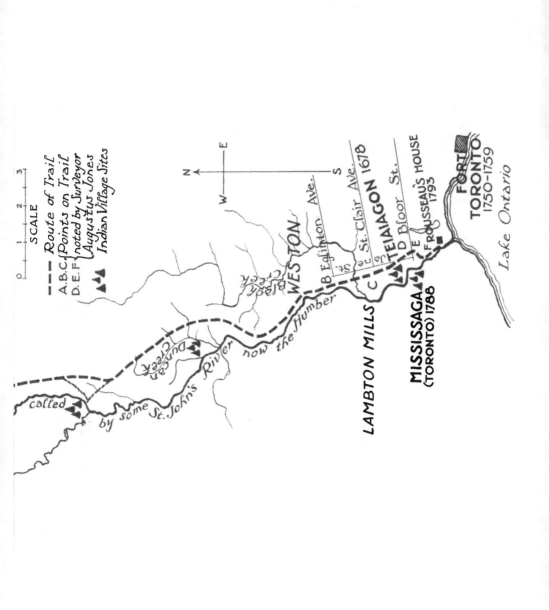

SCALE

0   1   2   3

--- Route of Trail
A.B.C. Points on Trail
D.E.F. noted by Surveyor Augustus Jones
▲▲ Indian Village Sites

N
W   E
S

called

by some St. John's River now the Humber

Duncan Creek

Black Creek

WESTON

B Eglinton Ave.

St. Clair Ave.

LAMBTON MILLS   C

TEIAIAGON 1678

D Bloor St.

E

F ROUSSEAU'S HOUSE 1795

MISSISSAGA
(TORONTO) 1788

FORT TORONTO
1750-1759

Lake Ontario

PREFACE

THE CENTENARY of the city of Toronto seems an appropriate time for gathering together whatever is known of the history of the region during the French régime and down to the founding of York in 1793. Dr. Henry Scadding, in his *Toronto of Old*, first published in 1873, sketched the outlines of this period. Only a few documents were at that time accessible. Since the appearance of his classic work, the publication of very many documents and maps, and the researches of numerous investigators, have made a more detailed picture possible. The plan adopted in the present study has been to record all known facts and wherever possible to allow the original documents to speak for themselves, bridging any gaps in the continuity of the narrative by historical comment. Except in one or two cases the original spelling and punctuation of the documents quoted has been retained. Only an arbitrary standard in the spelling of Indian place-names would reduce, for example, the fifty-five variants of Cataraqui to uniformity; the infinite and picturesque variety of the originals has not been sacrificed.

Younger by two hundred years than Montreal and Quebec, Toronto, at first sight, does not seem to possess that heritage of history and romance which flings a glamour about the traditions of the older cities. Nevertheless the Toronto Carrying-Place for a century and a half before the arrival of Simcoe, possesses a history which, though little known, is always dramatic and picturesque; it is the history of the wilderness, of the fur-trade, of the wars and cruelties of the Iroquois, of the adventures of explorers and missionaries, of the discovery of the Mississippi Valley and of the great North-West. Sometimes intimately, sometimes remotely, the Toronto Carrying-Place was touched by the struggle for the control of the continent waged so long between the French on the St. Lawrence and the Dutch and the English on the Hudson.

The reader will observe two omissions in this record. The

story of the Huron Mission has been told so often and told so
well that it does not require to be retold; but it ought not to be
forgotten that the events of that dramatic and tragic episode
took place within the Toronto region, for, as we shall discover in
the course of our study, the name "Toronto" was at one time
or another applied to all parts of the pass between the Georgian
Bay and Lake Ontario. Neither will the coming of the United
Empire Loyalists find a place in the narrative, except to mark
the limits of investigation. Very happily the hundred and
fiftieth anniversary of the arrival of the Loyalists in Ontario
coincides with the centenary of the city of Toronto. The
history of the Province of Ontario begins with that event, but
the Loyalists themselves did not settle in the Toronto region
till the founding of York. Their coming exercised too profound
an influence upon the destiny of Canada to be discussed within
the limits of a local history. It was, however, an eminent
Loyalist, Sir John Johnson, proposed by Lord Dorchester as
the first Lieutenant-Governor of Upper Canada, who in his
capacity of Indian Agent arranged the purchase from the
Missisauga Indians of the tract of land known as the "Toronto
Purchase," within which lies the city of Toronto, and to which
all land titles trace their legality.

Much of the present volume is composed of entirely new
matter. A continuous history of the locality from 1615 to 1793
is now for the first time possible. The site of the Seneca village
of Teiaiagon, visited by Hennepin and La Salle, has been
identified. Joliet is shown to have been the first to record the
position of Toronto Island, as Raffeix in 1688 was the first to
trace the course of the Don. The existence of a French post
at Toronto in 1720, hitherto unsuspected, and built by the
Sieur Douville, is now for the first time established by documentary evidence. The results of the recent discoveries of
M. E.-Z. Massicotte, the learned archivist of Montreal, proving
that two forts were built by the French at Toronto in 1750 and
1751 on different sites, have been included. Hitherto unpublished letters from Fort Rouillé have been translated. An

accurate restoration of Fort Toronto, officially called Fort
Rouillé, is now for the first time possible. Biographies of the
Sieur Douville, the Sieur de la Saussaye, Captain René-Hypolite
La Force, Captain J. B. Bouchette and Philippe de Rocheblave,
all connected in one way or another with Toronto, have
been prepared; as de Rocheblave was the first to point out the
value of the site of the city of Toronto, a special article by the
Hon. E. Fabre Surveyer of the Superior Court of Quebec, has
been included in an appendix. Surveyor Aitkin's account of
the first survey of the Toronto Purchase in 1788 is now published for the first time; this recently-discovered document
establishes the fact that Toronto was laid out by Lord
Dorchester as a town five years before York was founded by
Simcoe. Many new facts about Col. J. B. Rousseau, the
last of the French traders at Toronto, have come to light and
have been included. The etymology of the word "Toronto"
has been discussed from a fresh point of view, and a cartography
of the Toronto region has been prepared. The Toronto
Carrying-Place has been mapped and its course through the
city of Toronto indicated.

In collecting the details of our local history, sources of
information too numerous to mention have been laid under
contribution. More especially the writer is indebted to the
researches of Dr. Scadding, Miss Lizars, Mr. F. D. Severance,
the historian of Fort Niagara, and Professor Louis C. Karpinski
of the University of Michigan. Grateful acknowledgment is
made of the generous assistance of Mr. L. Homfray Irving of the
Ontario Department of Archives, Mr. N. A. Burwash of the
Ontario Surveys Department, Major Gustave Lanctot, M.
F.-J. Audet, Mr. N. Fee of the Public Archives, Ottawa, M. E.-Z.
Massicotte of the Montreal Archives, M. Ægidius Fauteux,
Chief Librarian, Montreal, and Mr. Justice E. Fabre Surveyer
of the Superior Court of Quebec. The author wishes to thank
Dr. F. N. G. Starr, of Toronto, for permission to reproduce
a photograph of the astrolabe found on Christian Island,
and Miss Margaret Rousseau and Miss Muriel Rousseau, of

Hamilton, for access to the papers of Col. J. B. Rousseau. Mr. J. M. Walton, of Aurora, by his knowledge of local topography, and Mr. A. J. Clark, of Richmond Hill, by his thorough acquaintance with the archaeology of the district, have rendered invaluable assistance. Professor W. B. Kerr, of the University of Buffalo, has given me the results of his examination of the Amherst Papers. The author is indebted to Mr. R. Home Smith for permission to reproduce several of the illustrations in Miss Lizars' *The Valley of the Humber*.

P. J. R.

CONTENTS

ILLUSTRATIONS

*From Miss K. M. Lizars' *The Valley of the Humber.*

Toronto
During the French Régime

I

THE east bank of the Humber, where it flows into Lake Ontario, is formed by a ridge whose steep sides are still clothed by vestiges of the original forest. Along the crest of this ridge Riverside Drive winds among the trees with scarcely room here and there for the houses. Occasional glimpses are to be caught of the river meandering as pleasantly through marshy ground for the modern motor boat as for the canoes of the Senecas and Missisaugas. Less picturesquely in the valley to the east and screened by a growth of trees, runs the Kingsway, pulsating with the traffic of a modern highway. Riverside Drive enjoys a peculiar seclusion. The forest seems to be making a last stand against the intruder. The hum of the adjacent city scarcely penetrates this isolated region, and when it does it is not loud enough to break the mood of musing and reminiscence so easily evoked. There is no monument to recall the past, but this is one of the most historic spots in the lake region, and here we may go back three centuries to the beginning of Canadian history. This is the foot of the Toronto Carrying-Place with memories of Simcoe and Joliet, of La Salle and Denonville, of Brûlé and St. Jean de Brébeuf.

In the centuries when all travel was by canoe and trail, the Carrying-Place was the link between Lake Ontario and the upper lakes. Running from the mouth of the Humber to the west branch of the Holland, it was always traversed on foot. It was a long portage, but the road was good and it saved the traveller a detour of hundreds of miles over the exposed waters of the Great Lakes. The oldest maps indicate that its course was always the same. This was no ordinary trail; it was a

1

main thoroughfare, a trunk line of communication with distant regions definitely determined by the contours of the country traversed. The Carrying-Place possessed a permanence very different from casual paths through the forest. It was as old as human life in America.

May we for a moment anticipate research and weave the shadows of this modern street into a brief pageant of forgotten traffic along the old trail? A midsummer night and moonlight would be the best setting for this reunion of the ghosts of bygone days, but the trail was trodden for so many centuries by human feet on so many errands, that if anything of outworn humanity clings to our material surroundings, here at least at any time imagination may evoke the past.

Along this street, when it was only a narrow foot-path in the woods, how many grotesque and terrible figures passed in the long years before and after the coming of the white man: war parties of painted braves; lugubrious trains of miserable prisoners destined to the stake; embassies from tribe to tribe on more peaceful errands; hunters wandering into the distant north in quest of furs; Hurons and Iroquois, Ottawas and Menominees, Shawanoes and Sacs and Foxes and last of all the debauched Missisaugas, spectators of the white man's progress and participating with him in cruel and dramatic events; raids into New York, the defeat of Braddock, the tragedy of Fort William Henry, the fall of Quebec, the massacre of Wyoming!

Traders, too, of every description knew the mouth of the Humber and bargained here for the precious peltries; Dutchmen from the Hudson before the French themselves had gained access to Lake Ontario; French traders from Fort Frontenac; English freebooters from Albany, they all knew the Carrying-Place, and with or without license robbed the poor Indian. How various and picturesque they were, these rascals from the Hudson and these lawless *coureurs-de-bois* from the St. Lawrence, wild hearts and children of the wilderness as truly as the aborigines whom they beguiled. To-day there is a dance-hall on the bank of the Humber on a knoll overlooking the lake; it stands

MOUTH OF THE TORONTO OR HUMBER RIVER
The Carrying-Place ran along the top of the bank on the right.

at the foot of the Carrying-Place; below it is a cove where hundreds of these gentry landed for their nefarious trade. Time has shifted the scene.

Here, too, in sombre contrast with the war-paint of the savages and the gay garments of the *coureurs-de-bois* were seen the black robes of the Jesuits and the less gloomy garb of the Récollets and Sulpicians. Hennepin was here, and Raffeix mapped the shore and traced the course of the Don as early as 1688; and Fénelon and d'Urfé came from the mouth of the Rouge to preach at Teiaiagon.

Du Lhut and Péré, Tonti and La Forest, Henry and Frobisher, and many of the French pioneers of the West passed this way. None of whom stand out so vividly as the great explorer of the Mississippi with his crowd of Shawanoes and his great canoes, three feet wide, to be carried over the long portage and the "high mountains" between Teiaiagon and *Lac* Toronto. Great days those for the old trail when the dream of empire was maturing in the brain of La Salle, a dream which in the end was to expel the French from America!

And there are memories of Pouchot exploring the shores of Lake Ontario and perhaps already dimly conscious that he would be the last to defend the flag of France at Niagara; of de Léry carefully mapping a region so soon to slip into the hands of the English; and of all who came and went to the fort to the east, the soldier-abbé Picquet, and that Captain Douville whose wife was a niece of Madeleine de Verchères. How many of these sojourners idled a summer afternoon on the Toronto river or wandered up the enticing trail into the unbroken woods!

How the Missisauga chiefs from their village near by must have wondered at the fallen fortunes of the French when they saw the smoke of the burning fort rising above the trees, and what tales of a new order did they bring back to the river after they had sworn allegiance to the British and to Sir William Johnson at Niagara! Strange subjects these of the Crown, these first citizens of a British Toronto!

Here, too, at the foot of the old trail, Surveyor Aitkin and Colonel Butler debated with the Missisaugas the limits of the land purchased the year before at Quinte. The Indians had sold more than they intended or they had forgotten the limits of the sale. Here they are, the white men strong in the destinies of their race, and the red men fated to disappear and relinquishing with reluctance the lands of their fathers. Herodotus loved local history and he would have made a striking picture of so dramatic an incident.

Yonder is Jean Baptiste Rousseau, the last citizen of the old French Toronto and the first of the new York, putting out in the early dawn of a midsummer morning from his house at the foot of the trail to pilot the *Mississaga* into the bay. The vessel carries Governor Simcoe and his lady and numerous officials. They have crossed the lake in state to found the new town. The band of the Rangers is on board, and for the first time British martial music is heard in these savage wilds.

A few weeks later, the Governor's gentle wife is to be seen taking her rides along the ridge where the trail ran; and in the autumn of the same year the Governor himself setting out with a well-equipped party on horseback to explore the communications to the north. And then the trail vanishes from history. The story of the Carrying-Place comes to an end, for a great highway called Yonge Street presently takes its place.

II

THE GATEWAY OF THE HURON COUNTRY
1615-1663

LIKE a huge spearhead, the peninsula of Ontario projects into the heart of the lake region. More than two-thirds of the isthmus between the Georgian Bay and Lake Ontario is intersected by navigable river and lake. A portage of thirty miles, known as the Toronto Carrying-Place, completes this historic communication. Near the northern end the French established themselves early in the seventeenth century at Fort Ste. Marie, and failed in their first attempt to control the interior. At the southern end, on Lake Ontario, Simcoe in 1793 founded his town of York, which was to grow into the city of Toronto.

Flanked on all sides by magnificent waterways, the peninsula of Ontario occupied a strategic position long before the coming of the French. With the advent of the fur-trader, the explorer and the missionary, the country of the Hurons became the key to the continent. Adjoining the Hurons on the south-west were the Petuns; north of Lake Erie were the Neutrals; further south on the southern shores of Lake Erie were the Eries, or Nation of the Cat; southward on the Susquehanna lived the redoubtable Carantouans or Andastes, old allies of the Hurons; east of the Hurons were the Upper Algonquins, the Ottawas and the Nipissings, differing from the Hurons in customs and language and independent one of another, but all of them united in a common hatred of the Iroquois, whose rich and populous country lay south of Lake Ontario and extended east to the Hudson River. "The Huron Mission," writes Bressani in his *Relation Abrégée*, "included all these countries. Our purpose was always to march on to the discovery of new peoples, and we hoped that a settlement among the Hurons would be the key."[1]

1 ROCHEMONTEIX, *Les Jésuites et la Nouvelle France*, Tome I, p. 321.

Champlain himself desired the establishment of this mission not only from the point of view of religion, but because he appreciated the immense advantages which the French would derive from it from the point of view of commerce and conquest. The Huron Mission was, in Champlain's opinion, an advance post towards the west, which was to assure to France the freedom of her communications in the heart of North America. He hoped to attach the fur-trade to the mission, and to make himself master in the Huron country of all the commerce with the peoples of the interior, to the exclusion of the English and the Dutch.[1] He was not long in allying himself with the Hurons and visiting their country.

Accordingly on the eighth of September, 1615, we find Champlain at the northern outlet of Lake Simcoe ready to set out with the Hurons on an expedition against the Iroquois, and accompanied by his interpreter, Étienne Brûlé, whom he despatched with twelve Hurons and two canoes to the Carantouans or Andastes to summon their assistance. It is at this point that the "Toronto Carrying-Place" comes into history, for it was by this route that Brûlé and his companions set out on their long and devious journey to the Andastes. We have, however, to rely upon inference and tradition, for Champlain has little to say about Brûlé, and the dotted line on Champlain's map, which seems to indicate Brûlé's trail to the country of the Carantouans, begins south of Lake Erie and gives no hint of the route followed before reaching that point. The tradition which connects Brûlé with the Humber has, however, the support of all historians, including Parkman and Butterfield; and since Brûlé parted with Champlain at the Narrows it is reasonable to infer that he would follow the most direct route to his destination.

Butterfield remarks: "There were two streams, one from the southward emptying into Lake Simcoe, another the Humber, from the northward flowing into Lake Ontario, which were to be their highway of travel, there being a short portage from one to the other, across which two canoes could easily be

---

1 ROCHEMONTEIX, *Les Jésuites et la Nouvelle France*, Tome I, p. 335.

carried."[1] Butterfield is mistaken as to the length of the portage; the Toronto Carrying-Place, twenty-eight miles in length, ran from the west branch of the Holland to the mouth of the Humber, and there is no indication that it was ever traversed otherwise than on foot. This, however, would be no obstacle to the nimble Hurons, nor to Brûlé, who had now been five years in their country, and was by this time as active and nimble as themselves.

We may follow, in imagination, Brûlé and the Hurons, swinging along at a rapid rate through the September woods with their canoes on their heads. Possibly they reached the mouth of the Humber some time after sundown on the ninth. Brûlé was the first white man to behold the site of the city of Toronto; and the scene which met his gaze as he and his twelve Huron companions emerged from the woods by the foot-path which until recent years still followed the east bank of the Humber, must have been a noble and impressive sight. East and west the forest clothed the shores, and before him, extending to the horizon, lay the lake which has borne in succession the names, Tadenac, Lac Contenant,[2] Lac St. Louis, Lac des Entouhonoronons, Lac des Iroquois, Cataraqui, Contario, Lac Ontario,[3] Lac Frontenac, but which the Iroquois themselves called "Skaniadorio"[4] or the "beautiful lake"—a fair scene of primitive and virgin beauty, very different from the animated picture which the bathing-beach at Sunnyside presents to-day with its Mediterranean brilliancy of colour backed by the skyscrapers of a modern city.

What route Brûlé followed from the mouth of the Humber to the country of the Andastes has been the subject of considerable conjecture. It has been thought that the party crossed Lake Ontario in their canoes; others have maintained that they

1 BUTTERFIELD, *Brûlé's Discoveries and Explorations*, p. 48.

2 VISSCHER'S map, 1680.

3 POTIER, *Radices Huronicae*, I, p. 156; *ontare*—ils appellent ainsi tous les lacs (à l'exception du Lac Superior, qu' ils nomment *okouateenende*) + *io*, "beautiful, good, large," ibid., II, p. 236.

4 CORONELLI, map, 1688.

followed the shore to the end of the lake and coasted the southern shore to the mouth of the Niagara River; others have asserted that Brûlé turned westward from the mouth of the Humber and followed the valley of the Thames to the neighbourhood of Detroit and then reached the Andastes by a long detour south of Lake Erie.   All this is conjecture; but it seems probable, if the dotted line in Champlain's map represents the route followed after the party had crossed Lake Erie, that Brûlé on this historic occasion took the trail which appears on the earliest Joliet map, from the head of the lake to the Grand River, and that Brûlé, descending that river to its mouth, crossed Lake Erie and followed the route indicated by Champlain.

Posterity has not done Brûlé justice; he was the first of Europeans to master the Algonquin and Huron languages; he was bold enough and hardy enough to risk his life among these tribes for many years; he was the first to make the long journey from Quebec to Lake Huron by way of the Ottawa River; the first to enter what is now the Province of Ontario; the first in all likelihood to sail Lake Ontario and to visit the Niagara Peninsula, and the first to cross over northern New York and to descend the Susquehanna River, passing on his way through parts of Pennsylvania and Maryland and touching the soil of Virginia; he was the first also to stand upon the shores of Lake Superior.   Although research has revealed much about this extraordinary man, he remains a shadowy figure; it is likely that his explorations covered a much wider area than we know. He was illiterate and possibly irreligious.   His contemporaries, with the exception of Sagard, do not speak well of him.[1]   Champlain, while making use of the information which Brûlé obtained, ignores his discoveries.   Brûlé's unpopularity with the Jesuits may be due to the fact that he "went native"; the missionaries alleged that his life among the Hurons was a disgrace to the French and to Christianity.   Brûlé avenged himself by siding with the Huguenot traders and afterwards with Kertk; he shared the infamy of Marselot, another of Champlain's "boys,"

1 DU CREUX, *Historia Canadensis,* pp. 119, 120, 161, 172.

in piloting the English from Tadoussac to Quebec. He was sharply rebuked by Champlain, and was murdered some years later by the Hurons; they killed and ate him when they heard that the French had returned to Quebec. Poor Brûlé! It is impossible to form a very just estimate of an adventurer whose character has been painted in the darkest colours by his contemporaries. The discoveries which he made alone and unaided in the interior of America are a title to honours which he has not received. The investigations of Dr. A. F. Hunter make it almost certain that the skull and bones of Étienne Brûlé, together with his weapons, his pipe and other personal belongings, lie buried according to the custom of the Hurons somewhere in Lot 1 of the 17th Concession of the township of Tay.

Du Creux's formidable indictment of Brûlé—more formidable still in the stately Latin—lies like a monument of obloquy upon the memory of the intrepid explorer.

It is clear that Brûlé was a bad man, and guilty of every vice and crime. He had served as interpreter for the French among the Hurons, and the wretch had not been ashamed to disgrace himself by betraying the French and passing over to the English when they took possession of the citadel of Quebec. Champlain taunted Brûlé with this perfidy, and pointed out how disgraceful it was for a Frenchman to betray king and country, and for an orthodox Catholic to ally himself with heretics, share their foul intoxication and eat meat on days when, as he well knew, Catholics were forbidden to do so. The impious man answered that he knew all that, but since a comfortable future was not before him in France, the die was cast, and he would live with the English. Brûlé returned to the Hurons. It cost him nothing to give up his country. Long a transgressor of the laws of God and man, he spent the rest of his wretched life in vile intemperance, such as no Christian should exhibit among the heathen. He died by treachery; perhaps for this very reason, that he might perish in his sins. Deprived of those benefits by which the children of the Church are prepared for a happy issue from this mortal life, Brûlé was hurried to the Judgment Seat to answer for all his other crimes and especially for that depravity which was a perpetual stumbling-block to the Hurons, among whom he should have been a lamp in a dark place, a light to lead that heathen nation to the Faith. Let us return to our story.[1]

It is not unlikely that there were others who travelled the trail early in the seventeenth century; French missionaries and traders or adventurous Dutchmen from Fort Orange on the Hudson. It is possible that Brébeuf and Chaumonot passed this way in the spring of 1641, on their return from the country of the Neutrals where they had spent the winter; they reached Fort Ste. Marie on March 19th, and since the *Relation* for that year informs us that Brébeuf broke his left shoulder-blade in a fall on the ice on Lake Simcoe, the missionaries may have returned to Huronia by the Carrying-Place and not by the long inland trail up the valley of the Grand River. The finding of an ovoidal stone on Lot 24 of the fifth concession of the township of Vaughan, inscribed with the date 1641 and now in the Royal Ontario Museum, seems to indicate that there were Frenchmen in that vicinity in that year.[2] Sagard, however, makes it plain that when the Petun chief conducted Father de la Roche d'Aillon[3] into the country of the Neutrals in 1626 the party followed the long trail across country and not the more direct route of the Carrying-Place. Although there were many Frenchmen in Ontario from 1610 to 1650, we learn little from the *Relations* about the geography of any part of the Province except that district in which the French were conducting their missions. Yet it is incredible that bold and adventurous spirits should face all the dangers of the journey from Quebec to Huronia and then remain inactive within the confines of that somewhat restricted area; there were at times as many as sixty men engaged in one way or another

1 DU CREUX, *Historia Canadensis*, p. 160. Consult also a paper by Mr. J. W. Curran, of Sault Ste. Marie, read at St. Catharines, June, 1932.

2 *Ontario Archaeological Report*, 1897-1898, p. 32.

3 "Many of our Frenchmen," says the Jesuit *Relation* of 1640-1641, "have in the past made journeys in this country of the Neuter nation for the sake of reaping profit and advantage from furs and other little wares that one might look for. But we have no knowledge of any one who has gone there for the purpose of preaching the Gospel, except the Rev. Father Joseph de la Roche Dallion, a Récollet."

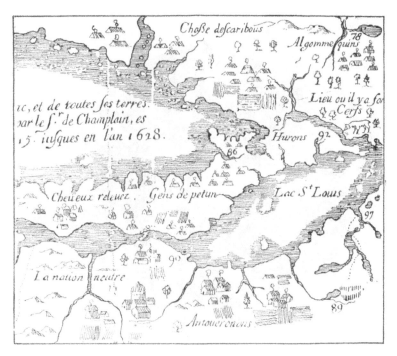

CHAMPLAIN—1632

The dotted line on the left is Brûlé's trail.

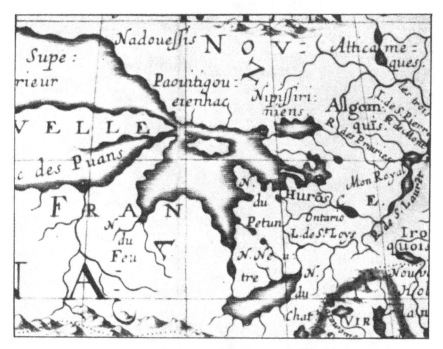

SANSON—1650

The two lines from the Georgian Bay to Lake Ontario are probably the Quinte and Toronto routes.

ASTROLABE DISCOVERED IN 1925 ON CHRISTIAN ISLAND,
GEORGIAN BAY, AND NOW IN THE POSSESSION OF
DR. F. N. G. STARR, TORONTO

This instrument was no doubt employed by the French missionaries in
constructing the earliest maps of the lake region. It bears the date 1595
and is 4¼ inches in diameter. Champlain's astrolabe, discovered on the
portage from the Ottawa River to Muskrat Lake in 1867, is dated 1613.
There are only two specimens of this rare instrument in America.

in the work of the mission, and Lake Ontario and the Toronto Carrying-Place must have had many visitors in the intervals of peace with the Iroquois.

To the Iroquois is due the fact that the country south of Lake Simcoe and along the north shore of Lake Ontario remained a no-man's land during this period, with no permanent settlements and traversed only by raiding parties from the north or from the south. The evidence seems to show that most of the attacks of the Iroquois upon Huronia came from the region of the Narrows above Lake Simcoe, and that the Iroquois availed themselves of the Trent Valley waterways as the most convenient approach; but it is more than probable that they occasionally employed both of the trails leading from Lake Ontario to the Holland River, and it is certain that, as soon as they had expelled the Hurons from the country, they began immediately to make use of these routes. We may suppose, too, that the Hurons often sent their raiding parties along both these trails, more especially when attacking the Senecas, the most westerly of the Iroquois. There is no record of the routes followed by the numerous embassies to and from the Andastes, but if the Toronto Carrying-Place was avoided, it was avoided because it was the obvious route and would be closely watched by the implacable enemies of the Hurons. The Toronto Carrying-Place was the front door of the Huron country, and the French, though compelled to follow the toilsome trail up the Ottawa, had learned at an early date of this route from Quebec to Huronia, for the Hurons informed them in 1632 that they knew of a trail by which they could come to the French trading place in ten days. So formidable, however, were the Iroquois who barred the St. Lawrence that not one single Frenchman ascended that river till the year 1657. Had it not been for the Iroquois it is probable that there would have been a French settlement at Toronto even before the founding of Montreal; the Jesuits would certainly have ascended to the Hurons by the shorter and more direct route, and the rich peltries which were collected at Fort Ste.

Marie would have descended to Quebec by *le passage de Toronto* instead of by the long and perilous portages of the Ottawa.[1]

From the first the fur trade determined the history of the Carrying-Place. The French had hoped by still further estranging the Hurons and the Iroquois to possess for themselves the peltries of the former, and the Iroquois had bent themselves to the destruction of the Hurons in the hope of acquiring the whole trade for themselves and the Dutch. Supplied by the latter with firearms, and stimulated with Dutch brandy, the Iroquois by a policy of terrorism expelled the Hurons, the Petuns and the Neutrals from the whole of the peninsula lying between the lakes, and acquired hunting grounds far richer than any south of the lake. Ontario appears on the maps for a century after the expulsion of the Hurons as "the beaver hunting ground of the Iroquois."[2]

In 1638, while these wars were raging, a people known as the Ouenrohronnons,[3] who lived east of the Niagara River, abandoned their country and took refuge with the Hurons. The *Relation* for that year informs us that they arrived in an exhausted condition and that many of them died on the way. As the statement is made that the distance which they had covered was more than eighty leagues, and since this corresponds roughly with the following route, we may assume that the Ouenrohronnons, escorted by the Hurons, skirted the western shores of Lake Ontario till they reached the mouth of the Humber, and then by way of the Carrying-Place arrived eventually at Ossossane, where they were to find a new home.

Between 1600 and 1663 the maps of the lake region are not numerous, but some of them are more detailed than the maps

1 "It is true that the way is shorter by the Sant de St. Louys and the Lake of the Hiroquois (Ontario), but the fear of enemies, and the few conveniences to be met with, cause that route to be unfrequented." Brébeuf, *Relation* of 1635.

"If once we were masters of the sea nearest the dwelling of the Iroquois we could ascend by the river St. Lawrence without danger, as far as the Neutral Nation and far beyond with considerable saving of time and trouble." Jérôme Lalemant, May 19, 1641, St. Mary's in the Huron Country.

2 WRAXALL, *New York Indian Records*, McIlwain, Introduction.

3 DU CREUX, *Historia Canadensis*, p. 238.

of the succeeding period. The Hakluyt map of 1600 merely indicates a great inland sea called "The lake of Tadenac whose bounds are unknown." This map is described by Hallam in his *Introduction to the Literature of Europe* as "the best map of the sixteenth century." It is in all probability the new map referred to by Shakespeare in *Twelfth Night*, Act III, Scene 2. More is to be learned from Champlain's map of 1612. No white man had as yet ascended the St. Lawrence above Montreal, and Champlain's information was derived from the Indians. In this map the falls of Niagara are indicated for the first time. Three villages are marked on the north shore of Lake Ontario. Champlain gives no name to Lake Ontario, but describes it as a lake of fifteen days' journey by canoe, *Lac Contenant 15 journées des canaux des sauvages.* The Dutch, supposing that *Contenant* was a proper name, perpetuated this error in their maps for fifty years. The Quinte Peninsula and the Trent Valley route are indicated.

In Champlain's smaller map of 1613, Lake Ontario appears for the first time as Lac St. Louis. In his much more detailed map of 1632 there are no place names or sites along the north shore; Lake Simcoe is shown, and the Humber River and Brûlé's trail to the Andastes south of Lake Erie. Jansson's map of 1636 shows that the Dutch knew the hills north of Toronto. Sanson's map of 1650 has lines which may be the Toronto and Quinte routes. His map of 1656 gives Lake Simcoe as Lake *Oentaron*. Du Creux in 1660 gives this lake as *lacus Ouentaronius* and marks the Holland and the Humber rivers and other streams flowing into Lake Ontario. Sanson and Du Creux probably based their maps upon Jérôme Lalemant's map of 1639, which has not been discovered. Du Creux's map is the more detailed in the Toronto region, and both these maps show a surprising knowledge of the lakes, although Lake Michigan and Lake Superior are still imperfectly delineated. We may believe that observations were taken in many places with the astrolabe found within recent years in the neighbourhood of Fort Ste. Marie II on Christian Island.

III

HENNEPIN AND LA SALLE AT THE CARRYING-PLACE
1663-1682

La Salle, "*un homme devenu grand par ses actes, par leurs conséquences et avant tout par le sacrifice de sa personne.*"[1]

IN 1663 Canada became a Royal Province; the period of romance was at an end; there were to be no more dreams of spiritual empire. But with the coming of the Carignan-Salières regiment in 1665 there was peace, and the French for the first time began to find their way to Lake Ontario, to explore its shores, and to lay their plans for recapturing from the Iroquois the fur-trade, which the latter had diverted to the English and the Dutch on the Hudson, and to the Swedes in New Jersey. The first steps had already been taken; for the Jesuits, abandoning the Huron country and the rest of Ontario to the Iroquois, had pushed farther into the west, and as early as 1660 had discovered Michilimackinac in the heart of the continent at the juncture of three great inland seas, where they established a post which was to continue for a century to be the citadel of the French in the interior. With the establishment of Fort Frontenac at the eastern extremity of Lake Ontario in 1773, the French found themselves at last in a position to impose an effective curb upon the Iroquois, and to collect at their leisure the peltries from the north and south sides of the lake. *Le passage de Toronto*,[2] which but for the Iroquois would have been the main avenue of approach to the Huron country, now became the link between Fort Frontenac at the base of the St. Lawrence and Michilimackinac and the Sault in the heart of the west, and began in a measure to replace the route by the Ottawa which had been the only available approach to the interior since the days of Champlain.

But hardly had the French resumed control of the fur-trade

1 MARGRY, Tome I, p. xii.
2 DENONVILLE, to M. de la Durantaye, June 6, 1686.

LA SALLE

Crossing the Toronto Portage, 1681, on his way to the Mississippi.

when France began to play a new rôle in America. With La
Salle and Frontenac, the empire-builder appears upon the
scene, and no longer content with the banks of the St. Lawrence,
the French conceived that grandiose scheme of securing the
valley of the Mississippi, which was to end in tragedy a century
later. It is an altered scene. If the old actors continue to play
a part, it is upon a larger and a more varied stage. *Le passage
de Toronto* becomes not only a link between Fort Frontenac
and Michilimackinac, but a highway to the Mississippi.

The Jesuit, Le Moyne, who undertook a diplomatic mission
to the Onondagas in the year 1654, was the first white man to
follow the St. Lawrence from Montreal to Lake Ontario. From
that time missionaries began to find their way into the Iroquois
country south of the lake. But it was not till the year 1668,
when the Sulpicians of Montreal began their mission among the
scattered Iroquois on the north shore of Lake Ontario, that the
district once so thickly peopled by the Hurons, the Petuns and
the Neutrals again comes into history. From the spring of
1650, when the miserable remnant of the Hurons fled northward
along the eastern shore of Georgian Bay, the whole of the
peninsula between the lakes had been in the hands of the
Iroquois. "Succurrebat animis," writes Du Creux, "Huronicos
tractus deinceps aliud nihil esse nisi locum horroris, et vastae
solitudinis, theatrumque caedis et cladium." For almost
twenty years the Iroquois, in the intervals of warlike expeditions, had gathered the rich peltries and sold them to the
Dutch and English on the Hudson. Gradually, too, after
1666, they had migrated in small bands to the north shore of
the lake, and had established themselves where the trails led
off into the interior, to the richer hunting-grounds of the north.
Beginning at the eastern end of Lake Ontario, the names of
these Iroquois villages are as follows: Ganneious on the site of
the present site of the town of Napanee, a village of the Oneidas;
Kenté on the Bay of Quinte, Kentsio on Rice Lake, Ganaraske
on the site of the present town of Port Hope, villages of the
Cayugas who had fled from the menace of the Andastes to a

securer position beyond the lake; Ganatsekwyagon at the mouth of the Rouge and Teiaiagon at the mouth of the Humber, villages of the Senecas who had established themselves at the foot of the two branches of the Toronto Carrying-Place and were thus in command of the traffic across the peninsula to Lake Simcoe and the Georgian Bay.[1] It is probable that there were other villages of the Iroquois here and there in the interior, but it is only possible to surmise their situation.[2] De Courcelles, who visited the eastern end of the lake in 1671, observed that the Iroquois never hunted the beaver on the south side of Lake Ontario for the very sufficient reason that they had exterminated them there long ago, and that it would be extremely difficult to discover a single specimen in the Iroquois country; they did all their hunting on the north side of the lakes, where the Hurons had formerly hunted.[3] On the first arrival of the French in Lake Ontario, they found the Dutch in possession of the trade. These enterprising traders from Fort Orange and Manhatte, *les Hollandois*[4] who appear so often in the records of the period, had long been *en rapport* with the Iroquois and could speak their language, and seem to have swarmed over the lake and the adjoining territory, debauching the savages and carrying off their furs. In the years between the fall of Huronia and the return of the French to the lake region, these Dutch traders must have frequented Ganatsekwyagon and Teiaiagon and the shore between these two villages where Toronto now stands.

1 "In the Huron-Algonquin era the north shore was without doubt more thickly villaged than the Sulpicians found it. The Iroquois desolation had swept over it, and we learn from a letter of Laval's that only in 1665 did the conquering race begin colonization." *Picturesque Canada*, Vol. II, pp. 635-6.

2 *New York Colonial Documents*, Vol. IX, p. 1056. "North of Lake Ontario" should read "south of Lake Ontario." On November 13, 1763, Sir William Johnson wrote to the Lords of Trade that the Five Nations claimed possession of Ontario, including the Missisauga country.

3 *Remy de Courcelles au Lac Ontario*, Margry I, p. 180; Lahontan, *Some New Voyages in North America*, p. 323, "They (the Iroquois) are in like manner forc'd to range out of their own Territories, in quest of Beaver in the winter time, either towards Ganaraské (Port Hope), or to the sides of the Lake of Toronto, or else Towards the greater River of The Outaouas; where it would be an easy matter to cut all their Throats, by pursuing the course I laid down in my letters."

4 MARGRY, I, p. 181-192.

Dollier de Casson, in his *Summary of the Quinté Mission*, describes its origin.

It was in the year 1668 that we were given the task of setting out for the Iroquois, and Quinté was assigned to us as the centre of our mission because in that same year a number of people from that village had come to Montreal and had definitely requested us to go and teach them in their country, this embassy reached us in the month of June. As, however, we expected that year a superior from France, it was deemed fitting that they should be asked to come back again, as it seemed inadvisable to undertake a matter of this importance without waiting for his counsel, so that nothing should be done therein save as he decided. In September the chief of that village did not fail to appear at the time set for him, to try and lead back into his country a number of missionaries. The request was placed before M. de Queylus, who had come to be superior of this community, and he gave his approval of the plan very willingly. After that we went to see the bishop, who supported us with his authority. As for the governor and intendant of the country, we had no difficulty in obtaining their consent, as they had from the first thought of us in connection with such an enterprise.[1]

M. de Trouvé, from whose letter the above extract is taken, and M. de Fénelon, the fiery half-brother of the famous Archbishop of Cambrai, and author of *Télémaque*, were the first missionaries; the latter, in company with another missionary, M. d'Urfé, passed the winter of 1669 and 1670 in the village of Ganatsekwyagon,[2] a fact which is commemorated by the name Frenchman's Bay, which clings to the inlet near the mouth of the Rouge.[3] This is the first recorded residence of white men in the neighbourhood of Toronto.

1 DOLLIER DE CASSON, *A History of Montreal*, translated by Flenley, p. 351; ibid., p. 359.

2 PROFESSOR LEWIS ALLEN suggests that *Gandatschekiagon*, as it is sometimes spelled, may mean "sand cut," i.e., opening in sand cliffs, from *gandechia*, "sand," and *gaiagon*, "cut."

3 "A little to the west of the Seneca village (Ganatsekwyagon) was a stream that gave kindly shelter to distressed canoes; and so by Indians of the next century and of a different race it was named Katabokokonk, or the "River of Easy Entrance." In making its way to the lake it pierced a hill of red tenacious clay, which sufficiently coloured its waters to justify the old French name, *Rivière Rouge*, ... It is still the Rouge and the name is interesting as the sole remaining trace now on this north-west shore of the old Sulpician Mission of Louis the Fourteenth's domain." Boyle, *History of Scarborough Township*, pp. 26 and 27, f.n., ibid. p. 24; *Picturesque Canada*, Vol. II, p. 624.

Frontenac, in his letter to the Minister under date of November 2, 1672, makes it very plain why the Sulpicians were selected for the new mission on Lake Ontario. It was felt that a new policy must be adopted with the Indians. The Jesuits had made no effort to turn them into Frenchmen or even to teach them the French language. It was hoped that the Sulpicians would render them more useful allies of the French.

It was in the year 1669, possibly before the arrival of Fénelon and d'Urfé in the village of Ganatsekwyagon, that two notable explorers, Péré and Joliet, camped for a time in that village before crossing *le passage de Toronto*[1] to the Georgian Bay. They were on their way to Lake Superior in search of the great copper mine reported to exist in that region. It has been thought that this was not the first visit of Péré to the locality, and that he visited the site of the city of Toronto in the preceding year;[2] he was the first French trader on Lake Ontario, and the few facts which have been ascertained about him serve to stimulate curiosity. On November 11, 1669, the sieur Patoulet wrote to Colbert from Quebec, "The sieurs Joliet and Péré to whom M. Talon has had paid 400 and 1,000 *livres* respectively, to go and find out if the copper mine which exists above Lake Ontario, and of which you have seen several samples, is a rich mine, and easy to work, and accessible, have not yet returned." They had left Montreal in May or June of 1669, and there is a legend on the Dollier-Galinée map attached to the village of Ganatsekwyagon, "It was here that M. Perray and his party camped to enter Lake Huron—when I have seen the passage I will give it; however, it is said the road is very fine, and it is here the missionaries of St. Sulpice will establish themselves." This information must have been obtained from Joliet and Péré, whom Dollier and Galinée met on September 24, 1669, at the village of Tinawatawa on the portage from

1 SEVERANCE, *An Old Frontier of France*, Vol. I, p. 29; *New York Colonial Documents*, Vol. III, p. 479; Margry, I, p. 81.

2 *Ontario Archaeological Report*, 1899, p. 183, article by General John S. Clark; *Bulletin de la Société de Géographie de Québec*, Vol. VIII, 1914, p. 325, article by Benjamin Sulte.

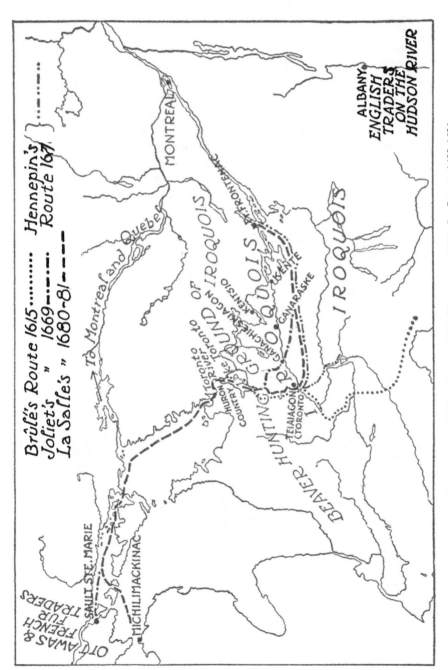

ROUTES FOLLOWED BY BRÛLÉ, 1615; JOLIET, 1669; HENNEPIN, 1678; LA SALLE, 1680-1681

the head of Lake Ontario to the Grand River.   Similarly at the
head of Matchedash Bay there is this legend on the Galinée
map: "I did not see this bay, where was formerly the country
of the Hurons, but I see that it is even deeper than I sketched it,
and apparently the road over which M. Perray travelled terminated here."   There is thus good evidence to prove that
Joliet and Péré passed over the *passage de Toronto* from Ganatsekwyagon to the mouth of the Severn River in the year 1669,
and that they found the road good and likely to prove an
excellent alternative to the long and dangerous route by the
Ottawa River.[1]   We may conclude also that the Abbé Fénelon
and the Sulpicians decided to establish themselves at Ganatsekwyagon because that village was situated at the foot of one
arm of the *passage de Toronto*.[2]   On several maps of this period
the Ganatsekwyagon portage is indicated and the Teiaiagon
portage is not marked, though the village itself is shown; the
French seem to have selected the former because it was nearer
to the eastern end of the lake, and for those travelling by canoe
there would be no need to go on twenty-three miles to the better
anchorage at the mouth of the Humber.   We shall hear once
more in Denonville's time of Ganatsekwyagon, and then the
preference seems to have been given to Teiaiagon and the
western branch of the portage, which became definitely known
as the Toronto Carrying-Place.

Péré and Joliet had been despatched not only to search for a
copper mine but also to find a new route to the west; they
were the first white men to pass through the straits at Detroit.
Dollier and Galinée had embarked on a similar errand in the
same year, but they tell us nothing about the Toronto region;
they followed the south shore of Lake Ontario and returned
next year by the Ottawa.   With the exception of Péré, the names

1 "The short communication from Montreal by the Ottawa River was
ever attended with so many inconveniences from the number of Carrying
Places that the French always preferred the Lakes."   Sir Wm. Johnson.

2 The length of the eastern portage, according to Raffeix, 1688, was 15
leagues, i.e., 36 miles, which would make the northern terminus Roche's
Point, which may have been the terminus in winter.

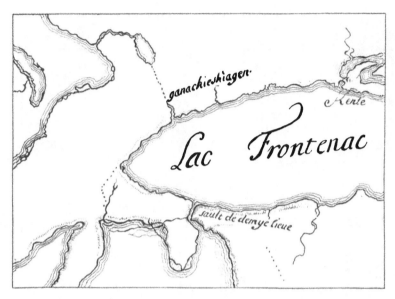

JOLIET—1674

This is the earliest map of the Toronto Carrying-Place.

DU CREUX—1660

In an inset map of the Huron country Lake Simcoe is *Lacus Ouentaronius*.

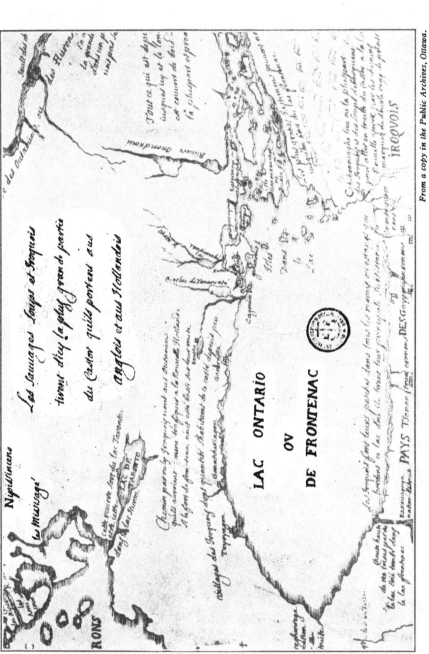

THE FIRST DETAILED MAP

This map (4044 B: No. 43, Service Hydrographique Bibliothèque, Paris.) has been ascribed to Joliet; it is not earlier than 1673. It is the first map on which the name *Taronto* appears, and the first to show Teiaiagon and Toronto Island. This map indicates that before 1673 the route of the English and Dutch with the Ottawas was round the eastern end of Lake Ontario to Ganatsekwyagon. The building of Fort Frontenac resulted in a new trade route from Chouéguen (Oswego) round the western end and of the lake to Teiaiagon, with the Senecas as middlemen.

of all these men are too well known to students of history to require further comment. Péré[1] remains a shadowy figure; choosing the life of a *coureur-de-bois*, he seems to have laid aside the loyalties as well as the restraints of civilization and to have conceived an ambitious plan for disposing of the furs of the *coureurs-de-bois* to the English at Albany. Arrested by the English and detained in England, he returned to America. There is ground for supposing that he was the discoverer of the Moose River flowing into Hudson Bay; it bears his name in some early maps. At any rate, he was one of those many Frenchmen attracted by the wild life of the woods who disappeared into the wilderness.[2]

On August 29, 1670, Talon sent to Colbert, by the hands of the Abbé Fénelon, a map showing the communication between Lake Ontario and Lake Huron. "Another missionary," he wrote, "also from the Seminary of St. Sulpice, has penetrated farther than he in order to find out for me about a river for which I was looking in order to establish a communication between Lake Ontario and Lake Huron where they say there is a copper mine. This missionary made a map of his journey a copy of which is in the hands of the said Abbé Fénelon. It will form *un assez juste sujet de vostre curiosité.*"

Hardly had the results of these explorations been ascertained when the Intendant Talon wrote to Colbert explaining his plans for curbing the Iroquois, who were hunting the beaver on the lands of those savages who had placed themselves under the protection of the king and plundering them of their own peltries. He proposed to establish two posts, one on the north and the other on the south side of Lake Ontario, and to build a small vessel which could be either sailed or rowed and

---

1 MARGRY, I, p. 296.

2 Ibid., p. 88; Severance: *An Old Frontier of France*, Vol. I, pp. 29 and 30; map 4040 B, 1699, Public Archives, Ottawa, which bears the legend attached to the Moose River, *Rivière par où la Sr. Perrayé a esté à la Baye de Hudson;* Franquelin map of 1688; Margry, Vol. VI, p. 38 *et seq.* Péré was retained by Governor Andros of New York with the design of sending him to open a trade with the Ottawas. Péré is perhaps the first to have conceived the scheme of using the Toronto portage for this purpose.

which could show itself wherever there was trading on the lake; he explained that the English from Boston and the Dutch from Manhatte and Orange secured from the Iroquois and other tribes in their neighbourhood more than 1,200,000 *livres* of beaver skins of the best quality, all of them secured on the dominions of the king, and that he thought he saw the way to direct the greater part of this commerce, naturally and without violence, into the hands of His Majesty's subjects.[1]   The two posts which he proposed to establish would protect the Ottawas when they came down with their rich beaver skins.   It is likely that Talon had in mind an establishment at Niagara on the south side of the lake and at Cataraqui on the north, for though the Ottawas were in the habit of employing the Toronto Carrying-Place, it was thought at first that these two posts would be sufficient.

In 1671, the year after Talon wrote to the king urging an establishment on Lake Ontario, the governor, de Courcelles, visited the lake.   It seemed to him *une pleine mer sans aucunes limites*, and he, too, speedily formed the opinion that the best means of preventing the trade between the Iroquois and New Holland, lately become New York, would be the establishment of a fort at the entrance of Lake Ontario, "which would occupy the passage by which the Iroquois passed on their way to trade with the Dutch when they had secured their furs."   He, too, observed that the Iroquois did all their hunting on the north side of the lake, and there were fresh expressions of indignation that the profits of this trade, drawn from what the French regarded as their own territory, should go to their rivals, the Dutch and the English.[2]

It was in 1672 that Frontenac, in writing to the Minister, proposed for the first time the erection of a post on Lake Ontario. He alludes to the post which de Courcelles had projected on the lake to frustrate the efforts of the Iroquois to capture the trade

1 "Talon au Roy" (November 10, 1670). Margry, I, p. 85.
2 "Récit de ce qui s'est passé au voyage que M. de Courcelles, gouverneur de la Nouvelle France, a fait au lac Ontario." Margry, I, p. 169.

with the Ottawas for the Dutch, and expresses the hope that
the Sulpician missionaries would prove of assistance. In
November, 1673, in writing to Colbert, he remarks: "You will
remember, my Lord, that several years ago you were informed
that the English and the Dutch were doing all they could to
prevent the Ottawas, the tribes from which we draw all our
peltries, from bringing them to us, and that they wanted to
get them to come to Ganacheskiagon, on the shores of Lake
Ontario, where they offered to bring for them all the goods
that they needed. The apprehensions of my predecessors that
this would utterly ruin our trade, and their desire to deprive
our neighbours of their profitable trade with the Ottawas
through the Iroquois, made them think of establishing some post
on Lake Ontario which would give them control." The
Governor then proceeds to describe the founding of Fort
Frontenac. It is plain from these remarks and from the legend
on the unsigned map shown on page 22 of this volume, that
Fort Frontenac was founded as a rival to the trade at Ganatsekwyagon, the Seneca village at the terminus of the eastern arm
of the Toronto Portage. In November, 1674, in writing to
Colbert, Frontenac returns to the same subject: "They (the
envoys of the Iroquois) have promised to prevent the Wolves of
Taracton, a tribe adjoining New Holland, from continuing their
hostilities with the Ottawas, of whom they had killed seven or
eight, which might have had grave consequences, and they
have given their word not to continue the trade, which, as I
informed you last year, they had commenced to establish at
Gandaschekiagon with the Ottawas, which would have absolutely ruined ours by the transfer of the furs to the Dutch."[1]
It is apparent, then, that the reason for the building of Fort
Frontenac was to destroy the trade of the English and Dutch
along the eastern arm of the Toronto Portage. It would seem
that the English and the Iroquois, foiled by Fort Frontenac in
their trade at Ganatsekwyagon, which they had reached along

1 "Lettre du gouverneur Frontenac au ministre Colbert, 14 novembre,
1674," *Rapport de l'Archiviste de la Province de Québec*, 1926-1927, p. 65,

the north shore of Lake Ontario, now began to trade at Teiaiagon, which they reached by following the south shore round the western end of the lake.

There was a serious obstacle, however, to the realization of these plans. The traders in Montreal discouraged every attempt to establish a post in the interior; trading was forbidden in the upper country and the Indians were encouraged to bring their furs to Montreal to a great annual market held there. The matter of a fortified post on Lake Ontario was deferred till 1673 when Frontenac, in the teeth of much opposition, founded his fort at Cataraqui.   Next year, in 1674, the seigniory of Fort Frontenac was granted to La Salle as a reward for discoveries already made, and, although Montreal continued to oppose the development of the west, La Salle held his ground. We shall find him almost immediately at the Toronto Carrying-Place.

The inhabitants of Teiaiagon,[1] the Seneca village on the site of Toronto, are not mentioned among those who sent envoys to confer with Frontenac at Cataraqui in 1673.[2] Possibly, being the farthest towards the west, they thought they might be excused from making the arduous journey. The deputies of Ganatsekwyagon, Ganaraske, Kenté and Ganneious had been rounded up by the missionaries, but too late to be present on the occasion when Frontenac addressed the Iroquois nations from the south of the lake, and the Governor seems to have been a little put out that he had to go through the performance again. However, after sharply rebuking them for their absence, he exhorted them to become Christians, to keep the peace and to maintain a good understanding with the French, all of which they promised to do with as much readiness as their kinsmen from the south of the lake, whose spirit and willingness to obey they professed to share. But though Teiaiagon was not represented on this important occasion, Frontenac and La Salle seem soon to have become aware of its

1 MARGRY, I, pp. 500, 514, 543; II, pp. 14, 115, 158.
2 "Le Comte de Frontenac au lac Ontario." Margry, I, pp. 233-235.

existence.   Its situation at the southern terminus of the Toronto
Carrying-Place was strategic, and accordingly, in the remarks
appended to the statement of expenditures incurred by La
Salle between 1675-1684, we find this statement:[1]

It (Fort Frontenac) has frustrated and will continue to
frustrate the designs of the same English, who had undertaken
to draw away to themselves by means of the Iroquois, the
nations of the Outawas.   They have to go to them by the road
which leads to Lake Huron from the village of Teiaiagon, and
they would have succeeded had not M. de Frontenac placed
this fort in their path; the whole country has felt the benefit,
not only in the protection of the trade and in maintaining
peace, but in checking the license of our deserters, who had an
easy road there by which to make their way to strangers.

We may be sure that La Salle, when he established himself
at his seigniory at Fort Frontenac, in 1675, took pains to
acquaint himself still more thoroughly with the shores of the lake,
and especially with the north shore, where the fur trade was
most active.[2]   It is likely that he visited the villages along the
shore and gathered all information available about the trails
leading into the interior.   He would, no doubt, accompany the
small vessels sent from the fort to collect the furs at these
places, and it would not be long before he would learn about the
Toronto Carrying-Place; he may even have passed over it on
some unrecorded exploring expedition prior to 1680.   It is more
than likely that he was quite familiar with Teiaiagon and the
Carrying-Place long before he employed that route in his
western explorations.   As we shall presently see, La Salle was
the first traveller to describe in his own words a trip over the
portage; he was also the first to record the place name "Toronto"
in its accepted spelling.[3]   Before La Salle, the maps indicate
that the eastern trail from Ganatsekwyagon was the route
usually followed.   La Salle's choice of the trail from Teiaiagon

1 MARGRY, II, p. 14.
2 Frontenac, in 1673, in selecting Cataraqui relied on a map of Lake
Ontario sent by La Salle. *Rapport de l'Archiviste de la Province de Québec,*
1926-1927, p. 37.
3 It has been stated that the spelling in the original documents in Paris
is Taronto. *Bulletin des Recherches Historiques,* 1899, p. 137.

must have been deliberate and may have been due to the fact that there was better anchorage for larger vessels. Experience had probably proved it the better path; also it may have been easier to elude the vigilance of the Iroquois at Teiaiagon than at Ganatsekwyagon, for La Salle was anxious to conceal the fact that he was carrying ammunition to the Illinois, with whom the Iroquois were at war. According to Raffeix's map of 1688, the western route from the Humber mouth was much shorter.

But before following La Salle on the various occasions on which he traversed the Carrying-Place, we have to recount the visit which Father Hennepin paid to Teiaiagon and the mouth of the Humber in the late autumn of 1678; for it is in the company of this remarkable person that documentary history arrives for the first time at the foot of the trail and at the site of the present city of Toronto. Hennepin had joined the Récollet mission at Fort Frontenac in 1675, so that in 1678 he was no stranger on Lake Ontario. The barefooted follower of St. Francis is famous for his thirst for adventure and glory, and for his lukewarm attachment to the truth. But on this occasion when he was visiting an obscure Indian village, there need be no reason to suspect his veracity. He will be allowed to tell his story in his own words; it is contained in the beginning of the fourteenth chapter of his *New Discovery of a Large Country in America*, which the author published in an English edition in London in 1698 with a dedication to "His Most Excellent Majesty William III," a fact which will not be without significance to those who recall the subsequent devotion of the city of Toronto to that monarch. Hennepin writes:

That same year, on the Eighteenth of November, I took leave of our Monks at Fort Frontenac, and after mutual Embraces and Expressions of Brotherly and Christian Charity, I embarked in a Brigantine of about ten Tuns. The Winds and the Cold of Autumn were then very violent, insomuch that our Crew was afraid to go into so small a Vessel. This oblig'd us and the Sieur de la Motte, our Commander,[1] to keep our course

1 SEVERANCE, *An Old Frontier of France*, Vol. I, p. 43 ; Margry, II, pp. 7-9.

on the North-side of the Lake, to shelter ourselves under the
Coast, against the North-west Wind, which otherwise wou'd
have forc'd us upon the Southern Coast of the Lake. This
Voyage prov'd very difficult and dangerous, because of the
unseasonable time of the Year, Winter being near at hand.

On the 26th, we were in great danger about two large
Leagues off the Land, where we were oblig'd to lie at Anchor
all that night at sixty Fathom Water and above; but at length
the Wind coming to the North-East, we sail'd on and arriv'd
safely at the further end of Lake Ontario, call'd by the Iroquoese,
Skannadario. We came pretty near to one of their Villages
call'd Tejajagon, lying about Seventy Leagues from Fort
Frontenac, or Catarokuoy.

We barter'd some Indian Corn with the Iroquoese, who
could not sufficiently admire us, and came frequently to see us
on board our Brigantine, which for our greater security, we had
brought to an anchor into a River, though before we could get
in, we run aground three times, which oblig'd us to put fourteen
Men into Canou's, and cast the Ballast of our Ship over-board to
get her off again. That River falls into the Lake; but for fear
of being frozen up therein, we were forc'd to cut the Ice with
Axes and other Instruments.

The wind turning then contrary, we were oblig'd to tarry
there til the 15th of December, 1678, when we sail'd from the
Northern Coast to the Southern, where the River Niagara runs
into the Lake; but could not reach it that Day, though it is but
Fifteen or Sixteen Leagues distant, and therefore cast Anchor
within Five Leagues of the Shore, where we had very bad
Weather all the Night long.

On the 6th, being St. Nicholas's Day, we got into the fine
River Niagara, into which never any such Ship as ours enter'd
before. We sung there *Te Deum*, and other Prayers, to return
Thanks to God Almighty for our prosperous Voyage. The
Iroquoese Tsonnontouans inhabiting the little Village, situated
at the mouth of the River, took above Three Hundred Whitings,
which are bigger than Carps, and the best relish'd, as well as the
wholesomest Fish in the World; which they presented all to us,
imputing their good Luck to our Arrival. They were much
surprized at our Ship, which they call'd the great woodden
Canou.

We have quoted at some length from Hennepin; he is an
interesting person whose talents have been somewhat obscured

by his lack of veracity, for did he not attempt to appropriate the glory of the discovery of the lower Mississippi, incorporating for that purpose in his own book a passage from Le Clercq's *l'Établissement de la Foy*, describing La Salle's journey from Fort Crèvecoeur to the mouth of the Mississippi in 1682 and so twisting it as to refer to himself? Nevertheless Hennepin's is a vivid personality; we can easily picture the barefooted, brown-habited friar, with the cord of St. Francis about his waist, in the autumn of 1678 at Teiaiagon. He confesses himself that he loved adventure and travel as much as religion, and in truth he is far removed from the earnest Jesuits who preceded him, who believed in the conversion of the Indians as a reality and a possibility, and were ready to suffer tortures to attain that object. Father Hennepin took his religion less seriously; it was all very well to preach the Gospel to the savages, but he tells us himself that it was idle to expect their conversion; the savages were too fickle and too degraded. Meantime he devoted himself to exploration. We find him on this occasion storm-stayed at Teiaiagon for nearly three weeks, and we may be sure he did not devote all that time to the spiritual welfare of the inhabitants. Very likely he had been in Teiaiagon before, as it was an outlying post of the mission at Fort Frontenac, and we can imagine him, when he had satisfied his conscience with a little mission work in the lodges, exploring the shore, or reading his breviary by the banks of the Humber, where he would be more sheltered from the wind which was lashing the lake, and impatient to proceed on his journey to the Niagara River and so on to the great falls, of which he was to give us the first detailed picture which we possess. While he tarries reluctantly and the ice begins to form in the Humber and the first scuds of snow chase one another over the black ice, let us try to see Teiaiagon as it must have presented itself to his eyes.

Indian villages as a rule did not remain longer than about twenty years in one place; a change would be necessary, not only for sanitary reasons, but also because the supply of wood for the fires in the lodges would become exhausted. But there were reasons why Teiaiagon should remain more permanently where it was. It was an Iroquois village and there were cultivated fields near by, and the labour of clearing away the forest would be too great to encourage frequent changes. Moreover, Teiaiagon was at the foot of the Toronto Carrying-Place and commanded the route by which the Iroquois from the south of the lake passed to the rich beaver hunting-grounds formerly enjoyed by the Hurons. Teiaiagon, once established, could never move far from the mouth of the Humber. It was tied to this locality by another excellent reason. Like their neighbours at Ganatsekwyagon at the mouth of the Rouge, the inhabitants of Teiaiagon depended for part of their sustenance upon the salmon fisheries which were especially abundant at the mouths of the Humber and the Rouge. Everything combined to give permanence to a village once established at so strategic a point, and indeed the name "Teiaiagon" appears attached to the mouth of the Humber on the best maps of the district for a hundred and thirty years after La Salle and Hennepin; though no mention of the place has been found in any document later than 1688.[1]

Would that the versatile friar had devoted some of his time to a more detailed description of Teiaiagon; undoubtedly he would have done so had he divined that a great city was one day to spread itself for miles along that sandy shore where the waves beat so mercilessly that autumn. There is no likelihood, however, that Teiaiagon differed very much, except in situation, from a score of other Indian villages with which Hennepin was familiar, and since he has told us a good deal about what he observed of the life of the savages during his two and a half years at Fort Frontenac, it will not be difficult to reconstruct the scene. We may be sure that Teiaiagon was protected

1 The way in which Teiaiagon on many maps wandered up and down the north shore of Lake Ontario led to curious mistakes. In one instance it carried the name Toronto with it. In 1834 Smith's Creek, now Port Hope, was on the eve of adopting the name Toronto which was resumed by the provincial capital hitherto called York. Consult *Picturesque Canada*, Vol. II, pp. 636-637, and the *Globe*, Vol. 23, p. 61.

by a stout palisade[1] and fortified with all the skill which the
Iroquois could command; this would be equally true of all the
Cayuga and Seneca villages on the north shore of the lake, for
they were outposts, cut off from assistance in case of raids from
the north.   Teiaiagon in this respect would have much to fear.
What was left of the Huron and Algonquin enemies of the
Iroquois had concentrated themselves at Michilimackinac and
the Sault where the French had recently formally declared their
ownership of the country; the Jesuits were there and the fur-
traders, and to all the savage hordes who roved the northern
wilderness Teiaiagon was within easy striking distance by way of
the Toronto Portage.   It would be well palisaded, and inside it
would not differ in general pattern from other Iroquois villages.
There would be long-houses[2] in place of the conical lodges of
the Algonquins, and there would be the usual filthy squalor of
those miserable abodes; the narrow streets would be a play-
ground for naked children; there would be groups of women
and girls gossiping or performing the simple tasks incident to
savage life; there would be young men gambling in the shade
and old men comforting their age with tobacco; possibly there
would be Dutch traders or furtive coureurs-de-bois, anxious
to escape the observation of the emissaries of La Salle; coming
and going there would be hunters from the woods, or old hags
bringing in faggots from the forest, or braves returning from a
scalping party with prisoners to be tortured; for in Teiaiagon,
no doubt, were enacted those horrible scenes of torture and
cannibalism which seemed to the missionaries so like their
imagined conceptions of inferno.   Hennepin does not say so,
but the hopelessness of reforming such places was due in large
measure to the traffic in brandy and to the loose living of the
white men who undid and gave the lie to all the efforts of the
missionaries.

1 Traces of a palisade were discovered on Baby Point in 1889 by Mr.
A. F. Hunter. These relics of a fortification might be ascribed to Teiaiagon,
the Missisauga village, or the Toronto Post of 1720. Consult also *Transactions Canadian Institute*, 1886-1887, p. 12; pp. 37-40; ibid., 1887-1888, p. 22.
2 The Raffeix map of 1688 shows these pergola-like structures.

Although the visit of Father Hennepin to Teiaiagon in 1679 is the first visit to Toronto personally recorded, it is not the first glimpse which history gets of the place. Some time in the '70's a party of La Salle's men from Cataraqui were at Teiaiagon and engaged in a drunken debauch; this is the first definitely recorded visit of white men to the site of the present city; a rather melancholy beginning for Toronto the good! The incident is recorded in an obscure tract entitled *Histoire de l'eau de vie en Canada*, under the heading, "Sad Death of Brandy Traders": "The Carnival of the year 167- six traders from Katarak8y named Duplessis, Ptolémée, Dautru, Lamouche, Colin and Cascaret made the whole village of Taheyagon drunk, all the inhabitants were dead drunk for three days; the old men, the women and the children got drunk; after which the six traders engaged in the debauch which the savages call *Gan8ary*, running about naked with a keg of brandy under the arm." The writer of the tract then proceeds to point out that each of the traders met a tragic end.[1] The same document mentions the fact that two women were stabbed at Tcheiagon (Teiaiagon) in 1676 as the result of a drunken brawl, possibly the same occasion. In 1682 the *Mémoire de la guerre contre les Iroquois* informs us that the Iroquois having resolved "to put Onontio in the pot," began the year by plundering three Frenchmen at Tcheyagon (Teiaiagon): Le Duc, Abraham[2] and

---

1 "Ils ont tous finis d'une mort misérable: Duplessis, est mort à la Barboude, où il a esté vendu par les Anglois. Ptolémée s'est noyé, tournant en canot sur un rocher auquel il a donné son nom, le Sault Ptolémée. Dautru s'est noyé dans la Barque de M. de la Salle, qui périt dans le Lac Huron. Lamouche s'est noyé à l'entrée de la Rivière Sainte Anne, avec un Lanodière. Colin a esté bruslé aux Iroquois, en 1692, accompagnant M. Le Chevalier d'Eau en ambassade. Cascaret est mort sans confession, chez un Chirurgien à Montréal, rongé de vérole, aussi bien qu'un nommé Lacauce, qui fut trouvé mangé des Aigles à la Pointe à Baudet dans le Lac Saint François. C'estoit un célèbre impudique et un fameux traiteur d'Eau-de-vie."—*Histoire de l'eau-de-vie en Canada*, p. 17. Three of them, Duplessis, Colin, Dautru, sailed with La Salle in the *Griffon*. M. Massicotte informs me that Laurent Cascaret, born in 1654, was buried in Montreal, May 20, 1684; that Charles Ptolémée, born 1639, perished in the Sault Saint-Louis in 1679; he had been a member of the 16th squad of Maisonneuve's militia and had been engaged by La Salle on July 1, 1669, to go with him "chez les nations sauvages tant du côté du sud que du côté du nord." Lamouche is probably a nickname.

2 RENÉ ABRAHAM, born 1645, who married Jeanne Blondeau about 1672. He lived at Three Rivers and Sorel between 1673 and 1680. E.-Z.M.

PART OF RAFFEIX'S MAP—1688
From a copy in the Public Archives, Ottawa.   This is the first map
to show the Don River.

Lachapelle.[1] Apparently Teiaiagon had the characteristics of a frontier post.

The exact position of the site of Teiaiagon has been the subject of considerable conjecture.[2] Several sites have been suggested, on all of which extensive remains of former habitation have been discovered. One of these lies close to the corner of Dundas St. and Shaw St.; this site was explored by members of the Denison family many years ago. Another site more recently explored is adjacent to the corner of Eglinton Avenue and Oriole Parkway. Another site is on Withrow Avenue, east of the Don. There are others in the Black Creek neighbourhood in York township. None of these sites, however, conform to

1 LA BARRE encouraged the pillaging of *coureurs-de-bois* without licenses.
2 *Picturesque Canada*, Vol. II, pp. 623 and 636.

the best maps of the period, the most reliable of which place Teiaiagon on the east bank of the Toronto River at the foot of the Toronto Carrying-Place.[1] Several of these maps indicate the distance across the portage in leagues from Teiaiagon to the west branch of the Holland River—a sure indication that the village was not far from the shore of Lake Ontario. There is one site, however, not already mentioned, which satisfies all the conditions, and which has a better claim than any other to authenticity. Baby Point on the Humber commands the foot of the Carrying-Place; the Humber can be forded at that spot; the river, impassable above, becomes navigable to the open lake; it is a high, commanding situation, easily fortified and far enough back from the lake for safety. On this site all kinds of relics of the aborigines have been found, indicating very ancient occupation; there are traces of all the tribes, and iron implements have been discovered showing occupation after the coming of the white man.[2] Hundreds of graves have been opened and are still encountered when excavations are made. Traces of a palisade were observed by Mr. A. F. Hunter in 1889. At least four distinct village sites have been discovered on Baby Point and there is an area of nine or ten acres full of mounds and isolated graves. Mr. J. N. B. Hewitt, of the Smithsonian Institute, Washington, informs me that the probable meaning of the name "Teiaiagon" is "It crosses the stream," and that the reference might be to a path, a log or a bridge. As a village on Baby Point would command the ford over the Humber, this explanation seems appropriate. Professor Louis Allen, to whom I applied for information, states that the word contains Bruyas' Mohawk root, *gaiagon*, to cut; *kaiahiagon*, to cross a river. Dr. Scadding gives as the traditional meaning of the word "a portage or landing-place," a meaning not in agreement with the explanations given above but very descriptive of Teiaiagon, since the Humber was navigable for canoes

1 DE LÉRY's map of 1728 places Terraiagon (*sic*) on the west bank of the Toronto river.

2 Relics have been discovered by Mr. R. J. Dilworth, Mr. A. J. Clark and others.

almost to the foot of the great bluff, and at this point the traveller began the long portage to the Holland River.

Teiaiagon must always have been a strategic point. The trail running east and west along the north shore of Lake Ontario would bend inland to ford the Humber. The site commanded the traffic in two directions, north along the portage to Lake Simcoe and east and west along Lake Ontario. In addition, Teiaiagon would be the natural terminus for those crossing the lake from Niagara. From Baby Point there is a magnificent view of the Humber Valley, a view which would not be greatly impeded by the forest which at that time clothed the banks of the river. It adds additional romance to the site to recall that the Hon. James Baby, the original owner of the land, and a member of Governor Simcoe's council, was a Frenchman from Detroit, a descendant of Jacques Baby de Rainville, an officer in the Carignan-Salières regiment, and a member of a family long interested in the fur trade and well acquainted with all the trade routes of the upper country. Baby's ancestors had traded at Toronto. Did he select this site from sentiment and a knowledge of its historic importance even before the coming of the white man, or was it because he expected further developments along the Carrying-Place? However that may be, Baby was successful in obtaining land where Frobisher, de Rocheblave, La Force, Bouchette and Rousseau failed. The Baby Point site has much to offer to those who like to reconstruct the past. Somewhere on the sunny hillside La Salle seated himself in 1680 to write the long letter dated from Teiaiagon which he composed in the autumn of that year during the delay occasioned by the difficulties of the portage. On the opposite side of the stream and just above the "Old Mill," has been placed the site of the Missisauga village of Toronto of Sir William Johnson's time. The Old Mill itself is, no doubt, on the site of the mill projected in 1751 by the Marquis de la Jonquière.

Whether the relics discovered by Mr. Wm. Mansell in 1924

on the brow of the hill behind his residence on Baby Point belonged to the Senecas of Teiaiagon or to the Missisaugas of Missisauga Toronto would be difficult to determine. These relics, which consisted of a large number of iron trade axes bearing the usual markings, some nondescript fragments of metal and two broken clay pipes of European manufacture, are proof that the site was occupied by the aborigines since the coming of the white man. The tomahawks were found on the crest of the hill where it overlooks the Humber sweeping down from Lambton Mills. At the foot of the hill there is a stretch of swampy land; the slope is still well wooded and intersected with numerous paths. Quantities of bones of every description, found on the slope of the hill, jawbones of deer, ribs of bears and fragments of partridge bones, indicate that the inhabitants of the village found the slope of the hill a convenient place for the disposal of refuse. Eight of the iron tomahawks discovered in 1924 were found in a cluster or circle, and suggest the gloomy thought that this lovely spot was at some time desecrated by one of those atrocities described so minutely by the early missionaries and explorers. In burning a prisoner, it was customary for the Indians to add to the torment of the victim by suspending from his neck a collar of axe-heads heated in the flames and held together by a withe. It is idle to conjecture whether the poor victim on Baby Point was a Huron or Iroquois captive or a prisoner from New England.

Hennepin, as we have seen, left Teiaiagon on December 15, 1678. He expected to meet La Salle at Niagara, where the latter was to spend the winter in preparations for fresh enterprises. There were already at this early date four vessels on Lake Ontario of from twenty-five to forty tons, but as yet there was no vessel on Lake Erie, and the winter of 1678 and 1679 was spent by La Salle in the construction of the *Griffon*. In this ill-fated vessel he set sail on August 7, 1679, for Michilimackinac and the country of the Illinois.

It will not be necessary to follow La Salle back and forth over the ground between the Illinois and Fort Frontenac in the numerous journeys which he made in his struggles to co-ordinate the various parts of his expedition.

But since historians have for the most part ignored the fact that La Salle crossed the Carrying-Place on three and possibly four occasions, and since the maps in our text-books represent him as following the traditional route by Lake Erie, I have thought it best to give several versions of the same episodes, informing the reader at the outset that La Salle crossed the Toronto Carrying-Place in 1680 from Teiaiagon to Michilimackinac, and in 1681 from Michilimackinac to Teiaiagon on his way to Fort Frontenac, and again in the same year on his way back to Michilimackinac. It is possible that La Salle crossed the Carrying-Place a fourth time in 1683, on his return from the Mississippi. With these facts in mind, the reader should have no difficulty in following the various versions of these events, each of which adds something to our knowledge of the locality.

We find La Salle, then, at Teiaiagon in the summer of 1680; he had left Fort Frontenac on the tenth of August on his second journey into the country of the Illinois. He had with him twenty-five men, including ship-carpenters and the materials necessary to complete the vessel which he had begun to build at Crèvecœur to serve for the descent of the Mississippi. "He arrived on the fifteenth at Teiaiagon, a village of the Iroquois situated sixty leagues from the fort, towards the extremity of the north side of Lake Frontenac. He remained there till the twenty-second, because of the necessity of transporting all his baggage overland to Lake Toronto,[1] which discharges itself into Lake Huron by a river which is navigable only by canoes and runs from east to west. He learned in this place (Teiaiagon) definite news of the loss of his ship from two deserters whom he was to arrest later, one of whom, Gabriel Minime, obtained permission to return with him as he complained that he had been misled by the others. The other escaped and carried off

1 Lake Simcoe.

the peltries which the Sieur de La Salle had had seized, and which he had left in the care of one of the savages. On the twenty-third, the Sieur de La Salle arrived at Lake Toronto, on which he embarked with all his people and descended the river which comes out into a bay full of islands. Thence he turned north to follow the north shore of Lake Huron because there are more harbours and places in which to shelter than on the south side, and because there is protection there from the great winds afforded by three long islands which are six or seven leagues from the shore. These islands extend towards the west to a great point of land which separates the straits of Mackinaw from the Sault Sainte-Marie."

The above extract is from the *Relation Officielle*, as given in Margry.[1] The same indefatigable collector of documents supplies us with a letter in which La Salle himself alludes to this episode.[2]

To resume my account of my journey, I set out last year from Teioiagon, on the 22nd of August, and arrived on the 23rd on the shore of Lake Toronto, where I arrested two of my deserters, one named Gabriel Minime and the other Grand-maison, who had escorted my people, and I had the peltries of the latter seized, but since I left the furs with a savage, and I did not keep the man with me, he has recovered them.[3]

From both these documents we learn that on this occasion, while La Salle took the shorter route over the Toronto Carrying-Place, he made the rest of his party, who were carrying the heavier baggage, go round by Niagara and Lake Erie. At Michilimackinac La Salle waited with some anxiety for the arrival of these persons. The *Relation* informs us, "He was waiting with much disquiet for the arrival of a blacksmith, two

1 MARGRY, Vol. I, pp. 500 and 501.
2 Ibid, Vol. II, p. 115.
3 MARGRY gives the names of others who passed over the Carrying-Place in 1680 with La Salle: "J'avois le sieur d'Autray, qui est un fort brave jeune homme, un chirurgien, les nommez You, aussy fort brave garçon, Tamisier mort depuis peu, Baron et André Henault, qui avec moy et le sauvage faisoient huit personnes." Margry, II, p. 127. "Le sieur d'Autray était fils du premier procureur general de Québec." Ibid., II, p. 125.

sailors, a corder and two soldiers who were to bring with them three hundred pounds of powder, lead, guns, iron, oakum, pitch and the sails and the tools with which to finish his ship.   He had given them orders to come by Lake Erie in order that they might meet the Sieur de Tonty, if he returned by that route, and also to avoid the transport of such heavy baggage over the thirty leagues, and the high mountains which have to be traversed in going from Teioiagon to Lake Toronto where the Sieur de La Salle had himself embarked."[1]   La Salle himself remarks in the letter already quoted, "I had left Monsieur La Forest behind with three soldiers, at Missilimakinak, to wait for the blacksmith, the two sailors, the two soldiers and a corder, who were coming by way of Lake Erie with the iron, the oakum and the pitch, the sails and the tools with which to finish the ship, and with three hundred pounds of lead, powder and guns for our defence; and since the winds had been violent during the autumn, although they had set out before me, they were unable to reach Missilimakinak; for the winds are much more dangerous in Lake Erie and Lake Huron on the south side than along the north side of Lake Huron, which I had taken, which was full of islands where one is always in shelter.   But I had made them take this route because there is a strip of land to cross thirty leagues in width from Teioiagon to Lake Toronto, where all baggage must be carried over the crest of very high mountains,[2] and being very heavily loaded they would have had trouble in doing this, and would have lost much time, besides, as I thought that Monsieur de Tonty might have returned by that route, I was very pleased not to miss him, and this obliged me for my part to take the other route by the north of Lake Huron, which is shorter but much more difficult, and where one must live entirely on Indian corn, as there is no hunting for more than a

1 MARGRY, Vol. I, pp. 513-514.

2 "In the parts north of Toronto we more frequently find pine and cedar on account of its vicinity to mountains. They are not as high as the Vosges, but covered with fine timber and good soil. They are not cold like those near Carillon." Pouchot, *Mémoire* (translation), Vol. II, p. 121.

hundred and fifty leagues.   Still they tried to prevent me from finding any."[1]

We find La Salle again at the Carrying-Place in the following year; he had been forced to return to Canada, to appease his creditors and to collect his scattered resources.   At Michili-mackinac he had expected to find the Sieur de La Forest, but the latter, contrary to La Salle's instructions, had lingered at Fort Frontenac in order to discharge some business, without considering the consequences of delay.   "This mishap caused much annoyance to the Sieur de La Salle, who was obliged to go to Fort Frontenac, by way of Lake Taronto.   He found there the Sieur de Tonty in good health, and letters from Count Frontenac instructing him to come down to Montreal to confer with him.   However, he did not meet him there, and this caused much useless waste of time.   Returning to Fort Frontenac, La Salle prepared for his journey.   He arrived in the beginning of August, 1681, at Teyoyagon, where he employed fifteen days in transporting all his baggage to the shores of Lake Taronto, upon which he embarked at the end of the same month of August as in the preceding year."[2]   La Salle on this occasion spent a part of his time at Teiaiagon in writing an account of what had lately occurred to a correspondent in France, concluding as follows:

This is all I can tell you this year.   I have a hundred things to write, but you could not believe how hard it is to do it among Indians.   The canoes and their lading must be got over the portage, and I must speak to them continually, and bear all their importunity, or else they will do nothing I want.   I hope to write more at leisure next year, and tell you the end of this business, which I hope will turn out well: for I have M. de Tonty,[3] who is full of zeal; thirty Frenchmen, all good men, without reckoning such as I cannot trust; and more than a hundred Indians, some of them Shawanoes, and others from New England, all of whom know how to use their guns.

1 MARGRY, II, pp. 125-126.
2 Ibid., I, p. 543.
3 SEVERANCE, *An Old Frontier of France*, Vol. I, p. 79.   "Returning west-ward in August, 1681, their (Tonty, La Salle and Membré) loaded barque sailed from Frontenac to Trajagon (Teiaiagon)."

It was October before he reached Lake Huron. Day after day and week after week the heavy-laden canoes crept on along the lonely wilderness shores, by the monotonous ranks of bristling moss-bearded firs: lake and forest; forest and lake; a dreary scene haunted with yet more dreary memories—disasters and deferred hopes; time, strength, and wealth spent in vain; a ruinous past and a doubtful future; slander, obloquy, and hate. With unmoved heart, the patient voyager held his course, and drew up his canoes at last on the beach at Fort Miami.[1]

From the extracts from Margry it is evident that La Salle traversed the Carrying-Place three times, once in 1680 from south to north and twice in 1681, first from the north and then, on his return from Fort Frontenac, from the south; it was, it appears, the usual short-cut between Lake Ontario and Lake Huron and a sheltered route in stormy weather. La Salle does not seem to have employed the alternative route by the valley of the Trent; the explanation would seem to be that by making use of the ships which he had at Fort Frontenac he could traverse the distance from that place to Teiaiagon in comfort and so shorten the journey. As to the mountains which he mentions and to which Tonti also alludes as the reason for not carrying heavy merchandise over the Carrying-Place, the term "mountains" can mean no more than hills, for the height of land in the township of King does not rise very much above eleven hundred feet above sea level; and the country, though rough in places, cannot fairly be described as mountainous. From the *Relation* of Nicolas de Salle[2] we learn that the canoes employed by La Salle were twenty feet long and three feet wide, and that each canoe carried about twelve hundredweight of merchandise, and that La Salle concealed his powder and lead from the Iroquois,[3] who did not wish him to carry any to their enemies, the Illinois. I have not been able to discover any indication of La Salle's route when returning to Quebec in 1683, after

1 PARKMAN, *La Salle,* p. 294.

2 MARGRY, I, p. 548.

3 "We were right in the Iroquois country at a little lake called Toronto." "Relation de Henri de Tonty." Margry, I, p. 593.

successfully descending the Mississippi; it is possible that he again crossed the Carrying-Place. However that may be, Toronto and the Carrying-Place may be proud of so many historic memories of this remarkable man. "Cavelier de La Salle stands in history," says Parkman, "like a statue of iron; but his unwilling pen betrays the man, and reveals in the stern, sad figure an object of human interest and pity." Here is his character, as sketched by his friend, Abbé Bernou, in a memorial to the minister, the Marquis de Seignelay: "He is irreproachable in his morals, restrained in his conduct, and a man who wishes order among his people. He is learned, judicious and politic, vigilant, indefatigable, sober and intrepid. He has a sufficient knowledge of architecture, civil, military and naval, as well as of agriculture; he speaks or understands four or five savage languages, and learns others with ease. He knows all their ways, and obtains from them what he wants, by address and eloquence, and because of their high opinion of him. On his voyages he enjoys no better cheer than the least of his people, and goes to much trouble to hearten them, and it is believed that with the protection of Your Eminence he will found more considerable colonies than all those which the French have established hitherto".[1]

On his return from the Mississippi in 1683, La Salle found that Frontenac had been recalled. For the soldierly Frontenac the Iroquois had had a wholesome respect. For his successor, the Sieur de la Barre, they had nothing but contempt. La Barre's expedition against the Iroquois in 1684 ended ignominiously in the fever-stricken camp at La Famine, where terms were practically dictated by the Iroquois themselves. What La Barre called his "army of the south" never advanced beyond Niagara. This picturesque flotilla had mustered at Michilimackinac and Detroit and had passed down Lake Huron and Lake Erie under the leadership of those great captains of the west, La Durantaye and Du Lhut. But when the feathered and painted savages found no one at Niagara to meet them except a

---

1 *Mémoire pour Monseigneur le Marquis de Seignelay,* 1682.

messenger with the news that the war was over, they were loud in their protests of indignation, the loyalty of the tribes to the French was shaken, and the six hundred Hurons, Ottawas, Pottawatamies and Foxes dejectedly retraced their steps over the difficult Niagara portage and dispersed to their distant villages.   Du Lhut did not accompany them.   Crossing to Teiaiagon, he took the road running north from that village. A letter from Du Lhut to La Barre is dated *au-dessous du Portage de Teiagon, le 10 septembre 1684*.[1]   The fame of Du Lhut is only inferior to that of La Salle, and his name must now be added to the list of those who used the Carrying-Place.

1 MARGRY, Vol. VI, pp. 50-51.

IV

FROM THE RETURN OF LA SALLE TO DE CALLIÈRES' TREATY WITH THE IROQUOIS: 1683-1701

WITH the news of the discoveries of La Salle the English colonies on the Atlantic immediately extended their boundaries in imagination westward to the Mississippi. Long before the English government discerned the importance of the impending struggle, Dongan, the Irish Catholic governor of New York, had assumed the aggressive. In America both the French and the English accused one another; Dongan maintained that the French intended to confine the English to the coast, and the French in their turn were convinced that the English were already plotting to confine New France within the territory bounded on the west by the Ottawa and on the south by the St. Lawrence, and that in the event of a war between the mother countries the French would be excluded from America. It was believed that the English in New York intended to employ the Iroquois in order to effect their purpose, and since the latter were at that time in possession of what is now Ontario, such a plan might easily have succeeded.[1] A chain of fortified trading-posts from Quebec to the mouth of the Mississippi seemed the only method by which the French could hope to maintain their hold upon their discoveries, and for the first time in 1686 we find the suggestion advanced that a trading-post or fort should be erected at Toronto.

Before, however, considering this historic proposal, which is contained in a letter from Denonville to M. de La Durantaye, the commandant at Michilimackinac, bearing the date of June 6, 1686,[2] and written from Montreal, let us briefly review the opposing forces in this contest for the possession of the fur

---

1 ROCHEMONTEIX, *"Les Jésuites et la Nouvelle France,* Tome III, pp. 217, 218 and 234; "Denonville à Seignelay, 12 juin, 1686"; Parkman, *Frontenac and New France under Louis XIV,* p. 127.

2 MARGRY, V, p. 22.

trade and the control of the interior.   From Fort Orange on the Hudson, lately become Albany, the English and Dutch traders had easy access to Lake Ontario by the Mohawk River and were accustomed to despatch their traders into the northern wilderness by this route in order to entice the Algonquin tribes of the north to barter their rich furs on the Hudson instead of at Montreal.   The Iroquois and their allies, the Wolves, to the south of Lake Ontario had long been the agents of the Dutch and English and were ambitious to secure the whole of the trade for themselves by crushing the Illinois and inducing the Ottawas and the Algonquin tribes of the north to ally themselves with the English rather than the French. · The latter, strongly entrenched at Michilimackinac, and rapidly extending their influence in the interior, could only hope to retain their hold on the trade so long as their Algonquin allies remained loyal; the prosperity of the French depended upon the adhesion of the Ottawas and the other tribes of the lakes, otherwise the huge trade which now centred at Michilimackinac would be lost.   The Toronto Carrying-Place now became the highway between the opposing camps.   If the Iroquois should succeed in crushing the Algonquins of the north as they had already crushed the Hurons and the Neutrals, or should they seduce them from their allegiance, they would be in a position to dictate terms to both the English and the French.   Should the English and Dutch traders discover a short and safe route to Michilimackinac, they would capture the trade by the prices which they could offer.[1]   The ambition of the Iroquois to crush competition and to secure the whole profits of the trade for themselves and their allies in Albany and Schenectady had to be frustrated by the French before the larger problem of the control of the Ohio and Mississippi valleys could be solved.

Between the years 1685 and 1687, Denonville conceived the project of securing the safety of the colony and of barring all

---

1 "Lettre de Frontenac à Colbert en date du 12 novembre, 1674."   Margry, I, pp. 274-275; "Talon au Roy, 1670."   Margry, I, p. 85; "Dépenses faites par La Salle de 1675 à 1684 au Fort Frontenac."   Margry, II, p. 11.

the avenues of approach against the Iroquois and the English, by a chain of forts which was to extend from Lake Champlain to Michilimackinac and the Illinois. Chambly, Cataraqui and Niagara were the first objects of his attention; Chambly, founded on October 19, 1686, was to guard the approaches to Lake Champlain and the Richelieu; Cataraqui seemed to him of the greatest importance in order to secure control of Lake Ontario, and Niagara would command the communication with Lake Erie and secure to the French the mastery of the Senecas and their fur trade, a great part of which passed over the portage on the Niagara River. It was part also of Denonville's plan to establish posts at Detroit and Toronto for the defence of the Ottawas, and to serve as places where they might take refuge if attacked by the Iroquois. "I should not be surprised," writes Margry,[1] "if the idea of these posts was suggested to Denonville by Father Enjalran,[2] a man of intelligence, who fifteen years later supported the project." Margry probably founded his conjecture upon the fact that Father Enjalran came down from Michilimackinac in 1686 to communicate to the new governor the deplorable state of affairs. Denonville writes to M. de Seignelay in the autumn of that year:

We may set down Canada as lost if we do not make war next year; and, yet, in our present disordered state, war is the most dangerous thing in the world. Nothing will save us but the troops you will send and the forts and blockhouses which it is necessary to build. Yet I dare not begin to work at them for, if I make the least movement in this direction, I shall assuredly draw all the Iroquois down on us, before I am in a condition to attack them.[3]

Apparently Enjalran succeeded in impressing upon the governor the need for action; he was a man of action himself, and next year, in 1687, we find him taking part in the great raid into the Seneca country at Irondequoit Bay and sustaining

1 MARGRY, V, Introduction, p. XXVIII.

2 ROCHEMONTEIX, *Les Jésuites et la Nouvelle France*, Tome III, p. 192.

3 *New York Colonial Documents*, Vol. IX, p. 299. "M. Denonville à M. de Seignelay, Québec 8 octobre, 1686."

a gunshot wound in the shoulder. If Enjalran advised the governor to take active steps against the Iroquois, he was following the policy recommended years before by Le Jeune[1] and Druilletes;[2] and if it was he who first proposed the establishment of a post at Toronto, it was a natural thing for a Jesuit missionary to do, for who knew better than the Jesuits the strategic importance of the Toronto Portage at the northern extremity of which their own fort had been established fifty years before?

While deferring for the present a fuller discussion of the origin and etymology of the word "Toronto," something should be said at this point. As a place-name the word does not occur on any of the maps prior to 1673; it seems to have come into use when the French returned to the lake region in the sixties. It is first used by La Salle, Denonville and Lahontan, who apply the name to Lake Simcoe, the Severn River and the southern part of the Georgian Bay. As the word does not appear during the period of the Huron missions while the Hurons themselves were still living in their own country, it is a fair conclusion that it was employed to describe a region which had assumed a new relation to the French and Hurons now established at Michilimackinac. Lake Simcoe had ceased to be the lake of the Hurons (*lacus Ouentaronius*), and Michilimackinac had become the centre of the rich fur trade of the upper lakes and the west, and the object of the envy and cupidity of the Iroquois and their allies, the Dutch and English on the Hudson. A new nomenclature would be used to describe a region which now owed its importance to a changed relation. There were two approaches to Michilimackinac, one by Detroit and the other by Lake Simcoe. The Hurons' name for Detroit, according to Potier, was *karontaen*, a pass, or gate, and since the word appears also in the form *tarontaen*, it may reasonably be assumed that this name was applied to the other pass and was the origin

1 ROCHEMONTEIX, *Les Jésuites et la Nouvelle France*, Tome II, *Pièces Justificatives* VII, and Tome II, p. 166, f.n.
2 *Jesuit Relations*, Cleveland Edition, Vol. XXXVI.

of the name "Toronto," a name which gradually extended itself over the whole pass from the mouth of the Severn to the mouth of the Humber.

We find the name of Enjalran in the letter written by Denonville to M. de La Durantaye, the commandant at Michilimackinac from Montreal, on June 6, 1686; and since this is the first recorded allusion to the project of a post at Toronto, we shall quote the passage in full:

Sir, I am writing to you by the Sieur de Juchereau whom I am sending to you, until the Reverend Father Enjalran can join you at Michilimackinaw, which depends upon the restoration of prisoners which is to take place at Cataracouy. In the meantime it is absolutely necessary for the service of the King and of the colony that you retain about you all the Frenchmen that you can, for I propose to have two posts occupied, one at the straits (le Detroit) leading from Lake Erie, and the other at the portage of Toronto. I desire that the first should be occupied by M. Dulhud, to whom you will give twenty men. I am writing to him to be ready to set out on the receipt of this letter for the said straits in order to select a suitable place there in which to entrench himself, and afterwards to have sent there a sure and faithful person whom he shall choose, and whom he will establish as commandant there.[1]

In his letter of the ninth of November of the same year, to M. de Seignelay, already quoted, Denonville refers to the project:

The letters I have written to Sieurs du Lhu and de La Durantaye, of which I send you copies, will inform you of my orders to them to fortify the two passes leading to Michilimaquina. Sieur du Lhu is at that of the Detroit of Lake Erie, and sieur de La Durantaye at that of the portage of Taronto. These two posts will block the passage against the English should they attempt to go again to Michilimaquina, and serve as retreats for our Indian allies either while hunting, or while making war against the Iroquois.[2] . . . The said Antoine L'Epinant assures, moreover, that a company of fifty men was formed to go to Missilimakina, that their canoes were

1 MARGRY, V, p. 22.
2 New York Colonial Documents, Vol. IX, p. 300.

purchased, and that the low state of the waters had prevented them starting; that they are waiting for the rain to raise the rivers, and that the Senecas have promised to escort them. I have heard of Sieur du Lhu's arrival at the post of the Detroit of Lake Erie, with fifty good men well armed, with munitions of war and provisions and all other necessities sufficient to protect them against the severe cold, and to render them comfortable during the winter wherever they will entrench themselves. M. de La Durantaye is collecting men to fortify himself at Michilimaquina, and to occupy the other passage at Taronto which the English might take to enter Lake Huron. In this way our Englishmen will find some one to speak to.

The expedition to which Denonville refers took place in the autumn of 1685 and is of importance since it was the first occasion on which white men other than French appeared in the upper lakes. Governor Dongan of New York had no intention of allowing the French to monopolize the trade at Mackinac. The party consisted of eleven canoes laden with trade goods and rum and was commanded by Johannes Rooseboom,[1] a young Dutchman of Albany; they made their way to Mackinac by the Niagara portage, the north shore of Lake Erie and Detroit under the guidance of Abel Marion Lafontaine, a renegade French trader well acquainted with the lake region. The English goods and the English rum proved very attractive to the tribes, and in three months Rooseboom was back in Albany. Dongan was delighted. He decided to try again next year. Denonville, on the contrary, was infuriated and gave orders to guard the pass at Detroit and the pass at Toronto. The English had not yet actually employed the Toronto Carrying-Place; but there was a danger. Next year they were at Toronto.

In the autumn of 1686 Dongan despatched a second expedition. The first division left Albany on the eleventh of September and was again commanded by Rooseboom, with Lafontaine as guide. They had twenty canoes and numbered thirty-four in all, most of them members of prominent Dutch families in

1 SEVERANCE, *An Old Frontier of France*, Vol. I, pp. 96-106.

Albany. The first division, after wintering in the neighbourhood
of Oswego, proceeded by the Niagara route in the direction of
Mackinac. As soon as the waterways were free of ice in the
spring of 1687, Dongan despatched a second division of the
same party, entrusting its command to a person whom he
describes as "a Scotch gent named McGregor." Colonel
Patrick MacGregorie had come to America in 1684 from Scotland
and had gained the confidence of Dongan, who had appointed
him earlier in 1686 "Muster Master General of the Militia of
the Province of New York." Severance gives some interesting
details of the subsequent experiences of MacGregorie, but he
seems to be at fault in his account of the adventures of the
"Scotch gent" and his party on this occasion. Severance and
Parkman, following Colden, state that the second division, like
the first, took the Niagara route and passed through Lake Erie
unharmed. The *Mémoire de la guerre contre les Iroquois* has a
different account:

1687. This year a palisade was built around Ville-Marie.
Meantime Dongan the governor of Manhatte, a catholic but a
very mischievous man, being persuaded by persons named
Du Plessis and Lafontaine Marion, *francs fugitifs du profit*,
that there was something to do at Missilimakinac, sent there a
man named Grégorie with a large party of sixty men and three
thousand pounds of goods; and having been warned that
M. Duluth was on guard at the pass of Toncharontio (Detroit)
which leads from Lake Erie to Lake Huron, they went by
Taronte, and were led by Lafontaine Marion, the person
named Gaustassy and Tegannenset. They arrived in the
neighbourhood of Missilimakina towards the month of May to
the number of sixty. M. de la Durantaye, a very brave and
prudent officer in command there, feeling that he must anticipate
the meeting of the Ottawas and the Dutch, set out ahead with
his company; all the savages set out at the same time fully
armed and form a numerous party in the woods a gun-shot from
the French. *Chose admirable!*—all the savages were inclined to
favor the Dutch on account of the cheapness of their goods;
Grégorie, however, was convinced that the savages came to
escort and support the French; M. de la Durantaye without

giving the savages time to declare themselves, being between them and the Dutch, advances with his company with gun pointed, compels the sixty Dutchmen to lay down their arms, binds their hands, and at the same time allows all the savages and French to pillage their goods winning over thereby those who perhaps would have rebelled.

The Grégorie of this narrative is of course Colonel Patrick MacGregorie. The first Englishman to visit Toronto was a Scotchman! MacGregorie and Rooseboom, whose division had shared the same fate, were carried prisoner to Niagara; they were subsequently released. Lafontaine as a French deserter was shot by order of Denonville at Cataraqui. Lahontan, in 1703, in a book published in Amsterdam, protested his execution, and describes him as "an active fellow who had travelled frequently all over this continent and was perfectly well acquainted with the country, and with the savages of Canada." The Du Plessis of the narrative is, no doubt, the same trader who some ten years before had been one of six to debauch the inhabitants of Teiaiagon; he died in the Barbadoes, where he was sold by the English. "It is certain," wrote Denonville, "that if the English had not been stopped and pillaged, the Hurons and Ottawas would have revolted and cut the throats of all our Frenchmen." *Chose admirable* for the French, *chose malheureuse* for Dongan and Patrick MacGregorie and the English! Had Dongan's expedition succeeded the French would have been confined to the St. Lawrence and the English would have held the continent. History forgets failures.

It has been assumed that de la Durantaye, in obedience to instructions, established a fortified post at the southern end of the Toronto Portage; if so, it must have been a very temporary structure. Several maps of the period show Duluth's fort on the site of the present town of Sarnia, but no map has as yet come to light which indicates that de la Durantaye made any fortification at Toronto. The Toronto Portage could have been blocked as effectually at the northern end as at the southern; it was at the mouth of the Matchedash Bay (*Baye*

de Toronto) that Lahontan placed his "Fort Supposé,"[1] a project
still under discussion when Deputy Surveyor-General Collins
made his report to Lord Dorchester in 1788,[2] and finally carried
into effect by the military post projected by Simcoe at Penetanguishene and established in 1816. There is a passage in
Denonville's report to de Seignelay written from Montreal on
June 8, 1687, which causes still further perplexity:

> I must inform you, My Lord, that I have altered the orders
> I had originally given last year to M. de la Durantaye to pass
> by Taronto and to enter Lake Ontario at Gandatsitiagon to
> form a juncture with M. du Lhu at Niagara. I have sent him
> word by the Sieur Juchereau who took back the two Hurons
> and Outaouas chiefs this winter, to join Sieur du Lhu at the
> Detroit of Lake Erie, so that they may be stronger and in
> condition to resist the enemy should he go to meet them at
> Niagara.[3]

As we have already seen, there were two trails from the
Holland to Lake Ontario; one from the east branch to Ganatsekwyagon at the mouth of the Rouge, and the other from the
west branch to Teiaiagon at the mouth of the Humber. Denonville, on this occasion, instructed de la Durantaye to use the
eastern trail to Ganatsekwyagon because it was nearer to
Irondequoit Bay, the gateway to the Seneca country. Had
Denonville intended to block the portage at the southern end,
it is not possible to be sure that he did not intend his post at
Toronto to be placed at Ganatsekwyagon rather than at
Teiaiagon. These two villages were twenty-three miles apart,
and in reality it would have been necessary to fortify both
places. On the other hand, what does Denonville mean by
instructing de la Durantaye "to pass by Taronto"? Does he
mean Lake Toronto as Lake Simcoe was then called, or does he
mean the village of the Missisaugas of that name which Carver
tells us was on Lake Simcoe? Raffeix's map of 1688 gives
fifteen leagues as the length of the eastern portage, which would

1 LAHONTAN, map of 1703.
2 *Ontario Public Archives*, 1905, p. 362.
3 *New York Colonial Documents*, Vol. IX, p. 327.

mean that its northern terminus was at Roche's Point and not at Holland Landing; probably in winter the trail would end at the former place and in summer at the latter.   In 1793 there was a village of the Missisaugas on Cook's Bay, opposite Roche's Point, and from this village a trail led on to the foot of Kempenfeldt Bay and on to Penetanguishene.   A post on Cook's Bay at this point would have blocked both of the southern trails.   So far as is known at present, the name "Toronto" had not in Denonville's time become localized anywhere on Lake Ontario; it was still associated with the Lake Simcoe region. Even so, it is not, outside the range of possibility that when Denonville stated that he intended to have the "portage of Toronto" occupied, he meant the southern end of the trail, distinctively known at a later date as the Toronto Carrying-Place; possibly, in spite of all the objections which may be raised, we shall be right in assuming with Margry that Denonville's proposed post was the origin of the present city of Toronto.

But before leaving this fascinating question, the spot which Denonville proposed to fortify, one more suggestion may be made.   The Jesuits in 1650 built a substantial fort on Christian Island, which they were compelled almost immediately to abandon on account of famine and pestilence.   It was apparently the strongest spot in the country, for it commanded the route by the Nottawasaga and that by the Severn; it was the only spot which could be said to control the passage from Lake Ontario to Lake Huron.   Lahontan suggested a fort at the mouth of the Bay of Toronto, and in his map the words Bay of Toronto run between Christian Island and the mainland; and though his *fort supposé* is usually placed on his maps at the mouth of the Severn, there is one version in which it is placed where the Jesuit fort stood.   Is it possible that this was the original Toronto?   On Du Creux's map of the Huron country (1660) there is a village adjacent to this spot marked *Taruen-tutunum*, a Latinized form.   Many names of French towns had Latin names ending in *-dunum*.   Was there a Taruentu?   The late Father Devine informed me that in his opinion the Jesuits had intended to remove their headquarters to Ste. Marie II on Christian Island some time before their forced removal in 1650.

The eastern trail to Ganatsekwyagon, which appears in the last half of the seventeenth century as the rival of the western trail or Toronto Carrying-Place, merits a more detailed description. It has been intimated already that it was at Ganatsekwyagon that the Sulpicians established themselves in 1669 and that it was by the eastern trail that Joliet and Péré crossed to Matchedash Bay in 1669, the first white men so far as is known, to pass that way since the expulsion of the Hurons. There are other indications that this trail was much used both by the Ottawas and the Iroquois in their trade with the Dutch on the Hudson during this period. Unfortunately there are in existence no maps comparable with the excellent maps of the western trail, which would enable us to determine the exact course of the trail from the mouth of the Rouge to the Holland Landing. Joliet's map and Raffeix's map seem to indicate that the trail did not follow the valley of the Rouge but ran in a northerly direction towards the village of Stouffville along the watershed to the end of the Little Rouge. If so, the trail probably passed close to the site of the fortified village east of Vandorf so well known to archaeologists, and from that point passed to the east of Newmarket on to the Holland Landing, from which point there would be an extension to Roche's Point, to be used in winter to escape the more exposed route by the Holland flats. Scadding, however, informs us that the Mississaugas set much store by a trail along the valley of the Rouge;[1] the existence of such a trail is corroborated by numerous village sites in that locality. There was also a trail parallel with Yonge St., running from Bond Lake to the eastern branch of the Holland, and this may have been the course of the eastern branch of the Toronto Carrying-Place so popular in the seventeenth century. It was by the trail from Ganatsekwyagon, as we shall presently see, that the savage allies of the French returned to the north after the raid into the Seneca country in

1 SCADDING, *Toronto of Old* (1873), p. 473.

1688. Which of the two trails would be used would depend upon the destination of the traveller; those travelling from the eastern end of the lake and from Fort Frontenac would naturally go north by the Rouge route, while those from the western end of the lake or from Niagara would follow the Humber trail; the distance by land in either case was the same, and both trails terminated in the north in the Holland River and Cook's Bay; at the south, however, they were twenty-three miles apart, and the southern end of the Humber trail was that much nearer to the mouth of the Niagara River, a fact which, joined to the proximity of an excellent harbour, must have contributed to the greater popularity of the western carrying-place.

On the fourth of July, 1687, Denonville embarked at Fort Frontenac for his campaign against the Senecas. With four hundred *bateaux* and canoes he crossed the foot of Lake Ontario, and moved westward along the southern shore. The weather was rough and six days passed before he saw the headlands of Irondequoit Bay. Far off on the glimmering water he saw a multitude of canoes advancing to meet him. It was the flotilla of de La Durantaye. Good luck and good management had so disposed it that the allied bands, concentrating from points more than a thousand miles distant, reached the rendezvous on the same day. This was not all. The Ottawas of Michili-mackinac, who refused to follow La Durantaye, had changed their minds the next morning, embarked in a body, paddled up the Georgian Bay of Lake Huron, crossed to Toronto, and joined the allies at Niagara. White and red, Denonville now had nearly three thousand men under his command.[1]

As for these allies from the upper lakes, Parkman tells us that most of them wore nothing but horns on their heads and the tails of beasts behind their backs. Their faces were painted red or green, with black or white spots; their noses and ears were hung with ornaments of iron; and their naked bodies were daubed with figures of various sorts of animals. As the rendezvous was Niagara, there can be little doubt that these fearsome savages followed the Humber trail; they returned after the

1 PARKMAN, *Count Frontenac and New France Under Louis XIV*, p. 154; *New York Colonial Documents*, Vol. IX, p. 447.

battle by the eastern trail from Ganatsekwyagon with their prisoners to Michilimackinac; they excelled, we are told, in cruelty rather than in courage.

After his campaign against the Senecas, in which the governor "although he tore down the nest failed to crush the wasps," Denonville proceeded immediately to the realization of his most cherished project. With a portion of his troops, he coasted the southern shore of the lake and, arriving at the mouth of the Niagara River on the thirty-first of July, he began at once the erection of a stockade on the site of the present fort. Fort Denonville had a brief and troubled existence; during the winter of 1688 and 1689 most of the garrison died of scurvy and the post was abandoned. Had it been possible for the French to remain permanently at Niagara, it would have been necessary for them to fortify the Portage of Toronto at a much earlier date; Niagara closed one door to Michilimackinac, but a fort there would have been useless had the pass at Toronto remained open. When the French, nearly forty years later, in 1720, resumed the project of a post at Niagara, we shall find that a trading post at the mouth of the Humber appears simultaneously, and that the history of the two posts is closely linked together.

In the summer of 1687, after the building of the fort at the mouth of the Niagara, Denonville embarked with his troops for Montreal; following the coast westward to the head of the lake, he returned along the north shore, and as this is the first occasion of a vice-regal visit to Toronto, we shall let the record speak for itself. In his official account[1] of the expedition against the Senecas, Denonville writes:

2nd of August—The militia having performed their allotted task, and the Fort being in a condition of defence, in case of attack, they set out at noon for the end of the lake, on their return home. 3rd.—The next day I embarked in the morning for the purpose of joining the militia, leaving the regular troops in charge of M. de Vaudreuil, to finish what was most essential,

1 *New York Colonial Documents*, Vol. IX, pp. 368, 369.

and to render the fort capable not only of defence, but also of being occupied by a detachment of a hundred soldiers, which are to winter there under the command of M. de Troyes, a veteran officer, now a full captain of one of the companies stationed in this country. We advanced 13 leagues and encamped on the point at the end of the lake, where there is a traverse of 4 leagues from the southern to the northern shore (Burlington Beach). 4th.—Fearing the day breeze we embarked in the morning as soon as the moon rose and accomplished the traverse of 4 leagues. We made 14 leagues to-day. (This would bring the party to the mouth of the Humber.)   5th July.—The storm of wind and rain prevented us leaving in the morning, but at noon, the weather cleared up and we advanced 7 or 8 leagues and arrived at a place (Ganatsekwyagon) to which I had sent forward our Christian Indians from below. We found them with two hundred deer they had killed,[1] a good share of which they gave to our army, that thus profited by this fortunate chase.

On the ninth the governor reached Cataraqui and on the thirteenth he was back in Montreal.

The morning spent at Toronto was windy and rainy, and it is not likely that Denonville saw very much of the surrounding country. Father Enjalran and de la Durantaye had taken part in the campaign against the Senecas, and without doubt the project of a fort at Toronto had been thoroughly discussed. If it had been the intention of the governor in his letter of the year before to fortify the southern end of the portage, he apparently abandoned the project, for though he was now on the very ground, he says no more about it. One cannot but ask whether the governor employed the morning spent at the mouth of the Humber in raiding and destroying the Seneca village of Teiaiagon; he had already dealt roughly with the inhabitants of Ganneious and, since we hear no more of the Iroquois villages on the north side of Lake Ontario after this memorable expedition, it is quite possible that Denonville conducted some military operations which he does not report. On the other hand, the Indians were always subject to panic,

---

1 DENONVILLE had also despatched Indians to Detroit to secure provisions for those returning to Michilimackinac by that route.

and the inhabitants of the five villages, or at least the most westerly of them, may have fled to the south side of the lake.

Imagination would like to dwell a little longer on the scene at the mouth of the Rouge, when the two hundred deer provided a rich feast for the victorious Indians and Frenchmen. The Christian Indians in question were, no doubt, the allies from the Sault whom Denonville had sent across the lake from Irondequoit Bay to Ganatsekwyagon, to return to the north by the easterly trail.

Denonville was followed a little later by the regular troops under the command of de Vaudreuil. The writer of the *Mémoire de la guerre contre les Iroquois* evidently belonged to this party.

He writes:

We crossed Lake Ontario from south to north where the lake is four leagues wide, with a light breeze which made waves like the sea. Where we landed we had a pleasant sight; for a quarter of a league along the shore all the trees had a skinned roebuck hanging from the branches. M. de Troye died there of dyssentry. The food had given everyone this sickness which had spread owing to the fresh pork and the beans (other writers say the green corn). After coasting past Téhiâgon and calling at Kenté and Ganeyousse, by the Tannahouté we reached Katarak8y the day after a great storm which compelled us to pass the night on a rock or little islet. We reached Katarak8y where M. le Marquis anxiously awaited us for we had been followed by the Iroquois.

But though the governor and his victorious troops celebrated a rude triumph on this occasion and looked across the waters of the broad lake with complacency towards the harried country of the Senecas, Denonville in reality only succeeded in rousing the fury of the Iroquois. Niagara and Fort Frontenac were abandoned, and next year the massacre of Lachine shook the allegiance of all the tribes of the lakes and almost placed in the power of the English and the Iroquois the great prize for which both they and the French were contending—the fur trade of the west.

Denonville had ruined for the time the fortunes of the French in America. With the return of Frontenac in 1689, confidence was gradually restored. Fort Frontenac was rebuilt. Phipps' attack on Quebec was repulsed, and the respect of the western tribes was regained by the raids which Frontenac made into New York and New England. We hear no more for the present of a chain of forts in the west; nor did the French government, having rejected Lahontan's plan of three posts,[1] one at Buffalo, another at Detroit and a third on the point at the mouth of the *baie de Toronto*, attempt any further fortifications till the founding of Detroit in 1701. In that year de Callières' great council with the Iroquois and the western tribes at Montreal brought to an end a long period of hostility and ushered in an epoch when the rivalries of trade were more peacefully pursued in the Great Lakes. During the next few years, allusions to Toronto and the Toronto Portage will be few. The band of Frenchmen who built Fort Pontchartrain in 1701, thereby laying the foundations of the city of Detroit, went thither by the Ottawa trail; and although there was an occasional passage by way of the Niagara, for some years the principal coming and going between the upper lakes and the lower St. Lawrence was by the northern route.

Some time during the period which we have been considering, the Missisaugas began to replace the Iroquois along the north shore of the lake. The campaigns of Denonville and Frontenac must have made the position of any of the latter who ventured to remain very insecure. The nefarious kidnapping of the inhabitants of Kenté and Ganneious must have made all who

---

1 "Avec ces moyens il se proposait de faire trois fortins en différents endroits, le premier à la décharge du lac Érie, le second au lieu où il avait commandé en 1687 et en 1688 et le troisième à la pointe de l'embouchure de la baie de Toronto. Quatrevingt dix hommes devaient suffire selon lui pour garder les trois redoutes." Margry, V, Introduction, p. LX. Lahontan's map places a *fort supposé* at the mouth of the Severn; but there is an edition of his map (1720) which places the fort on the site of Ste. Marie II. The Jesuits, in 1650, had established themselves there knowing that it was the only point which could command traffic from the mouth of the Nottawasaga as well as from the mouth of the Severn. Possibly this was the Toronto which Denonville intended to fortify. Islands north of this region are still called "The Watchers."

professed neutrality exceedingly apprehensive.[1] Teiaiagon and Ganatsekwyagon, if they still existed, lay right across the path of the Ottawas descending from the north. Indian tradition is notoriously inaccurate, but the fact that Copway, himself a Chippewa, in his traditional history of the tribe, asserts that it was in the latter part of the seventeenth century that the Missisaugas expelled the Iroquois from the country north of the lakes, may be allowed some consideration.[2] At any rate, when Toronto and the Portage again emerge into the light of history, the Missisauga Indians are in possession.

Here is the first documentary proof of the reappearance of an Algonquin tribe on Lake Ontario since the beginning of the seventeenth century. Champlain's map of 1612 indicates that at that time the Hontagounon—the Iroquois name for the Algonquins—had three villages on the north shore of the lake. On June 30, 1700, envoys from the Five Nations presented certain "Propositions for Ye Commisioners for Trade" at Albany. They said:

We must now give you an account of what the Dowaganhaes (Outawas) have said at Onondaga.

Some of the Dowaganhaes having had a conference with our Indians at their hunting last winter, conclude to desert their habitations and to come and settle upon Ye Lake of Cadarackqui, near the Sinnekes' country at a place called Kanatiochtiage (Ganatsekwyagon),[3] and accordingly they are come and settled there and have sent five of their people to Onondaga to treat being sent from three Nations who are very strong, having sixteen castles.

They say,—

"We have come to acquaint you that we are settled on Ye North side of Cadarachqui Lake near Tchojachiage (Teiaiagon) where we plant a tree of peace and open a path for all people,

1 "Assuredly the five villages will avenge our quarrel." Lahontan, *Voyages in North America*, Vol. I, p. 122 and 123; *New York Colonial Documents*, Vol. IX, pp. 362, 363 and 819.

2 "Colonel Strickland, in his explorations of the County of Peterborough, found near the Otonabee River the field that gave the Missisaugas the lordship of Rice Lake and Stoney Lake and the other lakes beyond." *Picturesque Canada*, II, p. 642.

3 *Handbook of Indians of Canada*, p. 234, "Kanatiochtiage."

quite to Corlaer's house (Schenectady)[1] and desire to be united in Ye Covenant Chain, our hunting places to be one, and to boil in one kettle, eat out of one spoon, and so be one; and because the path to Corlaer's house may be open and clear, doe give a drest elke skin to cover Ye path to walke upon."[2]

Peace was made with the Dowaganhaes and they were welcomed to Corlaer's house.   Thus it was that the Missisaugas, for it is they, established themselves at Toronto and became allies of the Iroquois.

1 The Indians often referred to the governor of New York as Corlaer as they called the French governor Onontio.
2 *New York Colonial Documents,* Vol. IV, p. 694.   Ibid., IV, p. 476.

V

FROM THE FOUNDING OF DETROIT TO THE BUILDING OF FORT TORONTO: 1701-1750

THE *Magasin Royal* AT TORONTO: 1720-1730

WE come now to a period in the history of Lake Ontario when records and exploits seem to vanish.[1] Denonville's raid into the Seneca country, followed by the massacre of Lachine and Frontenac's punitive expedition into the Iroquois country, closed the region to the French. The Iroquois, though cowed, were still formidable, and if the French came at all into Lake Ontario they came stealthily and avoided offence. Between 1687 and 1716 there is very little upon which to base the history of the Toronto district. The missionaries, the explorers and the soldiers seem to have passed it by, and although after 1701 there was a steady stream of settlers making their way over the Niagara portage to Detroit, they often followed the south shore of the lake, and in any case there is little record of these migrations. After 1713 there followed a period of comparative peace with the English. There were few war parties abroad, and the rivalries of trade compose the meagre records of the period.

Scanty though these records may be, they are picturesque, and we may feel sure, even without documentary proof, that no year passed without the presence of some vagrant *coureur-de-bois* from Quebec or some rival trader from Albany at the mouth of the Toronto River. It was in this period that the foundations of permanent settlement at Toronto were laid. The city of Toronto, instead of dating its existence from Simcoe and 1793, or Lord Dorchester and 1788, or from Portneuf and 1750, must now go back to the Sieur Douville and 1720. The evidence is complete. But while 1720 is at the present the earliest date at which permanent settlement at Toronto can be placed,

---

1 SEVERANCE, *An Old Frontier of France*, Vol. I, p. 146.

justifiable inference from existing documents makes it certain that there was regular trading at Toronto as early as 1715, and when the history of Fort Frontenac is written, it will, no doubt, be apparent that, with the exception of a short period between 1687 and 1715, there was continuous trading at Toronto from Péré in 1668 to Simcoe in 1793.

The history of the struggle between the French and the English for the control of the fur trade on Lake Ontario between 1695 and 1720 is obscure, but the main outlines are now apparent. The Iroquois had voluntarily withdrawn or had been expelled from the north shore, and as early as 1700 the Missisaugas were established in the western end of the lake; their villages, of which the most important was at Toronto, extended from the mouth of the Rouge to the mouth of the Niagara. They were thus in control of the approaches to Mackinac and of the immensely valuable trade there.

As a rule the Indians and the traders in their canoes followed' the shores of the Great Lakes, though the former on occasion would venture to cross the open water. Fort Frontenac had been established, as we have seen, to intercept the traffic along the north shore from Toronto to Albany carried on by the Dutch and their allies, the Iroquois. Unfortunately for the French, the route westward from Toronto and along the south shore was equally convenient. It is a question whether the Iroquois in their strength would have allowed both approaches to be blocked. When the Missisaugas established themselves at Toronto and the western end of the lake, the region, all of which was included by the French in the term *fond-du-lac*, at once proved to be of strategic importance and both the French and the English took steps to secure control. The Missisaugas in the *fond-du-lac* were within equal reach of Frontenac and Chouéguen. From the first, attracted by the potency of the English rum, the Missisaugas showed a distinct preference for trading at Albany.

In 1700, as we have noted in the conclusion of the preceding chapter, the Missisaugas introduced by the Onondagas were

THE STONE HOUSE AT NIAGARA

Built by de Léry in 1726 and now restored to its original condition. Toronto was a dependency of Niagara from 1720-1793.

BABY POINT

The site of Teiaiagon and the probable site of the Sieur Douville's *Magasin Royal* in 1720. Louis Thomas de Joncaire, Sieur de Chabert, was the first inspector of this post.

welcomed in "Corlaer's house" and indicated their intention of trading with the English. In the same year the New York commissioners, Schuyler, Livingston and Hanse, heard that the French intended to build five forts on Lake Ontario.[1] In 1706 it is recorded that the Indian allies of the French were trading with the English.[2] In 1715 the French heard rumours that the English were about to build a post in the end of the lake, and even in 1726 the English were still sending their canoes past the mouth of the Niagara to secure the trade with the Missisaugas in the end of the lake and along the north shore. It was this fact that induced de Léry to build his stone house, not at the foot of the portage at Lewiston, but at the mouth of the Niagara, where it stands to-day looking out over Lake Ontario.[3] The efforts of the French to frustrate the English resulted in permanent settlements at Toronto and Niagara very early in the century; these efforts will now be related in detail.

With the rebuilding of Fort Frontenac in 1695, the collecting of peltries along the north shore of Lake Ontario, at the foot of the important trails leading into the interior, was resumed. The Missisaugas were now established in the hunting grounds of the Iroquois north of the lake, and trading went on as before at Kenté and Ganaraske and especially at the mouth of the Toronto River where the Toronto Carrying-Place afforded easy access to rich and varied hunting-grounds.

The regular collection of peltries at these and less important places about the lake would be accomplished by the king's canoes or by the barks which were maintained for this purpose at Fort Frontenac. Apparently no permanent houses or magazines had as yet been constructed. Fort Frontenac or Cataraqui was the centre for Lake Ontario in the same way that

1 SEVERANCE, *An Old Frontier of France*, Vol. I, p. 334.

2 "I have observed with pain your representation of the trade which the Indian allies of the French carry on with Orange"—"M. de Pontchartrain to M. de Vaudreuil, 6th June, 1708." *New York Colonial Documents*, Vol. IX, p. 813.

3 De Léry remarks, "If they had built the stone house at the portage, it is certain the English would have built another on Lake Ontario."

Detroit and Michilimackinac were the centres for the collection
of peltries in the districts which they commanded.

That there were grave irregularities and much private
profiteering on the part of those in charge of these posts is
evident from the fact that Louis XIV, under the date of June 30,
1707,[1] issued instructions to M. de Clerambaut d'Aigremont at
Quebec to visit Fort Cataraqui, Niagara, Detroit and Michilimackinac and "to verify their present condition, the trade
carried on there, and the utility they may be to the Colony of
Canada." M. d'Aigremont left Fort Frontenac on June 20,
1708, and on the twenty-seventh he was at the mouth of the
Niagara River, after a week spent in visiting the various points
on the north and south shores of the lake dependent on Fort
Frontenac. There is no mention of Toronto in the long and
detailed report submitted by M. d'Aigremont to the king, but
it is likely that he visited the mouth of the Humber and inspected
the conditions under which the trade was conducted there.

Ten years later, in 1718, the author of an anonymous report
gives the following scanty information about the Missisaugas.
"On the opposite or north shore of Lake Huron you have
Matchitace; some Missisagues are there, whose manners are
the same as the Outaouaes. You have the Toronto Carrying-
Place, leading from Lake Ontario to Lake Huron fifteen leagues
long." This statement is incorporated with Chauvignerie's
Memoir on the Indians of Canada as far as the Mississippi
(1734)[2] with the additional statement, "The Missisagues are
dispersed along the shore at Kenté, others at the River Toronto
and finally at the head of the lake[3] to the number of one hundred
and fifty in all and at Matchedach. The principal tribe is that

1 SEVERANCE, *An Old Frontier of France*, Vol. I, p. 163; and *New York
Colonial Documents*, Vol. IX, p. 822.

2 *New York Colonial Documents*, Vol. IX, p. 889; Ibid., p. 1056.

3 The village called *Ganastogué Sonontoua Outinaouatoua* by Galinée in
1669, at the western end of Lake Ontario, may be identical with the *Ganadoke*
of the Homan-Danville map of 1756, and the Gannandoxe of 1676 mentioned
in the *Histoire de l'eau-de-vie en Canada*. The MS. map, 4044B, No. 43,
has a note stating that the western end of Lake Ontario is infested by Gan-
tastogeronons (Andastes?). Colden's map (1747) shows three villages, probably
Toronto, mouth of Credit, head of the lake.

of the Crane." This is the first time that the Humber appears as the Toronto River, and with the establishment of the Missisaugas at the mouth of the river we emerge into the era which preceded Simcoe; for the Missisaugas are the tribe which sold to the government the site of the city of Toronto, and, as we shall see, they were on the ground in 1788 to dispute with the first surveyor the limits of the purchase. It is likely that the Missisaugas established themselves on the site of the Seneca village of Teiaiagon on Baby Point; a site which has yielded proofs of long and varied occupation both before and after the coming of the white man. There are indications also that the Missisaugas had a village on the opposite side of the river. Possibly they alternated for sanitary reasons between these desirable sites, both of which commanded the Carrying-Place. But whether we place the Missisauga village of Toronto on the east or the west bank of the river, the name Toronto as the designation of a permanent settlement became now for the first time localized on Lake Ontario.

There are several references in the records of this period to the magnitude of the trade which was being carried on by the Indians of the upper country with the English at Albany or Orange,[1] and much of it must have come by way of the Carrying-Place. At the war-feast held in Montreal in August, 1711, the Indians from the upper country hesitated to raise the hatchet and to join in the war song in Onontio's name because they had all been trading with the English.[2] In 1717, Alphonse de Tonti, while crossing Lake Ontario on his way to Niagara, encountered nine canoes all going to Albany to trade; and two days later he fell in with seventeen more, all full of Indians and peltries and bound on the same errand.[3] In spite of the re-establishment of Fort Frontenac, the French had not yet solved the problem of excluding the English from the lakes; the English continued to divert a large portion of the fur trade

1 WRAXALL, *New York Indian Records*, McIlwain, Introduction.
2 SEVERANCE, *An Old Frontier of France*, Vol. I, p. 174.
3 Ibid., p. 178.

to Albany.   To the Marquis de Vaudreuil, Governor of Canada from 1703 to 1725, belongs the credit of the temporary success of the French on Lake Ontario.   The Governor's first experience of conditions in the upper country had been obtained when he accompanied Denonville on his memorable but fruitless expedition against the Senecas in 1687.   Vaudreuil had probably seen with his own eyes the value of the Toronto Carrying-Place and had had an opportunity of discussing with Father Enjalran the necessity of closing that approach to Michilimackinac.   As we shall presently see, store-houses were built simultaneously in 1720 in Quinte, Niagara and Toronto under instructions from Vaudreuil, and there is evidence that he had long had these projects in mind.   The post at Toronto, established in 1720, was thus a belated fulfilment of the post proposed by Denonville in 1686 and ascribed by Margry to Father Enjalran.   The solution of the problem of French ascendancy on Lake Ontario is to be credited, however, not so much to the foresight of the governor as to the astuteness of his subordinates, Joncaire and the younger Longueuil, who had been adopted by the Iroquois as "their children," and lived among them and were gradually able to obtain an ascendancy which the English were unable to shake.   Joncaire's story, so far as it is known, has been told by Severance.[1]   It is to be hoped that the researches of M. Aegidius Fauteux will reveal still more about this elusive agent of the French, who now assumes a new importance for local historians as the first governor or superintendent of the post established at Toronto in 1720.   Joncaire had married an Indian wife and through his popularity with the Senecas he obtained permission for the French to build at Niagara. Whether formal permission was given for the post at Toronto or not, it is to be observed that in 1726 the Senecas claimed the ownership of the land on the north shore of Lake Ontario opposite Niagara.[2]

From the lists of engagements of *voyageurs* in the district of

1 SEVERANCE, *An Old Frontier of France*, Vol. I, Chaps. X and XI.
2 Ibid., Vol. I, p. 252.

Montreal[1] a good deal is to be learned about the condition of the
fur trade on Lake Ontario in the early years of the eighteenth
century.   The number of those *voyageurs* whose destination
was Fort Frontenac or other parts of Lake Ontario is exceedingly
small.   Traders went to Michilimackinac, to the Illinois, to the
Mississippi and to Detroit, but it is not till 1702 that there is any
mention of Fort Frontenac or Lake Ontario.   In that year
Joseph de Fleury de la Gorgendière engaged ten *voyageurs* to
make the trip to Fort Frontenac and, we may assume, to trade
about the lake.   In 1703 eight men and one woman were
engaged to go to Fort Frontenac.   There is no further mention
of Lake Ontario till 1716, when we encounter names of great
interest in the history of Toronto.   On March 15, 1716, Jean
and Alexandre Dagneau-Douville and others engaged themselves
to Jean Baptiste Maurisseau to make the trip to *fond du lac,
autour du Katarakouy et au fort des Sables.*[2]   There is no further
mention of Lake Ontario in the *voyageur* agreements for several
years.

Jean and Alexandre Dagneau-Douville belonged to a family
very active both as soldiers and traders in the lake country and
the Ohio Valley, and since two members of the family were on
several occasions closely connected with Toronto, further
genealogical details are desirable.   Michel Dagneau-Douville,
the progenitor of this family in Canada, submitted evidence of
noble birth to the Intendant on June 25, 1708, and his claim
was allowed.[3]   He had come to Canada as an officer in the
marines, but did not rise above the position of ensign; he does
not seem to have been a very active individual.   His sons, on
the contrary, played a varied and important part in the rough
life of the west and possessed that vigour which so often accompanies the second generation of pioneers.   They were Jean

1 *Rapport de l'Archiviste de la Province de Québec*, 1929-1930, p. 195.
"Répertoire des Engagements pour l'ouest conservés dans les Archives
judiciaires de Montréal (1670-1778)" par E.-Z. Massicotte.

2 Ibid., p. 218.   Maurisseau was official interpreter.

3 *Rapport de l'Archiviste de la Province de Québec*, 1930; *Lettres de
Noblesse, I*, p. 127.

Dagneau-Douville, born 1694, Alexandre Dagneau-Douville, born in 1698 and known as the Sieur Douville; Philippe, born in 1700 and known as the Sieur de la Saussaye; Louis-Césaire, born 1704 and known as the Sieur Dagneau de Quindre; Guillaume, born 1706 and known as the Sieur Dagneaux de Lamothe. Of these brothers, whose surnames are so varied and perplexing —and the reader will find others listed in Tanguay—Alexandre and Guillaume served as officers in the troops; the others do not seem to have served.

In 1716, when Jean and Alexandre Dagneau-Douville appear for the first time in Lake Ontario, the elder, Jean, was a young man of twenty-two and Alexander was eighteen. Their engagement bound them to go to the *fond du lac* and, since this term was applied at this time not only to Burlington Bay but to Toronto, we may conclude that their chief destination was the latter place and that their employer intended to trade at the foot of the Toronto Carrying-Place. This is the first occasion of a definite visit to Toronto since Denonville's visit in 1688. Many of the maps of the period are inaccurate in their delineation of the western end of the lake; confusion seems to have arisen as to where the actual *fond du lac* was to be placed. In fact, the Iroquois prevented any proper survey of Lake Ontario till de Léry's survey of the south shore in 1728 and the north shore in 1744. Four years later, when a permanent post was built at Toronto, the post was officially known at first as *le fond du lac*, "the bottom of the lake." No more is heard of the Douvilles in Lake Ontario till 1720; but there is evidence that trading went on regularly between 1716 and 1720 at the mouth of the Toronto river although no buildings were erected there till the latter year. There is evidence, too, that the English from the south of the lake were trading along the north shore to the great annoyance of the French.[1]

Meantime Vaudreuil had been nursing his project of permanent posts around Lake Ontario. In 1716 he addressed the following request to the Regent: "The Marquis de Vaudreuil

1 *New York Colonial Documents*, Vol. IX, p. 976.

supplicates your Royal Highness to be pleased to permit him to establish among the Indians such posts as he will find adapted to the good of the service without being obliged to give notice beforehand, but merely to render an account thereof and of his reasons for establishing them, otherwise he will be obliged to postpone the establishment of these posts for two years, which might be very prejudicial."[1]   In the same year it was pointed out to the Council that the English also intended to establish posts and that it would be of advantage to forestall them by building posts in several places.   Vaudreuil received specific permission to establish the post at Niagara should the Iroquois desire it.

There is a letter from de Ramezay and Bégon to the Minister which describes conditions on the lake in 1715.[2]   The letter is from Quebec and is dated November 7, 1715:

M. de Longueuil has informed us on his return from the villages of the Iroquois that a small establishment is necessary north of Niagara on Lake Ontario about 100 leagues from Fort Frontenac, seven or eight days distant by canoe.   This post would prevent the Missisagnis and the Amikoes from going to trade with the Iroquois when they come back from hunting about Lake Erie.   But if His Majesty approve this establishment the trade must be for the King and the post must be managed as at Fort Frontenac, from which goods and necessary merchandise will be sent.   He proposes also to build a ship for transport from one post to the other, and thinks this would be a sure means of conciliating the Iroquois and obtaining most of the furs which go to the English which would be very profitable for His Majesty.   If this post were established we could in a measure prevent the *coureurs-de-bois* from trading in Lake Ontario by confiscating their goods and arresting them; the trade which they carry on being very injurious to that at Fort Frontenac. . . .   Three canoes of Mississages established at the foot of the lake Ontario about 100 leagues from Fort Frontenac and twenty from Niagara came down last May to Montreal on the invitation of the Sieur de St. Pierre who wintered among them; none of this tribe had

1 "M. de Vaudreuil to the Duke of Orleans, Regent, February, 1716." *New York Colonial Documents*, Vol. IX, p. 870.
2 *Archives des Colonies,* CII A, Vol. 35, pp. 43-44, 48-50.

come down for eight years. They told the Sieur de Ramezay that they had not come because of the dearness of the goods and the refusal to supply them with *eau-de-vie*. They gave him a handsome pipe and promised to come every year and smoke it. They assured him that Onontio was always their Father and that they would rather trade with the French than the English if the price of the goods were closer, and if they could get *eau-de-vie*, which they said they could not do without; and that if they could not get it at Fort Frontenac, where they could go in four or five days, they would go to Orange for it though it would be 70 leagues by land.

There was all the more need to grant the Indians what they demanded since it was in this village that the English from Orange had intended to establish themselves in order to be able to reach the Ottawa tribes from there. And they would have done so had it not been for the protests of the Sieur de Ramezay to M. Hunter the governor of New York as he had the honour to inform you, my Lord. Providentially, he replied to the said Sieur de Ramezay that he would acquaint the said merchants of Orange of his decision to oppose this enterprise and that he would tell them that he was right in having the goods confiscated of those who should go to the said village since, this village being on the north of this lake, they must not go there until the boundaries had been settled; and that it was on this occasion that the said Sieur de Ramezay had given instructions to the Sieur de Sabrevois and to the Sieur de Maunoir, his son, to pillage the goods of the English whom they might find in the upper country. . . . .

(Signed) DE RAMEZAY
BÉGON.

This letter, written during the absence of Vaudreuil in France, embodies the policy of the governor for the protection of the trade on the lake, and suggests that the first proposal for a post at Toronto was mooted in 1715, and that it was Longueuil who made the suggestion. Severance is, I believe, mistaken in making the first part of this letter refer to Niagara.[1] The

---

1 SEVERANCE, *An Old Frontier of France*, Vol. I, p. 175; Mr. Severance seems to have consulted the abridgement of this document which appears in the *New York Colonial Documents*, Vol. IX, p. 874, where marginal notes make it apparent that the authorities in Paris understood that a post at Niagara was recommended. The original document proves that the reference was to Toronto or to a village nearer the end of the lake.

expressions, "north of Niagara on Lake Ontario" and "this village being on the north of this lake" and "in order to be able to reach the Ottawa tribes from there," seem to refer to Toronto. It is certain, however, that at this time there were Missisaugas at other points as well as at Toronto, though their chief village was at the latter place. The Amikoes were the remnant of a tribe once resident about Lake Nipissing.

It is to Durant,[1] the renegade chaplain of Fort Frontenac, that we are indebted for our first definite knowledge of the existence of a *Magasin Royal*, or king's shop, at Toronto in 1720. Durant was present at Niagara in 1721 as a virtual spy in the English service. He describes himself as "a French Récollet priest of Huguenot family long desirous to leave his order and change his way of life and religion." In the same year, on the thirteenth of June, Durant abandoned his post at Fort Frontenac and, accompanied by an Indian guide, made his way to Albany, where he presented himself to Governor Burnet and conveyed to him a written record of what he had seen and heard at Niagara. Governor Burnet despatched him to the Lords of Trade in London with a recommendation that he be rewarded for his information, and no more is heard of him. Durant's memorial is to be found in the fifth volume of the *New York Colonial Documents*. There is no reason to doubt its authenticity, although the document is evidently a translation and nothing whatever has been discovered about its author. A Father Durant was rector in Annapolis, N.S., between 1704 and 1711; he was taken prisoner by the English and brought to Boston; in 1731 he was back in Quebec; nothing is known of him between these dates. Father Durant, born in 1699, was killed at Kaskaskia in 1724, according to Tanguay. As the archives of the Récollets are not available and are said to be in confusion, information must necessarily be incomplete. The name and office may even have been assumed as a protection from the consequences of espionage.

Durant's memorial contains the following statement: "In

1 "Durant's Memorial," *New York Colonial Documents*, Vol. V, p. 588.

the year 1718 came orders from the court of France to establish a Trade for the benefit of the King in the circuit of Lake Ontario and there to build Magazines as well upon the North as the south sides thereof." Durant proceeds to narrate for the benefit of Governor Burnet how he himself, in company with the Sieur de Joncaire, journeyed from Fort Frontenac to Quebec in 1720 and received instructions from Vaudreuil relative to the conduct of affairs in the Niagara region. They arrived in Quebec on September 3rd.

The next day the Sieur de Joncaire received orders to return immediately to Niagara with the title of Commandant which was given him for the first time. There was joined to this new dignity the inspection of the Magazine established in the Lake of Ontario. This Magazine is situate on the West of the Lake for the Trade with the Missasague, otherwise called the Round Heads, distant about thirty leagues from that of Niagara. The house at the bottom of the Lake was built by the Sieur de Anville (*sic*) a little after that of Niagara. Sieur D'Agneauz built also one on his side of the North of the Lake in the bottom of the Bay of Quinté to trade with the Outaouais. Quinté is about thirty leagues from the Fort Cataracuoy. They leave to winter in all their posts one Store Keeper and two Soldiers.

The Sieur de Joncaire, with whom Durant was so familiar, was the elder Joncaire. Father and sons, the Joncaires had been established among the Senecas for twenty years. It was through the influence of the elder Joncaire that the French succeeded at last in securing a foothold on the Niagara. In the end of May, 1720, a "Royal Magazine" was built on the site of the village of Lewiston, to be succeeded in 1725 by the stone house at the mouth of the river. According to Durant, Joncaire returned to Niagara in the spring of 1721 with the title of Commandant, and with the added duty of the inspection of a "magazine situate on the west of the lake for the trade with the Missasagues." This house, he tells us, was built a little after that of Niagara, that is, in June or July of 1720. There can be no doubt that the magazine referred to was at

Toronto.   By the shore, Toronto is approximately thirty leagues from Niagara.

That the French had a post at Toronto in 1727 and 1728 is confirmed by documentary evidence.[1]   That they had a post at *le fond du lac Ontario* between the years 1720 and 1726 is also well authenticated.   We shall now see that these two posts were identical and, that prior to 1726, the French were accustomed to allude to Toronto as *le fond du lac*, and that after that time this name was dropped and the post became known as Toronto.   A closer examination of the evidence is desirable.

Durant, in his memorial, informs us that definite orders came from France to establish posts, "as well upon the North as the south sides of Lake Ontario."   It is probable that the court designated the places where the magazines were to be erected, and what more likely places than Quinte, the abandoned site of the Récollet mission, and Toronto, already familiar from the explorations of La Salle and from the fact that Louis XV had always before him the Toronto Carrying-Place, clearly indicated on the great bronze globe constructed in 1690 for Louis XIV by the geographer, Coronelli.[2]   Since Durant describes a magazine situated "on the West of the Lake for the Trade with the Missasague otherwise called the Round Heads distant about thirty leagues from that of Niagara," it has hitherto been supposed by Severance and others that this magazine was at Burlington Bay.   Durant's description,

1 Consult also *Archives des Colonies,* CII A, Vol. 45, pp. 200-202 : "Estat des Pelleteries provenant de la Traitte faite au fort frontenac, à Niagara et dans le fonds du Lac Ontario pendant les années 1722 et 1723. . . . Gages des Employez pour la Traite."

2 "In the Grand Salon of the Ducal Palace at Venice in 1872 there was a large terrestrial globe some four feet in diameter, made in 1690 . . . Toiouegon was distinctly marked with the word 'portage.' "   Miss Lizars, *Valley of The Humber,* pp. 16, 17 ; Margry, II, p. 276. Demande de Renseignments pour tracer le cours de l'Ohio sur le globe terrestre de la bibliothèque du Roi. . . . "On travaille en cette ville à des globes qui ont quinze pieds de diamètre, dont on veut faire present au Roy. . . . On a peine encore à mettre sur ces globes la rivière d'Ohio dont vous avés marques la cours dans vostre carte.   On seroit bien aise de sçavoir s'il y a de bons fondemens de la marquer comme vous avez fait." . . . Lettre de M. de Tronson à l'abbé de Belmont, Paris, 2 juillet, 1682.

however, can apply only to the mouth of the Humber, which is thirty leagues from Niagara by the shore.   Nor does his next allusion to the magazine as "at the bottom of the Lake" destroy this theory.   M. d'Aigremont, reporting on the condition of the trade at the various posts for the year 1727, describes the post at Toronto as "a leasehold at the foot of Lake Ontario exploited in the King's interest in past years as a dependency of Fort Niagara."[1]   If M. d'Aigremont could describe Toronto in 1727 as "at the foot of Lake Ontario," then the references in the records of the period between 1720 and 1726 to the post at *le fond du lac* must refer to Toronto.   In these accounts, Frontenac, Niagara and *le fond du lac* are grouped together. After that date *le fond du lac* disappears and Toronto takes its place.   Again, it is to be observed that M. d'Aigremont in 1727 describes Toronto as a dependency of Fort Niagara; this would agree with the powers conferred upon Joncaire in 1720.   In 1729 the President of the Navy Board, writing to M. Hocquart,[2] speaks of the post at Toronto as a post "which *for all time* has been carried on as dependency of Fort Niagara."   In many of the maps of the period Lake Ontario appears without any indentation at the west end; the shore is made to run in a northerly direction from the mouth of the Niagara River.   To the French at Fort Frontenac, Toronto would be in the west of the lake, and since the Toronto Carrying-Place led from there to Lake Huron, it might properly be described as the *fond du lac*.   On no map which has come under my observation is there any indication that the French ever had a post at Burlington Bay.   Nor could they have hoped for much trade at that point in comparison with the trade drawn from the region to which the Toronto Carrying-Place gave access.   The country to the west of Burlington Bay would be adequately served by the post at Detroit.   It would hardly have been worth while for the French to establish a post at Burlington Bay for the benefit of the few Missisaugas who lived there and for the sake of the

1 SEVERANCE, *An Old Frontier of France*, Vol. I, p. 271.
2 *Archives des Colonies*, Série B, Vol. 53-2, pp. 338-9.

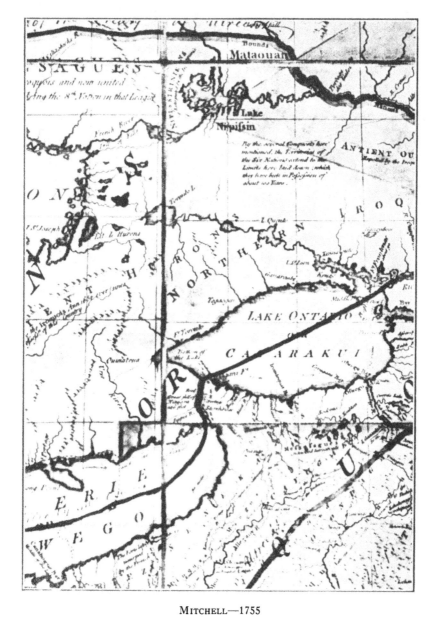

MITCHELL—1755

This map belongs to the group which placed Fort Toronto in the *Fond du Lac* or Bottom of the Lake.

traffic which occasionally passed over the Grand River Portage. With the English from Albany it was another matter.   There is reason to think that they intended early in the eighteenth century to place a post at the end of the lake.   But final and conclusive proof of the identity of *le poste du fond du lac* with *le poste de Toronto* is to be found in an extract from a legal document discovered by M. Fauteux among the unpublished notes of the Abbé Faillon.   This document is entitled *Cession du poste du fond du lac par le Sieur de la Saussaye—II aout 1728;* in the body of this document the post is described as *le poste de Toronto.*[1]

To return to Durant.   He tells us in his memorial that the Sieur Douville spent the winter of 1720 and 1721 with another Frenchman alone in the bark cabin at the mouth of the Niagara gorge waiting for Joncaire, who did not arrive till spring.   On May 19, 1721, Charles Le Moyne, Baron de Longueuil, the Lieutenant-Governor of Montreal, with an important retinue, which included Chaplain Durant, arrived at Joncaire's house at Lewiston.   Longueuil was under orders to visit the Senecas, to distribute presents and to thank them for permitting the erection of the *Magasin Royal*.   The distinguished company of Frenchmen gathered for diplomacy and pleasure on this occasion at the mouth of the Niagara River was still further augmented on the twenty-first by the arrival of the Jesuit, Charlevoix. Charlevoix has enriched Canadian literature and history by his *Histoire de la Nouvelle France*, the materials for which he collected during his first residence in Canada between the years 1705 and 1709.   He had returned to Canada in 1720 to report on the best route for an overland expedition in search of the western sea.   He visited the western posts and returned to France by way of Mobile.   Charlevoix tells us nothing of Toronto, but Bellin's map, which accompanies Charlevoix's *Voyage dans l'Amérique Septentrionale*, is remarkable for its accurate delineation of the shores of Lake Ontario and especially of the two trails leading from the mouths of the Humber and

1 See p. 86.

the Rouge to Lake Simcoe.   On his arrival at Niagara, Charlevoix would meet Joncaire and the Sieur Douville, who would
have accurate knowledge of the north shore.

The day after Charlevoix's arrival, a party which included
Chaplain Durant set out from the mouth of the Niagara River
and turning west made their way along the north shore to
Fort Frontenac.   Durant, in his memorial, writes:

> Monsieur de Cinneoil & Mr. de la Cavagnale had undertaken
> the voyage only out of Curiosity of seeing the fall of water at
> Niagara.   Mr. de Laubinois, Commissary of the Ordinance,[1]
> had orders to take an account of the effects remaining in the
> Magazine at the Fort of Cataracuoy, of the Post of Niagara,
> and of the Bottom of Ye Lake, and of that of Quinté, which he
> executed in making the Tour of Lake Ontario   .   .   .   On the
> 22nd, M. de Longueuil departed for to go to the Seneka villages
> with the Sieurs de Joncaire and La Chavinerie. And (he
> repeats himself) we embarked the same day, M. de Cinneoil,
> Monsieur de Cavagnale, Mr. de Noyen,[2] M. de Laubinois &
> myself for to return to Cataracuoy by the North side of the
> Lake Ontario we having come to Niagara by the south side.[3]

There is no document in existence showing that the king
ordered the construction of posts at Quinte, Niagara and
Toronto in 1720, as claimed by Durant, but there is a letter
approving of Vaudreuil's initiative in sending Joncaire to build
Niagara, which approval amounts to an *ex post facto* order.[4]
There seems no reason to doubt Durant's statement that the
post at Toronto was built in 1720, as we have statements of

---

1 i.e. *Commissaire Ordonnateur.*

2 SEVERANCE, *An Old Frontier of France*, Vol. II, p. 229.

3 *New York Colonial Documents*, Vol. IX, p. 590.

4 Consult, *Archives des Colonies*, CII A, Vol. 41, pp. 156-157. M. Bégon
in making his report for the trade at Fort Frontenac for the year 1717, which
he had forgotten to send in 1718, remarks: "La traitte du Lac Ontario et
celle du fort Frontenac sont tellement confondues qu'on n'en peut faire
aucune distinction, ainsy que le Conseil a marqué le souhaitter, parce que
toutes les marchandises traittées *dans ces deux postes* sortent du même
magasin." Ibid., Vol. 40, pp. 28-29, "Vaudreuil et Bégon au ministre 26 octobre,
1719"; Ibid., Vol. 42-2, pp. 273-274, "Mémoire du Roy aux Srs. Vaudreuil
et Bégon, Paris, 2 juin, 1720."

CHARLEVOIX-BELLIN—1744

The most accurate of the printed maps.

DANVILLE—1755

This remarkable map of the Huron country appeared a century after the expulsion of the Hurons. The mapmaker has moved the R. de Taronto and the L. Taronto too far to the east. This map is the source of the mistaken statement that the name "Toronto" was applied to the Trent Valley region.

goods sent there in 1722-1723,[1] as to a regular post, and the appointment of a permanent clerk during the same year at a salary of 350 *livres*, without mention that it is a new establishment. The clerks at Frontenac received 900 *livres*, the clerk at Niagara 400, while the clerks at Toronto and Quinte each received 350 *livres* for the years 1722 and 1723. Six soldiers were employed to assist in the trade at the various posts and received 30 *livres* apiece. The profits of the trade for two years were 5,700 *livres*, 11 *sous*. As the accounts for all the posts on Lake Ontario were included in one schedule, it is impossible to estimate the comparative importance of these places.

The *Magasin Royal*, built by Joncaire at the foot of the Niagara portage at Lewiston in 1720, soon became a blockhouse, forty feet by thirty, musket-proof, with portholes and surrounded by a palisade. The house built at Toronto by the Sieur Douville was, no doubt, a similar structure, possibly with an attic in which to store trade goods and the peltries acquired in exchange. Since the Niagara *Magasin Royal* was placed at Lewiston at the foot of the portage, there is every reason to believe that the Toronto *magasin* was similarly situated. Two sites suggest themselves: one at the mouth of the Humber on the site afterwards occupied by Rousseau's house; the other on Baby Point, where the remains of a palisade were observed in the eighties. The latter site is also the site of Teiaiagon. When Portneuf in 1750 built his first fort at Toronto, he built it, as we shall presently see, not on the site marked by the monument on the Exhibition Grounds, but on the east bank of the Humber.

I have before me a schedule of goods offered in exchange for the furs of the Indians at the four posts on Lake Ontario in the year 1726.[2] The number and variety of the items suggests that these frontier posts of two centuries ago resembled the

---

1 Ibid., Vol. 45, pp. 195-199: "Etat des vivres munitions et marchandises qui ont été traitées au fort frontenac, à Niagara, au fond du Lac Ontario et à la Baye de Quinté pendant les Années 1722 et 1723. . . . Fait à Québec le trentième octobre, 1723.—Bégon." Ibid., pp. 200-202.

2 Ibid., Vol. 48, pp. 243-248, "Dupuy au ministre, 26 octobre, 1726."

country shops of to-day; they sold everything from buttons and shirts and ribbons to combs, knives, looking-glasses and axes; flour and lard, pepper, prunes, raisins, olive-oil, tobacco, vermilion, powder and shot, caps of various sizes all mingled confusedly in this curious inventory.   It is plain that even in 1726 Toronto had assumed that commercial character which still distinguishes her inhabitants.

Having established and stocked these emporiums, the authorities were naturally impatient of competition, whether it came, as it often did, from the English in New York, or from unlicensed *coureurs-de-bois* from Quebec.   In 1726 the Intendant Bégon issued the following regulation:

Concerning the illicit trade in the neighbourhood of the posts on Lake Ontario and Lake Erie pertaining to the King.— Being informed that several private individuals are carrying on trade in Lake Ontario, Lake Erie and other places to the prejudice of that carried on for the King at Fort Frontenac, at Niagara, at the foot of Lake Ontario (Toronto) and elsewhere, we forbid all persons to trade in the aforesaid lakes Ontario and Erie, in their environs or anywhere else, on pain of confiscation of canoes, merchandise and the peltries with which they are laden, and a fine of five hundred *livres*, to which the said traders will be liable as well as those who outfit them; the said fines being awarded to those who lay the information or to whom it shall seem suitable, and the merchandise shall be confiscated to the profit of His Majesty.   And to this intent we order that all those passing Fort Frontenac, Niagara and the other posts where the trade is conducted for His Majesty, whether on the way up to the Upper Country or on the way down from the said country, shall be required to present to the store-keepers or other officers in charge of His Majesty's trade in the said posts, the licenses under which they go up, and on their return to present the same licenses granting them permission to go to the Upper Country; and if they fail to present the said licenses, we instruct the said store-keepers and other officers in the said posts, to seize the said canoes, goods and peltries and to draw up indictments to be forwarded us for execution.   We beg those in charge of the said store-keepers and others employed in the same trade always and as often as they shall be required to do so, to keep all traders and those also under their authority in hand in the execution of this ordinance, which will be issued in due form, published and posted in the cities of Quebec, Three-Rivers and Montreal, for the information of all. Ordered and done at Quebec the fourteenth day of September one thousand seven hundred and twenty-six.[1]

This edict was one of the last of the official acts of the Intendant Bégon, as the following despatch to the Minister was among the first official communications of his successor, the Intendant Dupuy. Both documents are concerned with the same subject, the difficulties of the trade on Lake Ontario. Dupuy's despatch bears the date of October 20, 1726, one month after the edict issued by Bégon, who was at the moment on his way back to France. The Intendant Dupuy wrote as follows:

My Lord,
    I have the honour to send you herewith the statement of account of the skins purchased at Fort Frontenac and at Niagara and at the *fond du lac Ontario* (Toronto) and also of the provisions, merchandise and munitions given in exchange for the said skins, by which you will see, My Lord, by a comparison of the profits of the sale of these skins and the goods given in exchange, transport to Fort Frontenac and wages of clerks employed in the trade, that there is a loss of 5003 *livres* 18 *sld*. Those which could not be sold have been put back in the warehouses of the King and will not make up the loss of the 5003 *livres* 18 *sld*. This trade has been so bad only because all spring and a part of the summer the English were in the neighbourhood of Niagara and secured all the best skins there. There have also been *coureurs-de-bois* from Montreal who have wintered in the trading ground of Fort Frontenac; they have done much harm there. Added to all this there has been a great decline in the price of skins.
    I have the honour to be with profound respect, my Lord,
          Your very humble and very obedient servant,
                                              DUPUY.
Quebec the 20th October 1726.[2]

1 *Ordres des Intendants*, 1726-1727, pp. 1-2.
2 *Archives des Colonies*, CII A, Vol. 48, pp. 243-248. "Dupuy au ministre, 20 octobre, 1726."

The simultaneous establishment in 1720 of magazines at Toronto, Quinte and Niagara, in addition to Fort Frontenac, had given notice to the English that the French intended to close Lake Ontario to their rivals and to secure all the profits of the lake trade for themselves. For a short time these efforts were successful. The profits of the trade at New York declined almost one-half. It was not long till the challenge was accepted. The energetic Burnet, Governor of New York, protested the post at Niagara, and by erecting a fortified stone house at Oswego in 1726 he established the first English permanent post and settlement on the lakes; and again the French were unable to prevent the Indians from going to Albany to trade. That the efforts of the French were futile is apparent from the report of the younger Longueuil to his father, the baron, in 1725, concerning his mission to the Onondagas; he wrote that he had seen more than a hundred canoes on Lake Ontario making their way to Oswego. And returning from Onondaga he encountered many canoes, propelled by Nipissings and Saulteurs from the Huron regions, making their way into Lake Ontario by the Toronto river and all headed for the mouth of the Oswego. He was of the opinion that the new *barques* which the French were constructing at Fort Frontenac would put a stop to this.[1]

In their turn the French now endeavoured to frustrate the English at Oswego by the erection of a more permanent structure at Niagara. In 1725 the Intendant Bégon notified the Minister that, in view of the importance of doing everything to prevent the English from driving the French from Niagara, he had determined to build two *barques* at Fort Frontenac to serve in case of need against the English and to serve also for carrying materials to Niagara for the erection of a stone fort. These vessels were not in commission till the spring of 1726, when they began the task of transporting stone and other building material to Niagara. On October 17, 1727, de Léry was able to report to the Minister that the stone house at Niagara was

1 SEVERANCE, *An Old Frontier of France*, Vol. I, p. 265.

entirely finished and surrounded with palisades to protect it from the savages. The French had now realized their dream of a permanent fortress on the Niagara River. From the erection of Fort Niagara there is a thread of continuous history which runs down to the present. This building, the oldest in America west of the Mohawk, is still standing and has recently been restored to the condition in which the French maintained it. From its windows the visitor may look out across the lake —as its isolated garrison did two centuries ago—and recall in imagination the feeble trading post at Toronto, which remained during all its history, whether as magazine or fort, an outpost and dependency of the great fort at Niagara, whose fall in 1759 was the occasion of national rejoicing in Great Britain. Nor did the connection of Toronto with Niagara terminate then; for another fifty years the connection was maintained under British auspices and it was from the mouth of the Niagara River, while Fort Niagara was still in British hands, that Simcoe sailed in 1793 to establish a town destined to become the capital of the new Province of Upper Canada on a site which had borne the name of Toronto for at least a century. The poet, Moore, had ample justification for attaching the epithet "old" to the name when he wrote in 1804,

> Where the blue hills of old Toronto shed
> Their evening shadows o'er Ontario's bed.

Oswego, or, as the French called it, Chouéguen, began at once to be a serious competitor. It was found necessary to lower the price of goods in the king's posts on Lake Ontario to a dangerous point in order to retain the trade. The profits began to shrink and disappear. It was decided to adopt the policy of leasing the posts.[1] Graft and incompetency seem to have ruined the enterprise from the first. In 1727 we find Beauharnois complaining of Dupuy's management of the posts.

1 Ibid., Vol. I, p. 265-276.

Under the date of September the 20th, he wrote to the Minister:[1]

That was his (Dupuy's) first manoeuvre at Montreal; the second was not to my taste, having found it contrary to the good of the service. He has leased for four hundred francs the post at Toronto to a young man who is not at all fit. M. d'Aigremont to whom M. Dupuy sent the lease for signature refused to sign it, saying that he would speak of it to the Intendant. He did so, representing to him that it would do much injury to the trade at Forts Frontenac and Niagara. In spite of that he sent the lease back to him the next day to make him sign, which he refused. The Intendant went on just the same. M. d'Aigremont to whom I spoke about the matter told me his reason was that a man of the city had offered a thousand crowns (about $600) for it some years ago, and M. de Longueuil told me the same thing two days later in his office; M. d'Aigremont was there at the time.

The person who secured this very advantageous lease at Toronto was Philippe Douville, Sieur de la Saussaye; we shall see presently that he secured also the post of *garde-magasin* at Niagara, and that the appointment provoked a scandal.

Dupuy seems to have appealed to the President of the Navy Board. We have the latter's reply under date of May 18th, with reference to the lease at Toronto.

I agree with you that the leasing of the Post at Toronto ought not to prejudice the trade at Forts Frontenac and Niagara, but it seems to me that the price of 400 *livres* a year at which you have leased this post is very moderate since several years ago a man offered 3000 *livres* for it, which makes me sure that you have been overreached. You ought to put right what could have been avoided if you had consulted M. d'Aigremont, who has been in the country for twenty-eight years and knows it well. Besides, it would not be right to lease this post without first informing M. le Marquis de Beauharnois, on account of the Indians.[2]

1 *Archives des Colonies*, CII A, Vol. 49-1, pp. 98-99. "Beauharnois au ministre, 20 septembre, 1727."
2 *Archives des Colonies*, Série B, Vol. 52-1, p. 143. "The President of the Navy Board to Dupuy, May 18, 1728."

A copy of this letter seems to have been sent to M. d'Aigremont. On October 15, 1728, M. d'Aigremont wrote to the Minister from Quebec.

My Lord, I have received your letter of the 18th of May last to M. Dupuy. The letter being almost entirely concerned with the differences between M. le Marquis de Beauharnois and M. Dupuy, I have nothing to reply. I had the honour to explain to you in another letter that the lease of the post at Toronto was very prejudicial to the trade at forts Frontenac and Niagara carried on there for the King, and the reasons that there are for cancelling the lease given by M. Dupuy which had still a year to run. I have the honour to be very respectfully and gratefully My Lord, your very humble and very obedient servant,—D'AIGREMONT.[1]

There is no mistaking the tone of this letter. D'Aigremont was an old and experienced official, thoroughly acquainted with the Indians and the fur trade. Dupuy, the Intendant, was a man of ability, who during his brief period of office was involved in constant quarrels with the Governor and the Bishop. Both Beauharnois and Dupuy assumed office in 1726, and neither of them could have known very much about conditions on Lake Ontario. Beauharnois continued in office as Governor for twenty-one years. Dupuy was superseded in 1728. The quarrel between the two officials over the Toronto affair was terminated by instructions from France to cancel the lease. M. d'Aigremont, finding that Dupuy had not only leased the post at Toronto at a nominal rate to Douville, but had in addition appointed the same person store-keeper or *garde-magasin* at Niagara, drew the attention of the Minister to this impossible situation in his report on the trade of the various posts for the year 1728. M. d'Aigremont's report, to which he refers in his letter of May 18, 1728, has been preserved, as well as the reply addressed to M. Hocquart, the Intendant, by the

1 *Archives des Colonies*, CII A, Vol. 50, p. 131, "M. d'Aigremont au ministre, 15 octobre, 1728."

President of the Navy Board, which bears the date of April 19, 1729.[1]

In his report M. d'Aigremont explained that there had been incompetency at Niagara and that the official in charge of trade at Niagara, Le Clerc, had died and had left his accounts in confusion, and that he was afraid he would have no better report to give for the following year:

M. Dupuy having sent to Niagara to replace the Sieur Le Clerc, a man who is scarcely able to read and sign his name, notwithstanding representations which I have made regarding it. This man is Rouville la Saussaye (*sic*), to whom was leased last year the post at Toronto for one year for 400 *livres*.   He still has that lease which is not compatible with his employment as clerk (*commis*) and store-keeper (*garde-magasin*) of Niagara. This lease-hold which is at the foot of Lake Ontario and which has been exploited in past years in the King's interest as a dependency of Fort Niagara, ought not to be leased to the store-keeper in charge of trade at Niagara, because of the abuses which may spring from it—this man may send off to the Toronto post the Indians who come to Niagara, under pretext that he has not in the storehouse there the articles they ask for.   Furthermore he might make exchanges of good peltries for bad ones, and besides he could intercept all the Indians in Lake Ontario and so utterly ruin the trade at Forts Frontenac and Niagara.

The result of these representations was the cancelling of the lease at Toronto; and since the post does not appear again in the reports for the period, it may be inferred that the schemes of M. Douville were responsible for its abolition.   In 1750 it reappeared as Fort Toronto.[2]   The text of the order will be given in the original French:

Je vous observeray que le Poste de Toronto qui est dans le fonds du Lac Ontario et qui a esté de tout Temps Exploité pour

---

1 *Archives des Colonies*, Série B, Vol. 53-2, pp. 338-339.   "The President of the Navy Board to Hocquart, April 19, 1729: 'Je vous observeray que le Poste de Toronto qui est dans le fonds du Lac Ontario et qui a esté de tout Temps exploité pour le Compte du Roy. . . .' "

2 Fort Toronto was seldom called Fort Rouillé.   The name appears only once or twice in official documents.   On the maps it is always Fort Toronto. The place was Toronto long before the fort built by Dufaux in 1750-1751.

le Compte du Roy comme dependant du fort de Niagara a esté
donné a ferme par M. Dupuy en 1727 et 1728 moyennant 400
livres par an au nommé Douville.   M. d'Aigremont m'a marqué
a ce Sujet qu'aprés la mort du Sr. Le Clerc qui estoit commis au
Poste de Niagara M. Dupuy avoit donné cette Commission à
Douville qui ne Scait ny lire ny écrire et par consequent hors
d'Etat de l'exploiter, que dailleurs il y avoit incompatibilité
entre cette Commission et la ferme de Toronto à cause des
abus qui pouvoient s'ensuivre en ce que la personne qui ex-
ploiteroit ces deux Postes pourroit renvoyer au poste de Toronto
les Sauvages qui Iroient travailler à Niagara, sous pretexte
qui'il n'auroit pas dans ce magazin ce qu'ils demanderoient, que
d'ailleurs ils pourroient échanger toutes les bonnes pelleteries
contre de mauvaises, qu'il pourroit aussy arrester à Toronto
tous les Sauvages du Lac Ontario et par ce moyen ruiner les
Traites de Niagara et de frontenac toutes ces raisons l'ont engagé
a retirer ce Commis du Poste de Niagara et à Supprimer la ferme
de Toronto; ce que j'ai aprouvé, vous agirez Sur le mesme
principe.[1]

The President of the Navy Board seems to repeat the
phrases of M. d'Aigremont, but there are one or two variations;
the name of the holder of the lease at Toronto, M. d'Aigremont
calls him Rouville la Saussaye; the President of the Navy Board
speaks of him as "a man called Douville."   According to the
former, this person was "scarcely able to read and to sign his
name"; according to the latter, "he could neither read nor
write."

M. Aegidius Fauteux, Librarian of the Public Library of
Montreal, has placed at my disposal the following extract from
a deed drawn in 1728 between Philippe Dagneau de la Saussaye,
the holder of the lease at Toronto and the clerkship at Niagara,
and his brother, Alexandre Dagneau Douville.   M. Fauteux
informs me that the extract is taken from manuscript notes of
the Abbé Faillon, but that the abbé or his scribe had not thought
it worth while to mention where the original was to be found;
it is probably buried in the Montreal Archives.   The extract
bears the number (74) with the heading, "August 11, 1728—

1 *Archives des Colonies,* Série B, Vol. 53-2, pp. 338-339.   "The President
of the Navy Board to Hocquart, April 19, 1729."

Transfer of the post at the head of the lake by the Sieur de la Saussaye," and reads as follows:

We the undersigned, Alexandre Dagneau Douville and Philippe Dagneau, have agreed in good faith to the following, to wit: that I, de la Saussaye, not being able myself to exploit the lease of the post at Toronto for the year commencing July 2nd, last, on account of the employment which I have at Niagara, and not being even free to withdraw my effects from the said post, to have them returned to the Sieur Desruisseaux who has stayed for the trade and to have them brought to this city to satisfy my engagements, of my own accord and under the good pleasure of Monsieur l'Intendant transfer and hand over to Douville all my rights and claims in the said lease as much for the year ending the 2nd of July last as for the current year from the same date and in consequence arrange and dispose at his discretion conjointly with the Sieur Desruisseaux that he shall have a share in the interests of the said lease as well as in the beaver skins and furs which are actually received by the Sieur Desrivières.

Have appeared (before me) the Sieurs Alexandre and Philippe Douville, the Sieur Julien Trottier Desrivières mentioned in the above agreement who have stated and admitted that they have made the above bargains and agreements.

As we have already seen, the Sieur de la Saussaye was not able to retain his lease at Toronto.   His efforts to continue the exploitation of that post by delegating his rights to his brother were not successful.   The illiteracy of the Sieur de la Saussaye was probably exaggerated.   M. Fauteux is of the opinion that he has seen some of his letters among the manuscripts of St. Sulpice and that they are no worse than those written by his contemporaries.   Alexandre Douville, his brother, became an ensign in the army in 1735 and eventually became captain. He was in command of the garrison of Fort Toronto when it was abandoned and burned in 1759.

Severance, in his *Old Frontier of France*, Volume I, p. 184, makes the suggestion that the builder of the post at the head of the lake, whom Durant in his memorial calls the "Sieur de Anville," and the builder of the post at Quinte in the same year, whom Durant calls "the Sieur d'Agneaux," and the "Sieur D'Ouville" who, according to Durant, spent the winter of 1720 and 1721 at the *Magasin Royal* at Lewiston in company with the young La Corne, are the same person. This is an assumption which may or may not be true. If true, it would still leave us in doubt as to the builder of the magazine at Toronto in 1720. Durant may have meant the same person in each case, but still there would be nothing to indicate which member of the Douville family was intended. The members of the Douville family bore a variety of appellations which make identification difficult. The Sieur Michel Dagneau Douville is described in a document of 1734 as "*Sr. Dagneaux Douville Enseigne en second*"; he was an inferior officer in the Marine troops serving in Canada. In that year he was permitted to retire from the service and his commission was transferred to his son, Philippe Dagneau de la Saussaye, by mistake,[1] the latter not being in the service; this mistake was rectified next year and another son, Alexandre Dagneau Douville, was appointed. The father of the Douvilles, the Sieur Michel Dagneau Douville, had, as we have seen, a large family of sons. The builder of the post at Toronto may have been the father, the Sieur Michel Dagneau Douville, or any one of the three elder sons, Jean, Alexandre or Philippe. Until further information is forthcoming, it is not possible to accept or disprove Severance's suggestion,[2] and the name of the builder of the first post at Toronto must remain in doubt, except that he was a Douville.

What influence Philippe Dagneau de la Saussaye was able to bring to bear upon the Intendant Dupuy does not appear. The terms on which he obtained a lease of the post at Toronto, and his subsequent appointment as *garde-magasin* at Niagara,

1 *Archives des Colonies*, Série B, Vol. 61-1, p. 107.

2 M. Aegidius Fauteux has corrected some of the mistakes made by historians in regard to the Douvilles: "Philippe Dagneau de la Saussaye, who died about 1754, was never an officer, and Alexandre Douville, who was an officer, was not killed, but died in his bed in Montreal about 1773. The Dagneau who was killed in 1755 was a son of Philippe Dagneau de la Saussaye."

led to a change in the administration of the post. His subsequent career deserves a more extended notice. Closely associated on several occasions with both the elder and the younger Joncaire, it is not quite certain whether he is to be regarded as a confidential agent of the government of the Joncaire species, or as a simple trader. There is evidence that the governor, Beauharnois, employed his services on several occasions, and that his influence with the Indians, especially the Chaouenons or Shawnees, made him an important person in the wilderness. Such men were indispensable to the French in their efforts to control the interior. If La Saussaye never attained the same importance as Joncaire, like de Rocheblave and Rousseau, who will come into the story a little later, he played a useful part in the control of the tribes.

After 1730, Philippe, known as La Saussaye, and his brother, Alexandre, seem to have been engaged in the fur trade at Green Bay and among the Miami. In 1730 he was at Detroit, and in 1731 at the River St. Joseph. From 1735 to 1743 he was continuously employed among the Chaouenons on the Ohio. At this time the latter were established on the Ohio some miles below the modern city of Franklin. It was to this region that the elder Joncaire was despatched after he had finished his work among the Senecas and had enabled the French to establish themselves at Niagara. The Joncaires and La Saussaye were pioneers on the Ohio, preparing the way for the formal occupation of the Ohio Valley in 1749. In 1735, oddly enough, La Saussaye was employing Jean Rousseau *dit* St. Jean among the Chaouenons, probably the same Rousseau who was later established at Toronto. In 1736 we find La Saussaye and the elder Joncaire partners in some trading enterprise on the Ohio. In 1739 La Saussaye conducted a band of Shawnees to Montreal for a conference with Beauharnois, and on this occasion he brought with him the news of the death of the elder Joncaire at Niagara. In 1739 Beauharnois employed La Saussaye in connection with a migration of the Shawnees and in the autumn of that year he was wrecked on Lake Ontario and the Governor

commended him to the Minister.[1] In 1749, when Céloron led
his famous expedition into the Ohio region, it was La Saussaye
who served as guide over the Chautauqua portage. The names
of La Saussaye and of his brother, Alexandre Douville, are
attached to the statement of independence made by the Iroquois
chiefs at Quebec in 1749. It is plain that they had great
influence with the Shawnees and with the Iroquois. Possibly
he was the M. Douville to whom the Hurons of Detroit gave the
name *Andououtore*. It is to be noted that it was the Shawnees
who contributed most to the defeat of Braddock, and that
Tecumseh belonged to this tribe. Evidently the work was
well done and La Saussaye, whether he was the builder of the
first post at Toronto or not, was a person of some consequence
in the wilderness. His name will remain associated with
Toronto.

The effect of the English post at Oswego had been felt at
once.[2] The profits of the French in 1725 were less than a third
of what they had been in 1724. Again in 1726 the English had
the best of it; the French sustained a loss of 5,000 *livres*. After
the building of the stone house at Niagara, matters improved,
but only temporarily. The competition of unlicensed traders
from Quebec and the English colonies, and even as far as
Louisiana, and the French prohibition of the liquor trade,[3] made
it difficult for intendants alternating between energy and
slackness to show a profit. The region was rich in furs. A
schedule of furs received from the Lake Ontario posts in 1727
enumerates 7,124 skins of a great variety of animals, of which
the beaver far outnumbers the rest. It was, in fact, chiefly
for the skin of this animal that the trade was conducted, a
beaver skin being worth twice as much as a bear or an otter.

1 In November, 1739, Beauharnois, in a letter to the Minister remarked,
"Le Sieur Douville de la Saussaye que j'avais chargé de nos ordres chez les
Chouanons pour l'execution de mon projet. . . ." *Rapport de l'Archiviste de
la Province de Québec*, 1922-1923, p. 186.

2 SEVERANCE, *An Old Frontier of France*, Vol. I, p. 220.

3 "The one thing that killed the trade at Niagara and Frontenac was the
restriction put upon the sale of brandy." Severance, *An Old Frontier of
France*, Vol. I, pp. 267-268.

Since the most valuable beaver hunting-ground was north of the lakes, it is a fair deduction that much of this trade came from Toronto.[1]

Following the dispute about La Saussaye's lease of the post at Toronto, the name "Toronto" disappears from the records. For the twenty years between 1730 and 1750, there was not, so far as is known, a regular post at Toronto.   The place continued to be served from Niagara.   The English from Oswego probably came frequently to the foot of the Carrying-Place, and we know from the complaints of the French that the Missisaugas were frequent visitors at Oswego.   On October 1, 1728, Beauharnois intimated his intention of adopting measures which would render Oswego or Chouéguen useless to the English; he proposed to issue orders obliging the canoes of the *voyageurs* on their way down from the upper country to pass along the north shore of Lake Ontario.   It became customary after 1739 to insert in the licenses of those traders who obtained permission to go to the upper country the words, "*défense de prendre d'autre route que celle du nord du lac Ontario.*"   Between 1739 and 1748 I have found fifty *congés* in which these words appear.   There must have been many jolly parties at the mouth of the Toronto river during this period.

Early in the forties the fur trade in Lake Ontario was leased for a period of six years to the French Company of the Indies, and under this company the lessee of the trade was the Sieur Chalet.   In the summer of 1743 Chalet made the round of Lake Ontario to learn the requirements and conditions of the trade.   There was at this time no establishment at Toronto, but Chalet sent to Toronto that summer several *voyageurs*, who camped at the mouth of the Toronto or Humber River and carried on a considerable trade with passing Indians, most of whom, had they not found the French there, would have gone with their furs to Oswego.[2]   In 1746 Chalet relinquished his lease of the Lake Ontario posts.

1 SEVERANCE, *An Old Frontier of France*, Vol. I, p. 273.
2 Ibid., Vol. I, p. 388.

In 1749 the younger de Léry, acting under instructions from Galissonnière, made a journey from Montreal to Detroit, making astronomical observations at certain points along the route. The party was under the command of Captain de Sabrevois, who was on his way to assume command at Detroit; it consisted of traders and several families intending to settle there. On the afternoon of the 29th of June, the canoes came to shore at the mouth of the Rouge. Embarking again about midnight, they reached Toronto Island towards dawn. Here they breakfasted, and, resting again at the mouth of the Credit, they reached the end of the lake that night. The first of July they were wind-bound, but on the second they paddled fourteen leagues and reached Niagara. As they made nineteen leagues on the thirtieth, they could not have stayed long at Toronto, where they did not enter the river, nor at the mouth of the Credit, where they ate their dinner. At the Credit, de Léry found a village of Missisaugas and gathered some inaccurate information which led him to suppose that the foot of the trail from Lake Huron was at that place. In his diary he suggests the establishing of a trade-house at the mouth of the Credit to prevent the Indians from the north going to Chouéguen. On his return to Quebec, on the twenty-fifth of September, de Léry found that Galissonnière had set sail for France. He made four copies of his report, one of which he handed to Jonquière, the new governor, another he forwarded to Galissonnière, another to the Minister of Marine, and the fourth he retained. On the ninth of October Jonquière wrote to the Minister, recommending the establishment of a post at Toronto.[1]

In the autumn of 1728, Chaussegros de Léry made a map of Lake Ontario which is preserved in the archives of Laval University, Quebec. This map has the following legend attached to the Oswego River, *R. Chueguen ou des Onontagues ou se sont établis les Anglais.* There is nothing to show that there were any establishments along the north shore of the lake at that time, except at Kenté and the mouth of the Humber. At the

1 *Rapport de l'Archiviste de la Province de Québec,* 1926-1927, pp. 334-348.

latter place the village of Teiaiagon is indicated, though mis-spelt, "Terraiagon," and wrongly placed on the west bank of the river.   In the map which de Léry drew in 1744, he tells us that in the earlier map he had embodied the results of an exploration of the south shore; he had not at that time explored the north shore.   In the 1744 map the Humber appears as R. Toronto.

VI

FORT TORONTO OR FORT ROUILLÉ: 1750-1759

EVEN in a record of fact, imagination may occasionally be permitted to point a contrast and to emphasize the rapidity with which great changes have taken place. Brûlé, at the mouth of the Humber in 1615, beheld a scene which bore no resemblance to the summer pageantry of Sunnyside. The Humber of Hennepin and La Salle is now the Humber of golf clubs and dance-halls. Douville's first magazine of 1720 could only faintly prophesy by the variety of its wares the palatial shops of to-day. Toronto has forgotten Teiaiagon. But nowhere is the contrast between what is and what has been more striking than in the grounds of the Canadian National Exhibition, where a monument was erected in 1878 on the site of Fort Rouillé. Here, where world championships are won and the wealth of half a continent is annually displayed, the more reflective may remember that two centuries ago French couriers paused on their way from Louisiana to Quebec, and the Missisaugas brought in the scalps of their English enemies south of the lake and claimed their reward. An inscription on a huge boulder contains these words:

This monument marks the exact site of Fort Rouillé, commonly known as Fort Toronto . . . established A.D. 1749 . . . on the recommendation of the Count de la Galissonière 1747-1749. Erected by the corporation . . . 1878.[1]

This inscription is at fault. Fort Toronto was built by the Marquis de la Jonquière, and the fort on the site indicated by the monument was the second fort and was not completed till the spring of 1751.

As we have seen in the preceding chapter, Oswego, or

1 This is the inscription on the boulder marking the original site; the monument bears the following: "Fort Toronto, an Indian Trading Post, for some time known as Fort Rouillé, was established here A.D. MDCCXLIX by order of Louis XV."

Chouéguen, had become a formidable menace to the French
trade. It is to this fact that Fort Toronto owed its origin, or
rather its re-establishment. Although English traders had been
active at Oswego for more than twenty years, the French had not
been awake to the reality of the menace. They were now faced
with a much more desperate struggle. The building of Fort
Toronto, intended primarily as an offset to Oswego and as a
place at which to sell liquor to the Indians, was also part of a
much more ambitious scheme conceived by the Comte de la
Galissonnière for the possession of the Ohio Valley and the
exclusion of the English from the west.[1]

Hardly had the Count arrived in Canada, according to the
anonymous author of the *Mémoire du Canada*, when he embarked
upon the project of defining and determining the limits and
boundaries of the French possessions in North America. His
design was just; but the interests of the colony demanded
peace, and as the Comte de la Galissonnière succeeded in
imposing his views upon the French Court and upon his successor, the Marquis de la Jonquière, his policy must be held
responsible for the outbreak of hostilities in America long before
the formal commencement of the Seven Years War in Europe.
It was in 1749, the year after the Peace of Aix-la-Chapelle,
that the Comte de la Galissonnière sent one of his officers,
Céloron de Blainville, to establish the claims of the French to the
Ohio River and the region which it drained, and it was in the
autumn of the same year that the Marquis de la Jonquière, his
successor, intimated to the Minister in Paris his intention of
establishing a post at Toronto.

The new post did not actually come into existence till the
next year, and the part which it played in the history of the
dramatic years which preceded the capture of Quebec is entirely
insignificant; but the remote origin of a great modern city
cannot be without interest, and if the actual events which

1 "After the conquest the importance of Oswego steadily waned: the
last remaining trader was driven out in 1778. . . . For a few years after
the conquest the trade at Oswego exceeded that at any other point on the
continent." Cruikshank, *Transactions Canadian Institute*, 1891-1892, p. 261.

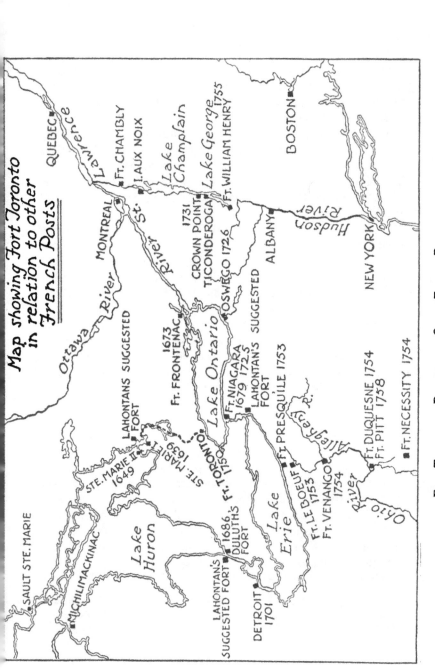

Map showing Fort Toronto in relation to other French Posts

QUEBEC
St. Lawrence
Ft. CHAMBLY
I. AUX NOIX
Lake Champlain
Lake George 1755
Ft. WILLIAM HENRY
BOSTON
MONTREAL
St. River
Ottawa River
1731
CROWN POINT
TICONDEROGA
OSWEGO 1726
ALBANY
Hudson River
NEW YORK
1673
Ft. FRONTENAC
LAHONTANS SUGGESTED FORT
Lake Ontario
Ft. NIAGARA 1679 1725
LAHONTAN'S FORT
SUGGESTED
Ft. PRESQU'ILE 1753
Allegheny R.
Ft. DUQUESNE 1754
Ft. PITT 1758
Ft. NECESSITY 1754
SAULT STE. MARIE
STE. MARIE II 1649
STE. MARIE I 1639
Ft. TORONTO 1750
MICHILIMACKINAC
1686's
DULUTH'S FORT
LAHONTAN'S SUGGESTED FORT
Lake Huron
Lake Erie
DETROIT 1701
Ft. LE BOEUF 1753
Ft. VENANGO 1754
Ohio River

FORT TORONTO IN RELATION TO OTHER FRENCH POSTS

transpired in the neighbourhood of Toronto at this time are of no
historic importance except to the student of local history, the
inhabitants of this lonely post were spectators of a series of
episodes which determined the destiny of the American continent.   In 1753, Washington, still an unknown young officer,
was sent to protest the incursion of the French into the valley
of the Ohio, and in the next year was forced to surrender
ignominiously to de Villiers, brother-in-law of Captain Douville
of Toronto.   In 1755 occurred the disastrous defeat of General
Braddock, and a year later Oswego fell to the French.   In
1757 Montcalm captured Fort William Henry, and then came
calamity, for in the next year Louisbourg and Fort Frontenac
and Fort Duquesne all fell to the English.   In 1759 Fort
Niagara was taken by Johnson, Ticonderoga and Crown Point
by Amherst, and then came the battle of the Plains of Abraham
and the end.   Such was the martial panorama unrolled on
distant horizons for the feeble garrison of Fort Toronto during
the troubled years of its existence.   As we shall see, echoes of
these events reached the lonely trading-post in the wilderness;
Indian runners carried news quickly, and there were Missisaugas
from Toronto in the army of Montcalm.

While the name of Fort Toronto hardly appears in the
military annals of the period, everything that transpired at
Toronto was connected in one way or another with the distant
struggle and reflected the current of events.   That de la Galissonnière included the post in his plan for the control of the
lakes and the west seems probable from the account contained
in the *Mémoire du Canada*, and since the writer of this document,
after describing the re-establishment of the post, proceeds at
once to the question of the control of the Ohio Valley, it is
apparent that Fort Toronto in his judgment was part of this
ambitious policy.

Here is what the *Mémoire* has to say:

The English had built upon the south shore of Lake Ontario
a fort which they called Oswego, or in Indian, Chouaguin.
The situation of the place was very advantageous, for it was in

the midst of the country of the Five Nations and it attracted them to it and kept them in check. For though we had Niagara on the same side of the lake and Frontenac on the other, these two forts were not sufficient for the needs of the savages; they did not find there the *eau-de-vie* and the rum which they were accustomed to find at Couaguin or Chouaguin, and this was a very great disadvantage. The priests had made the sale of liquor a matter of conscience, and had placed it among the sins that incur excommunication. They had the Governor on their side so that it was a crime to sell it. This was a good rule in the towns where the savages might indulge in license and so stir up trouble; but it is quite a different matter at the posts. It is the liquor which attracts the Indians and thanks to the drink Chouaguin had maintained itself and we had against us the tribes who resorted there. The Governor thought that the re-establishment of Fort Toronto would catch all the Mississaugas and the tribes of the North who passed that way on their road to Chouaguin; and as M. Rouillé was the Minister of Marine it received the name Fort Rouillé. This fort was directly opposite Fort Niagara. It had a palisade and mounted four small cannon. A large quantity of merchandise was sent up yearly. The commandant was instructed to maintain a good understanding with the savages and to divert them from trading at Chouaguin.

The author of the *Mémoire* then proceeds to remark that the Governor, having assured himself in this direction, began to think of enforcing the prohibition of English trading in the Ohio Valley which the Comte de la Galissonnière had sent M. de Céloron to proclaim.

While it was apparently the restless and ambitious de la Gallissonnière who conceived the project of a fort at Toronto, it was the penurious Marquis de la Jonquière who put the project into execution. Jonquière's despatch to the Minister, informing him of his intention to erect a fortified trading-post on the site of the former magazine of the king, bears the date of October 9, 1749.[1] It is of special interest since it indicates that the Intendant Bigot, who also signed the document, was

1 *Archives des Colonies,* CII A, Vol. 93, pp. 46-47.

already watching with attention this new opportunity for enrichment. It begins:

Quebec Oct. 9 1749.

On being informed that the Indians from the north generally stop at Toronto on the west side of Lake Ontario 25 leagues from Niagara and 75 from Fort Frontenac on their way to Chouaguen with their furs, we have felt it would be advisable to establish a post at this place and to send there an officer, fifteen soldiers and some workmen to build a small stockaded fort. The expense will not be great for there is timber at hand and the rest will be brought by the Fort Frontenac boats.   Too much care cannot be taken to prevent the said Indians from continuing their trade with the English and to see that they find at this post all that they need as cheaply as at Chouaguen.

We shall permit some canoes to go there on license and shall employ the funds for a gratuity for the officer in command.

Instructions will have to be given to those in command at Detroit, Niagara and Fort Frontenac to be careful that the traders and shopkeepers in these posts furnish goods in future at the same price as the English for two or three years.   In this way the Indians will lose the habit of going to Chouaguen, and the English will be forced to abandon the place.   If anything else occurs to us likely to hasten the downfall of Chouaguen we shall act.

LA JONQUIÈRE,
BIGOT.

Jonquière would have established other trading-posts on Lake Ontario and still others on Lake Erie. He has been accused, perhaps falsely, of an interest in the liquor trade.[1] He had to be content with the new post at Toronto. "More posts," wrote the President of the Navy Board, "would mean merely more expense and a scattering of the forces of the colony." In 1750, traders at Toronto were warned not to encroach on the territory tributary to Niagara.

It was not till the fifteenth of April, 1750, that M. Rouillé

---

1 The author of the *Mémoire du Canada* accuses Jonquière of complicity in the liquor trade with the Indians: "Débaucher les nations, telle était la politique des deux gouvernements. . . . Il était temps que M. le Marquis de Jonquière mourut." *Rapport de l'Archiviste de la Province de Québec*, 1925, p. 102.

approved the project of the new post at Toronto; his reply did not reach M. de la Jonquière in Quebec till the early summer. Meantime the Governor, assuming the approbation of the Minister, had given instructions early in the spring of 1750 to proceed with the construction of the fort. The officer entrusted with this task was M. Pierre Robineau, the Chevalier de Portneuf, an ensign in the marines on duty at Fort Frontenac, who was ordered to Toronto with a sergeant and four soldiers. Portneuf belonged to an old and distinguished French family, and had it not been for the British conquest, he would in all probability share with the Douville of 1720 the honours usually accorded to the founders of cities. The builder of Fort Toronto was the second son of René, third Baron de Portneuf and a descendant of that Maître Pierre Robineau, "councillor of the King and treasurer of the light cavalry of France," who in 1651 had been suggested as Governor of New France; although the first Baron de Portneuf did not become governor, he shared with M. de Longueuil the distinction of being among the first to be ennobled in New France. M. Pierre de Portneuf, the founder of Fort Toronto, was born on August 9, 1708, at Montreal; he held the rank of ensign in the marines when instructed to proceed to Toronto, and attained his captaincy in 1757. Later Portneuf saw considerable service in the Ohio Valley, where he was in command of Presqu'Ile from 1756 to the fall of Niagara. The winter of 1756-1757 was severe; provisions ran short at Presqu'Ile, and Portneuf despatched a sergeant and forty-three men to subsist on the bounty of Fort Niagara, which was itself none too well stocked with provisions. Montcalm records in his journal: "M. de Portneuf carried too much brandy and too little flour."[1]   He was not at the defence of Niagara; for some reason he remained at Presqu'Ile where it had been his task to assemble the Indians of the west. After the fall of Niagara we find him sending a flag of truce to Johnson, and a little later burning Presqu'Ile and retiring along with the garrisons of other French posts to Detroit. In 1761 he sur-

1 *Journal du Marquis de Montcalm,* pp. 195-196.

rendered to the British and, in company with many others who were reluctant to take the oath of allegiance, he embarked in the autumn of that year at Quebec on the *Auguste* for France. On November 15th this unfortunate vessel, described by the Abbé Faillon as "a floating Babylon," on account of its cargo of swindlers and grafters, was wrecked on the coast of Cape Breton, and of her 121 passengers, 113 were drowned, including the Chevalier de Portneuf.

On May 20, 1750, de Portneuf arrived at Toronto. The Intendant Bigot, acting in concert with the Governor, de Jonquière, had dispatched at the same time from Montreal a party with the necessary goods for the trade at the new post, which was to be a King's Post. Teiaiagon had disappeared, but there was a village of Missisaugas somewhere near the mouth of the Humber, then known as the Toronto River. It is likely that the Missisauga Toronto, which is shown on the Johnson map of 1771, was either on Baby Point or on the west bank of the Humber above the Old Mill. De Portneuf began at once, and in less than two months a small palisaded enclosure had been erected and a small storehouse, in which to store the King's goods. On July 17, 1750, M. de Portneuf and the trader sent thither by Bigot left Toronto, the former for Fort Frontenac and the latter for Montreal. During their brief sojourn of less than two months, they had obtained seventy-nine bundles of peltries, valued at 18,000 *livres*. Portneuf's small fort erected in 1750 was called Fort Toronto. It is now known that it stood, not on the site subsequently occupied by Fort Rouillé at the foot of Dufferin St., but on the east bank of the Humber. There is no record that it was burned in 1759, and it is quite possible that this was the building subsequently occupied by the Rousseaus, whose site is well known.

A letter from Jonquière to the Minister, written from Quebec, August 20, 1750, gives further details and informs the Minister of his intention to build another and a larger fort at Toronto. The trade had far exceeded expectations; Portneuf's Fort Toronto proved too small. To this second fort Jonquière

asked permission to give the name Fort Rouillé. The new
fort was not built on the old site, but it continued to be known,
except occasionally in official documents, as Fort Toronto.
The name Fort Rouillé does not, I think, occur on any contemporary map. Jonquière wrote:[1]

My Lord,
    I learned by your honoured letter of April the 15th last that
you approve the proposal which I made to you in the letter
signed by myself and the Intendant on the 9th of September last
for the establishment of a post at Toronto. I have the honour
to submit an account of the trade there.
    To avoid expense to the King I undertook to instruct the
Sieur Chevalier de Portneuf, ensign on duty at Fort Frontenac
to report at Toronto with a sergeant and four soldiers. He set
out from the said fort on the 20th of May last, and at the same
time a clerk appointed by the Intendant left Montreal with
the goods necessary for the said trade for the King.
    On his arrival at Toronto the Sieur de Portneuf had his
men build a small stockaded fort and a small house for the
safe-keeping of His Majesty's effects. He remained there with
the said clerk till the 17th of July last. The said Sieur de
Portneuf then left to rejoin his garrison and the clerk-trader
went down to Montreal with the bales of furs.
    They traded with most of the tribes who called at the said
post. This trade has not been altogether bad; they made
seventy-nine bales valued at about eighteen thousand *livres*.
    The trade-clerk assures us that he would have made more
than 150 bales if he had had more cloth, *eau-de-vie* and bread
for the Indians, and this would have been provided had we
expected such success.
    Since the tribes from the north have promised the said
Sieur de Portneuf to come next year in much greater numbers
and to give up the English altogether, it is very essential, my
Lord, to profit by their friendliness and to establish the said
post firmly.
    The house which the Sieur de Portneuf had built is too
small and it might have been feared that the King's effects
would not have been safe in as much as the large numbers of
Indians of various tribes who will probably go there to trade
next year (most of whom have been guilty of the worst conduct

1 *Archives des Colonies*, CII A, Vol. 95, pp. 171-177.

during the late war) could easily overpower the Sieur de Portneuf and plunder all the goods.

To avoid any risk I shall have built a double-staked fort (*fort de pieux doubles*) with curtains of eighty feet not including the gorge of the bastions, with a lodge for the officer on the right side of the gate of the fort, and a guard-house for twelve or fifteen soldiers on the left.

The warehouse will be along the curtain facing the entrance; the trade-clerk will lodge there; a bakery will be built in one of the bastions.

This fort will be placed on the point of the bay formed by the peninsula (*Sur la pointe de la Baye de la Presqu'Ile*) at about a quarter of a league to the north of the Toronto river where the boat (*la barque*) from Fort Frontenac can anchor safely quite close to land and bring there all that is needed for the fort and for the trade. A pilot who has navigated before in the said river undertakes to bring the boat there without any risk. This anchorage is sheltered from all the winds except from the south where it could be protected by having a small pier built.

It is of importance that this fort should be finished early in the year so that the Sieur de Portneuf can move there in the month of April with his party. It is certain that the trade will be best if we are there early. In view of this the Intendant and I have despatched a carpenter with three men to cut and square the timber. The trade-clerk has gone with them, also a baker, a tanner and five or six hired men to help him in the trade which he will be able to carry on during the winter with about ten Indians who are good hunters and live in the neighbourhood of the said post.

During the autumn I shall have delivered by ship planks from Fort Frontenac and by *bateaux de cent* the provisions, merchandise, liquors and other necessaries, so that there may be no lack at the said post.

In this way the said fort will be built without trouble and there is room to hope that this establishment will be in every way profitable. My Lord, I beg your approval, for my naming it hereafter Fort Rouillé. Your honoured name will attract in great numbers all the tribes, and will give it all the importance we should wish.

In fact all the tribes from the north who go to Chouaguen and pass the said post will be stopped there; and finding in abundance all that they need and especially *eau-de-vie* and cloth, they will naturally do their trading there and not go to Chouaguen.

The English will be deprived of the visits of these Indians and will find from that time a great decrease in the revenue which they have been accustomed to draw from their furs. This might help hereafter to make them give up the said post which would become useless.

Besides, if we succeed in making these tribes trust us and have nothing to do with the English, on the one hand we shall be quiet and nothing will hinder the French in their trade in the north; and on the other hand it will be very easy to persuade these tribes that it is in their interest not to allow the English to have a post at all beside them because they are enemies always at hand to harm them; and little by little we shall be able to make the Indians decide to destroy Chouaguen by force of arms. They are malicious, and once they form a decision, they are sure to carry it out.

The destruction of Chouaguen is a powerful motive for which I neglect nothing to accomplish its downfall one way or another. I am in earnest about this, but in time of peace I can do no more than try to bring over to our side the tribes loyal to the English.

I venture to assure you, my Lord, that if unhappily we should have a new war with them, Chouaguen would have to be well defended to prevent my becoming master there, having devoted myself to find out all I can about this post.

I am, with deep respect, my Lord, your very humble and very obedient servant,

LA JONQUIÈRE.

Four days later Jonquière again wrote to the Minister:

The pass at Toronto is not the only one which the savages from the north use in resorting to the English, they employ also the portage at the Sault Ste. Marie situated at the entrance to Lake Superior. This post has been almost neglected hitherto and as we can draw great advantages from it, especially by stopping these tribes and preventing them from going to trade at Chouaguen, I am determined to have it guarded.[1]

This extract is an indication of the wide circuit from which Oswego drew its trade and of the remote tribes who crossed the

1 *Archives des Colonies*, CII A, Vol. 95, pp. 178-179, Ibid., Série B, Vol. 91, p. 86.

Carrying-Place. From the days of Rooseboom and Mac-Gregorie, the Dutch and English of Albany had hankered after the trade with the Ottawas of the upper lakes. The Dutch were using the Toronto Carrying-Place before the French had Fort Frontenac on Lake Ontario, and it is of interest to note the large number of Dutch names among the first inhabitants of York.

It is at this point that a great deal of light has been thrown upon the history of the building of the second Fort Toronto by a series of documents recently discovered by M. E.-Z. Massicotte in the Archives of the District of Montreal. By the courtesy of the learned Archivist, I have been able to consult the original documents, but since the *résumé* published by M. Massicotte in *La Presse*, Montreal, on April 1, 1933, contains everything of importance, I shall translate the essential parts of the published summary. After pointing out that M. de la Galissonnière had nothing to do with the construction of the fort, having left the country in August, 1749, and that it is from the letter signed jointly by MM. de la Jonquière and Bigot of October 9, 1749, that our first knowledge of the project is derived, M. Massicotte proceeds to make abstracts from the newly-discovered documents and to summarize the less important parts. It now appears that the small stockaded fort built by the Sieur de Portneuf in the spring of 1750 was erected on the banks of the Humber, or as it then was, the Toronto River; that this structure was not rebuilt but that an entirely new building was constructed during the winter and spring of 1750 and 1751 about three miles to the east of the original fort on the site made familiar by the monument erected in 1878; that Portneuf's stockaded fort of 1750 never bore the name Fort Rouillé, and that the second fort, although so designated by Jonquière, is more correctly denominated *le fort royal de Toronto*. The plans for the second fort were prepared in whole or in part by M. Rocbert de la Morandière, the king's engineer in Montreal, who was associated with M. Varin de la Marre, the commissary (*commissaire ordonnateur*), in the same city in

issuing instructions for its construction to Joseph Dufaux, a
contractor of Montreal, who was to erect the building at Toronto
under the oversight of M. Du Chouquet,[1] the shopkeeper at
Toronto. Dufaux arrived at Toronto in September, 1750, and
though hindered by illness went to work energetically. From
the first there was friction with Du Chouquet, who seems to
have done his best to alienate the workmen and to impede the
work. In the spring Du Chouquet dismissed Dufaux a month
before the completion of the fort; it would seem that the latter
was not paid for his work. In April, 1752, a year later, the
contractor, Dufaux, and several of his loyal workmen signed
a series of sworn statements before a notary in Montreal alleging
that the delay at Toronto had been occasioned by sickness
among the men, the obstinacy and interference of Du Chouquet
and the misconduct of the workmen, Delorme and Gascon, who
had sided with Du Chouquet, the shopkeeper. As nothing has
so far come to light giving the other side of this dispute, it is
not possible to apportion the blame; nor is it yet known whether
the contractor was successful in securing his money. The
counter-accusations against Dufaux seem to have been that
he was disobedient and engaged in the fur trade while at Toronto.

Since the records of this dispute shed light on many points
in local history, M. Massicotte's summary is given in translation.
The sworn statements are five in number and include the
allegation of Dufaux and the testimony of his workmen, as
follows:

1st. The statement of Joseph Dufaux, contractor, master
carpenter, husband of Marie-Anne Harel, residing at the
corner of St. Gabriel street and Ste. Thérèse street, Montreal.
(His son born in Montreal in 1752 took orders in 1778 and
became *grande vicaire* of the Bishop of Quebec at Sandwich,
Ontario, in 1785. He died there in 1796.)

1 According to M. E.-Z. Massicotte there were two Lefebvre Du Chou-
quets attached to posts on Lake Ontario in 1750 and 1752: first, Louis Joseph,
born 1704, store-keeper at Fort Frontenac between 1746 and 1752; second,
Pierre, born in 1702, brother of the preceding, who was store-keeper at
Toronto in 1750, 1751 and 1752. In 1731 Philippe Dagneau made an engagement with Louis Lefebvre Du Chouquet to go to the river St. Joseph.
(*Archives de Québec*, 1929-1930, p. 286.)

2nd.   The dispositions of Joseph Latour, master joiner of faubourg S.-Laurent, and of Joseph Roy, mason of the faubourg S.-Joseph.

3rd.   —Of François Latour, joiner apprentice of the faubourg S.-Laurent.

4th.   —Of Joseph Larche, master mason of the faubourg S.-Laurent, and of Pierre Du Plessis (Bélair), master tanner of Coteau S.-Louis.

5th.   —Of Sebastien Laville, carpenter of l'île Jésus.

Statement of the Sieur Joseph Dufaux.—April 14, 1752, Joseph Dufaux, contracting carpenter, signed a long statement which begins, "I am compelled to make known the truth that an effort was made to cause me to lose all chance of success during my stay at Toronto   . . ." We summarize the remainder of his record.

The Sieur Dufaux set out from Fort Frontenac in his *bateau* (in the summer of 1750). Among those who accompanied him there was a sick man which obliged Dufaux to replace him; he was not well himself.

The ninth of September Dufaux camped a long league on this side of the fort of M. Du Chouquet. The same day he went to visit the old fort (*le vieux fort*). Not having considered the place suitable, he came back by the woods, examining the ground. Next day, the tenth of September, having found a good place, he planted a stake and set all the men to work. His zeal in discharging his duty added to the fatigue which he had given himself caused an eruption with fever. Without a doctor or good food, he was very ill; in addition, at the same time eleven of his men took sick. All this did not decrease Dufaux's eagerness to do his duty. Remaining on his *bateau*, he oversaw all that was done.

"The work being in hand," Dufaux said to Delorme *fils*, "that it was not much to cook for the workmen," but Delorme *père* was not of this opinion.

From that time they leagued themselves with Gascon against Dufaux, drew over the storekeeper, Du Chouquet, to their side and did all they could to injure the contractor.

The eighteenth of November, M. Du Chouquet, setting out for Niagara with his wife, ordered six of M. Dufaux's men to accompany him. These men were absent thirty-two days. Soon after, he sent the same men to Fort Frontenac, and this voyage took seventeen days. Then Du Chouquet made Delorme and Gascon dig a useless ditch, etc.

These annoyances prevented the contractor, Dufaux, from putting up the commandant's house and the guard-house before the end of January. He began also four undertakings, namely, two curtains, the baker's house, the blacksmith's house and the gate of the fort.

At this moment a fresh revolt of Gascon and Delorme, who took with them a group of workmen. These malcontents injured the work done, cut the posts, etc., and all this in the sight of M. Du Chouquet.

Dufaux resolved to write to the commissary (Varin) to inform him, but on the order of the shopkeeper no one would take Dufaux's letters, even those addressed to his wife.

M. Dufaux attributed the commencement of the quarrel between the shopkeeper and himself to the fact that when he was sick he had asked M. Du Chouquet for some wine, knowing well that he had a barrel for the sick. Dufaux could get only a pint and his workmen none. Dufaux had brought some himself, and he was then obliged to use his own (for the workmen), although it had been promised to him. Furthermore, M. Du Chouquet borrowed eight cans of it from him from a barrel of sixteen cans, and for this gave him an order on his brother at Cataraqui. During an absence of M. Du Chouquet, a detachment commanded by M. de la Ronde[1] stopped at Toronto. This detachment needed provisions to return to Niagara, and he wanted some.

Now M. Dufaux had been forbidden to give provisions to any one; however, to get rid of a detachment which kept his men from working and to avoid all disputes with an officer, he let him take some.

M. Du Chouquet on his return made a noise about this.

Finally M. Du Chouquet ordered Dufaux to leave in three days. He proceeded to obey, the twenty-first of March, at a time when he hoped to finish all his work within a month, and to be able to have the honour of presenting himself with his workmen to pay his respects to the commissary and to M. de la Morandière.

Depositions of J. Latour, Tessier and Roy.—April 14, 1752. Joseph Latour, J. B. Tessier and Joseph Roy, engaged to work

1 M. MASSICOTTE has the following note: "I think the officer may have been François-Paul Denys de la Thibaudière, Sieur de la Ronde, but M. Ægidius Fauteux is of the opinion that it is rather Charles Denys de la Ronde, brother of the former, whose name is not in Tanguay. Charles became lieutenant in 1759, and was killed in the battle of Ste. Foye in 1760."

at their trade in the construction of the fort for the King called Fort Rouillé, otherwise called Fort Toronto, declare that M. Dufaux, although sick during the undertaking, left nothing undone to push forward the work vigorously.

The sole cause of the delay of the works was occasioned by the obstinacy of the shopkeeper, Du Chouquet, and by the men called Delorme and Gascon. The latter wasted time in useless undertakings.

That the Sieur Dufaux had not traded with the Indians, that he had not disposed of any of the effects of His Majesty, that M. Dufaux had given provisions to M. de la Ronde and his detachment, but that he did so to prevent the pillage of the store.

That it is true that M. Dufaux had some buck skins in his possession, but that he had been entrusted with them by a man named Arcand and another named Latulippe to take to Montreal.

Deposition of F. Latour.—April 16, 1752. François Latour declares that he has read the depositions of the Sieurs Dufaux, Joseph Latour, Tessier and Roy and that they agree with the truth, for the Sieur Dufaux showed himself in all his work at Fort Toronto a true and zealous servant of his prince.

That the cause of the disputes with M. Du Chouquet, with Delorme and Gascon, proceeded only from his freedom in finding fault with them when the works were neglected.

That M. Du Chouquet resorted to several devices to make the workmen admit that M. Dufaux was a trouble maker (*un séducteur*), but that none had been ready to agree.

That M. Du Chouquet had deceived the Récollet Father Couturier,[1] and that the latter believed wrongly that Dufaux was a rascal and a bad servant.

Depositions of J. Larche and of P. Duplessis.—April 16, 1752. Joseph Larche and P. Duplessis on their soul and conscience declare that all the above is true, that it is within their knowledge that Gascon and Delorme declared that they would set about making the Sieur Dufaux leave the fort and that he would not be master to boss them.

That after the departure of the Sieur Dufaux, M. Du Chouquet and others "tried to intimidate the workmen in the

1 Father Nicolas Albert Couturier, born at Montreal May 17, 1703, was almoner at Fort Frontenac from 1750 to 1752, according to our archives. E.-Z. M.

shop, saying that whoever took his part would lose his wages and even that someone would hang for it."

In spite of this, the workmen declared that M. Dufaux's conduct had been discreet and without reproach.

Deposition of S. Laville.—April 20, 1752. Sebastien Laville confirms all the above.

Before discussing the inferences which may be drawn from M. Massicotte's summary relative to the sites of the various posts at Toronto, one or two additional fragments of information, drawn from the documents themselves, must be included. It is plain that there were horses at Toronto, for there are two complaints in the depositions of the shortage of hay for the horses, as well as of provisions for the men. One at least of the buildings in the fort had a cellar, which had filled with water. M. Dufaux remarks that he would have finished the buildings in a month. He proceeds,

At the time of my departure from Toronto the storehouse was not finished, the officer's house was up, the guard-house was up, the four bastions were hewed (*taillé* I take to mean smoothed off with the broad-axe) except two flanks, on account of these annoyances. I took from my shop the few people who were not well and I hewed the fronts of the houses of the commandant in the enclosure, the chief part of the work, where all the windows and doors are, that of the shopkeeper and the guard-house, the two curtains and the two houses namely those of the baker and the blacksmith which I hewed entirely and a bastion, except the two flanks which were not hewed which is a small matter. (This was towards the end of March.)   Loss of time prevented me from hewing and raising the officer's house and the guard-house until the end of January as soon as there was some timber ready.

This, however, does not exhaust what is to be learned or inferred from M. Massicotte's documents. The journey from Fort Frontenac in canoes and *bateaux* would occupy eight or nine days. M. Dufaux would have with him his workmen and their tools and necessary supplies. Heavily loaded, he would proceed at once to the spot where the fort was to be built. From Jonquière's letter of August 20th, written from Quebec, we learn that the site of the proposed fort had been already selected. It was to be the point of land at the entrance of the bay formed by the peninsula. The only spot adjacent to this site where *bateaux* could anchor in safety was the mouth of the small creek somewhat to the east, known later as Garrison Creek. It was a small stream and has long since disappeared into a sewer. Here, on the ninth of September, Dufaux established himself. As he states that he camped *"une grande lieue en deça du fort de M. Du Chouquet,"* it is a reasonable assumption that M. Du Chouquet's fort, the small stockaded fort of Portneuf, was on the east bank of the Humber at the foot of the Toronto Carrying-Place, on the site occupied in the eighties and nineties by the house of the trader Rousseau. Forty years is not a long life for a log building if continuously occupied. Left alone, such a building speedily falls into decay. There was, however, intermittent trading at the mouth of the Toronto River from 1750 down to Simcoe's time, and Rousseau's father, who was at the river mouth in 1770, may have fallen heir to the old structure.

On this occasion we may conjecture that Dufaux, who was not himself very well, went by boat from his camp to what he calls the "old fort." He did this the day of his arrival. Not considering the place suitable, he returned through the woods, examining the ground, and the next day, having discovered a suitable place, he planted a stake and set all hands to work. Next day, owing to over-fatigue, he was sick.

There is just a possibility that by *le vieux fort* Dufaux meant not Portneuf's fort on the Humber mouth, but the site of the Douville post of 1720, whose history we have already traced from 1720 to 1730 and which must now be regarded as the first permanent settlement at Toronto. There is reason to suppose that this fort or post was at Baby Point on the site of the Seneca village of Teiaiagon, and further evidence will be awaited with interest. Meantime, it is sufficient to observe that de Léry, who was at Niagara during the period, indicates the post at Toronto by "Terraiagon," an obvious mistake for

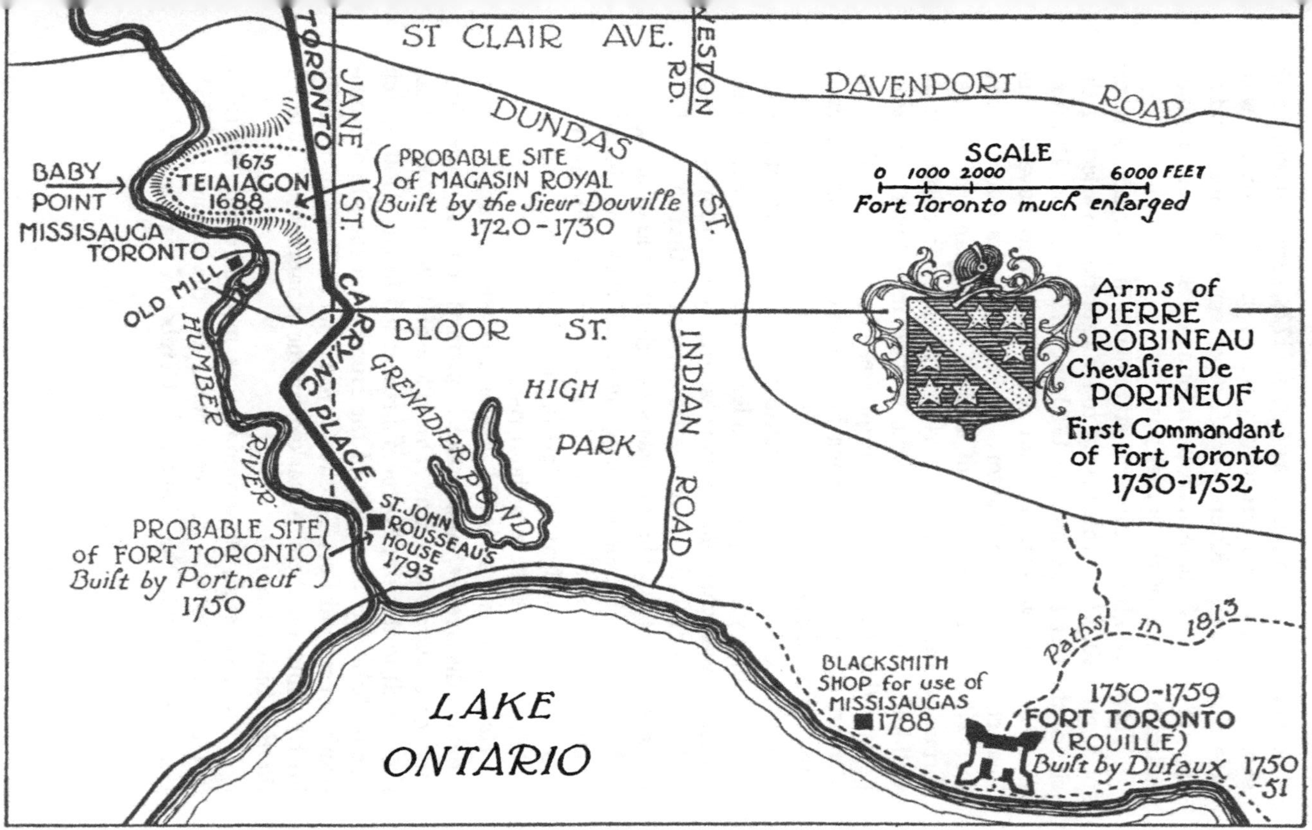
ST CLAIR AVE.
WESTON RD.
DAVENPORT ROAD
TORONTO
JANE ST.
DUNDAS ST.
SCALE
0 1000 2000 6000 FEET
Fort Toronto much enlarged
BABY POINT
1675
TEIAIAGON
1688
PROBABLE SITE
of MAGASIN ROYAL
Built by the Sieur Douville
1720-1730
MISSISAUGA TORONTO
OLD MILL
CARRYING PLACE
BLOOR ST.
INDIAN ROAD
Arms of
PIERRE
ROBINEAU
Chevalier De
PORTNEUF
First Commandant
of Fort Toronto
1750-1752
HUMBER RIVER
GRENADIER POND
HIGH PARK
ST. JOHN ROUSSEAU'S HOUSE
1793
PROBABLE SITE
of FORT TORONTO
Built by Portneuf
1750
paths in 1813
BLACKSMITH
SHOP for use of
MISSISAUGAS
1788
1750-1759
FORT TORONTO
(ROUILLE)
Built by Dufaux 1750-51
LAKE ONTARIO

Map Showing Position of the Three French Posts at Toronto

"Teiaiagon"; he had not, as yet, in 1728, surveyed the north shore of the lake and erroneously places this place on the west side of the Toronto River. Trade pipes, similar to one found on the site of Fort Rouillé, have been found on Baby Point and may indicate the site of the earlier post.

There are also certain mis-statements in Jonquière's letter of August 20, 1750, which seem to indicate that in selecting the site of the fort to be built in 1750 and 1751—that is, Dufaux's fort—he had two sites in mind and that he may have left the final choice to his contractor. Jonquière states that the new fort will be on "the point of land at the entrance of the bay formed by the peninsula," a perfectly accurate description of the well-known site. But his next remark introduces confusion; he says that the fort will be a quarter of a league north of the Toronto River. This is wrong in two ways; the fort, officially named Fort Rouillé, was two and a half miles, that is, about a league, to the *east* of the Toronto River. Baby Point, on the other hand, is just a quarter of a league north of the spot on the Toronto River where navigation ceased. It was from the village of Teiaiagon on Baby Point, as La Salle says, that the road ran to Lake Toronto. The site was strategic, the end of navigation and the beginning of the long overland route to the north. There is confusion again when Jonquière speaks of employing a pilot who "has navigated before in the said river and undertakes to bring the boat there without risk."

However this may be, M. Massicotte's documents, added to previous discoveries, now make it plain that there were three forts or posts at Toronto: Douville's of 1720 to 1730, whose site is still in debate; Portneuf's stockaded fort of 1750, which was probably at the mouth of the Humber on the site of Rousseau's house; and Fort Toronto, *le fort royal de Toronto*, officially Fort Rouillé, on the site marked by the monument of 1878 on the Exhibition Grounds.

As we have seen, the second fort, or, more correctly, the third fort at Toronto was not completed till the spring of 1751. Jonquière wrote to the Minister in October of that year, giving

an account of the building of the new fort which now officially
at least bore his name.[1]   He says nothing about the difficulties
of the contractor, except that the work had been interrupted
by sickness; but he adds interesting details of the success of the
French in alienating the Indians from the English.

Quebec October 6, 1751.

My Lord,

Trade at Fort Toronto.

I had the honour to inform you in my letter of August 20th
last year that the trade-house established at Toronto being too
small to hold the King's goods, I intended to have built there
a stockaded fort, a lodge for the officer in command, a guard
house, a storehouse and a bakery.

Work went on all winter.   The Sieur Chevalier de Portneuf,
an officer in the garrison at Fort Frontenac, arrived there on the
23rd of April.   He found that the work was fairly well on
(*assez avancés*).

The fort is of squared oak timbers.   (*Le fort est de pièces
sur pièces tout de chesne.*)   It is entirely enclosed and the shopkeeper housed.   The other buildings are not finished, most of
the workmen having been unable to work steadily on account
of the illnesses they have had.

Since there is no proper place in the fort for the powder, the
said Sieur de Portneuf has had stone prepared for building a
little powder-magazine.

He has observed to me that the situation of the place is very
suitable for a saw-mill, the stream furnishing water in abundance
all the year.   On this point I shall confer with the Intendant
and we shall have the honour of receiving your orders, if we
think that this mill will be useful to the King's service.

All these undertakings have been accomplished with great
economy, and it is certain that at the high price at which the
goods have been sold, the trade this year with the Indians will
repay the King's outlay upon the fort and upon the goods for
the store.

This trade cannot but increase in future.   In fact, the
tribes in the regions about Toronto who hitherto had resorted
only to the English, have not been to Chouaguen at all; they
have preferred to barter their furs at Toronto.

1 *Archives des Colonies*, CII A, Vol. 97, pp. 107-111.

The inhabitants of Toronto have had at heart the establishment of the fort. One can only attribute their docility to the protection with which you honour this colony, in which protection they profit especially. They even sent messages to all their allies and to the other tribes to divert them from Chouéguen and to invite them to go and trade at Fort Rouillé. They did more; they refused their canoes to several Indians from the Upper Country who wanted to buy them in order to go to Chouéguen. This secured us their peltries.

The growth of this trade causes inexpressible jealousy to the English and the Five Nations. In their anxiety they have done everything to entice the inhabitants of Toronto, but without success.

The Sieur de Portneuf discovered that the Five Nations last year sent four collars to a Fort Frontenac Indian who was on an embassy to the Montagués (Onondagas) who had passed them about among different tribes and that one of them remained with the Toronto Indians along with a flag. The English had given these collars and these flags to the Five Nations to engage the Indian tribes to go to Chouéguen to trade and to let them know that they would be very well treated there.

The said Sieur de Portneuf had no trouble in having this collar and flag sent back. The inhabitants begged him to send them to me, and told him that they wanted this same collar to serve to bind them very closely to the French and as a more particular proof of their loyalty they added their flag.

I replied to this message with a similar collar by which I testified to them my satisfaction in the sacrifice they had made of what they had received from the English, and I bound myself to them. At the same time I gave them a flag and exhorted them not to recognise any other than that of the King my master.

When the trading was finished the Sieur de Portneuf called the chiefs and the inhabitants together; he told them to be sure to keep an eye on the bad thoughts of the other tribes. He returned to Fort Frontenac to go on duty there.

I am with deep respect, my Lord,
Your very humble and very obedient servant,
LA JONQUIÈRE.

Jonquière's suggestion of a saw-mill at Toronto is of interest. There still seems to be confusion in his mind as to the two sites. No mill would be likely or possible on the Garrison Creek.

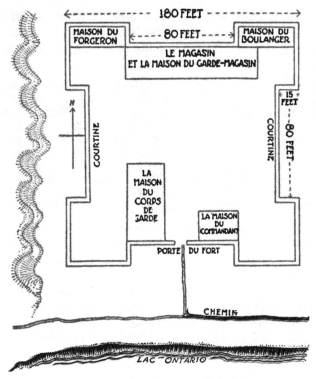

FORT ROUILLÉ OR TORONTO, 1750-1759
The materials for this reconstruction are drawn from various sources; the
dimensions are given in French feet.

One of Simcoe's first acts was to authorize a king's mill on the
Humber just below Baby Point on a site still marked by the
ruins of a later erection and by the Old Mill Tea Room.

It is now possible for the first time, with the aid of the
various letters of Jonquière, the depositions of Dufaux and his
workmen, the description of the fort contained in Pouchot's
memoir, and the numerous maps of the ruins, to reconstruct
Fort Toronto as it existed between 1751 and 1759, when it was
burned by Captain Alexandre Douville in obedience to
instructions from de Vaudreuil.

In his *Memoir upon the Late War in North America, in 1759-1760*, Captain Pouchot, the last French commandant of Fort Niagara, supplies precise information as to the form and size of the fort at Toronto. He writes:

The Fort of Toronto is at the end of the Bay on the side which is quite elevated and covered by a flat rock,[1] so that vessels cannot approach within cannon-shot. This fort or post was a square of about thirty *toises* (180 feet) on a side externally, with flanks of fifteen feet. The curtains formed the buildings of the fort. It was very well built, piece upon piece; but was only useful for trade. A league west of the fort is the Toronto river, which is of considerable size. This river communicates with Lake Huron by a portage of fifteen leagues, and is frequented by the Indians who come from the North.

Further information may be obtained from the map drawn by Captain Gother Mann and dated Quebec, December 6, 1788, which shows the ruins of the fort. From this map it is learned that there were five buildings within the enclosure. Traces of these buildings and of the palisade which surrounded them could be observed as late as 1878, when the ground was levelled and appropriated for the use of the Toronto Exhibition. In addition to these buildings, Dr. Scadding observed the mark left in the side of the bank where the flag-staff had stood, and the remains of an outside oven.[2]

Of the other existing maps the most definite and precise is that drawn in 1813 by George Williams and now in the Public Archives in Ottawa. This map indicates that the fort stood on the familiar site at the foot of Dufferin Street, near the steep bank of the shore which later crumbled away under the action of the waves and obliterated much of the area formerly occupied by the buildings. Williams' map shows that the lake-shore trail ran along the front of the fort on the edge of the bank and that the gate of the fort was on the lake side. To the west a ditch or ravine is indicated, possibly Du Chouquet's

1 i.e., protected by rocky shoals.
2 *History of the Old French Fort and Its Monuments*, by Henry Scadding, D.D., Toronto, 1887.

useless canal. The accompanying reconstruction, which is substantiated by Pouchot's measurements, must leave one small point in doubt; were the curtains and bastions, where not formed by the buildings themselves, formed of a double row of stakes placed upright, or were they, too, composed of squared timbers superimposed horizontally one upon another?

In that summer of 1751, the first year of the history of Fort Rouillé, we catch two brief glimpses of life at Toronto. The first is contained in a letter of the Chevalier de Portneuf, addressed to the commandant either of Frontenac or Niagara. The original French of this document is quaint and the spelling suggests that even a nobleman in Canada in the first half of the eighteenth century had little time or opportunity to acquire that difficult art. Evidently the malady which interrupted the work of Dufuax continued during the summer and assumed the proportions of a malignant epidemic.

Sir:

The sickness we have had here for a long time compels me at last to have recourse to you to beg you to be so kind as to send us your doctor for a few days. If it had been possible to have our numerous invalids conveyed to you I should have done so; but of all the garrison and all the employees we have only three soldiers left who are well and the three Canadians by whom I am asking you to be so good as to aid us in our present need.

You will oblige me for I myself will be ready to get cured since I am not at all well myself again after the fevers which left me some days ago. There must be some bad air to contend with, for the strongest are among those struck down among the first comers.

If you have a soldier, sir, in your garrison who knows how to cook I beg you to send him to us till our's recovers; he and his wife are very sick.

You see we cannot be more reduced, so I flatter myself you will consider our situation. This will be another reason for my subscribing myself with all respect possible sir
        Your humble and obedient servant,
                    CHEVALIER DE PORTNEUF.
Fort Rouillé,
    August 20th 1751.

Our second glimpse of life at the fort is the Abbé Picquet's account of his visit earlier in the summer of the same year. In June, 1749, Picquet had founded his famous mission of La Présentation, now the city of Ogdensburg, and in order to gain recruits for this establishment, he set out early in the summer of 1751 on a tour around Lake Ontario.   A record of this interesting journey is preserved in Lalande's memoir of Père Picquet, contained in *Lettres édifiantes et curieuses*.[1]

In the month of June, M. Picquet made a trip around Lake Ontario, with a King's boat and a bark canoe carrying five savages; his object was to entice native families to the new establishment at "La Présentation."   An account of this trip was found among his papers, from which I give an extract.

His first visit was to Fort Frontenac or Cataracoui, twelve leagues west of La Présentation.   He found no savages there, although it used to be a resort of the Five Nations.   The bread and the milk were bad; there was not even brandy to dress a wound.—He visited Fort Toronto seventy leagues from Fort Frontenac, at the extreme west of Lake Ontario; there he found good bread and good wine, and all that was necessary for the trade, although there was a scarcity at all the other posts.   He found there some Mississaguas who gathered around him; they began to say how fortunate their young people and their wives and children would be if the King would be as kind to them as he had been to the Iroquois for whom he procured missionaries: they complained that instead of building them a church they had only been provided with a brandy-shop. M. Picquet did not let them finish, and replied that they had been treated as they had deserved, they had never shown the least interest in religion, their attitude had been quite hostile, and that the Iroquois had shown their love for Christianity; but since he had no instructions to entice them to his mission, he avoided further explanations.

This is all the abbé has to say about Toronto, but after his visit to Niagara he had evidently formed the opinion that a post at Toronto was only necessary so long as Chouéguen continued to exist.   Of the latter much-detested establishment he writes:

1 Paris, 1783, Vol. XXVI.

This post has been much more prejudicial to us by the facility which it afforded the English of maintaining relations with all the Indian tribes in Canada, than by the trade carried on there with the French from Quebec as well as with the savages; Chouéguen had goods to sell to the French, as well as goods for the savages; which shows that illicit trade went on. Had the instructions of the Minister been followed Chouéguen would have been almost ruined, at least with the savages of Upper Canada; we ought to have stocked Niagara and especially the Portage[1] rather than Toronto.   The difference between the two first posts and the latter, is that three or four hundred canoes can come loaded with peltries to the Portage, and only those canoes can go to Toronto which cannot pass by Niagara and on to Fort Frontenac, such as the Ottawas from the head of the lake and the Missisagues; so that Toronto could not but impair the trade of these two old posts which would have been more than sufficient to stop all the Indians if their stores had been provided with the wares which they like.   We should have imitated the English in the matter of the trinkets which they sell to the savages, such as silver bracelets, etc.   The savages compared them and weighed them, according to the store-keeper at Niagara, and it was found that the bracelets from Chouéguen weighed as much and were purer silver and more attractive and cost them only two beaver skins, while they wanted to sell them for ten skins at the King's magazines.   So we were discredited and these silver articles remained a dead loss in the magazines of the King.   The French brandy was better liked than the English; but that did not prevent the savages from going to Chouéguen.   To destroy the trade there, the King's posts should have been furnished with the same goods as Chouéguen and at the same price; and the French should have been prevented from sending there the savages belonging to the settlements; but that would have been difficult.[2]

It is evident from these extracts that the Abbé Picquet did not think the post at Toronto necessary;[3] the truth is that he did

1 i.e., the Niagara Portage.

2 *Lettres édifiantes et curieuses*, Vol. XXVI, pp. 38 and 39.

3 "Nous avons dit que les officiers et aumôniers des forts Frontenac et Niagara se nourriraient au moyen des gratifications qui leur seraient payées, qu'il n'était point besoin de garnison à la Présentation, qu'à Toronteaux qui n'aurait qu'un détachement pendant l'été tiré de la garnison du fort Frontenac." *Mémoire sur les postes du Canada, par le chevalier de Raymond,* publié par M. Aegidius Fauteux, Québec, 1929.

not think any of the posts in the interior desirable or necessary. The account of his tour around Lake Ontario is appended to a statement of his views; the garrisons and the shop-keepers demoralized and defrauded the savages, estranged them from the missionaries and alienated them from the King.

Before the missionaries had won over the tribes of Upper Canada, the Indians conspired in all the posts against the French; they looked for opportunities to cut their throats. Those who were for us were hardly any support in time of war. We had not more than forty of them in the first years of the war of 1755.

In the opinion of the abbé, the missionaries were the only persons who could attach the savages to the King and induce them to serve against the English. He observed that where there had at one time been flourishing Indian villages in the vicinity of the forts in the interior, these villages were now deserted and the inhabitants had gone over to the English. Picquet was given an opportunity to test his theories in his mission of La Présentation; he rallied the wavering Indians to the support of the French and he and his mission proved such a thorn in the side of the English in the final war that he decided not to face the victors but fled away down the Mississippi to Louisiana, where he received a triumphal reception; when he reached Italy the Pope rewarded him with a gift of 5,000 *livres*.

Holding such views, it is hardly to be expected that the abbé would have much good to say about the new post at Toronto.   It had been established only a year, and he probably saw in Fort Toronto another evil influence in the interior. The Missisaugas had accused the French of giving them *un cabaret d'eau-de-vie* rather than a chapel, and no doubt they were right; in a *Mémoire sur l'état de la Nouvelle France*, bearing the date 1757, Toronto is described as "situé au nord du lac Ontario vis-à-vis de Niagara, établi pour empêcher les sauvages du nord d'aller commercer a Chouéguen; Chouéguen n'existant plus, ce poste devient inutile," and in a list of posts attached to this memoir there is this note: "Toronto ou Saint-Victor, petit fort de pieux sur le lac Ontario, pour vendre l'eau-de-vie aux sauvages afin de contre-balancer le commerce qui se faisait a Chouéguen."

We learn from this brief note that the post was occasionally referred to as Saint Victor.   There were at least two saints of that name: a Victor who was Pope from 190 to 202 A.D.; the second was a martyr of the third century, specially revered at Soleure in Switzerland; both are obscure saints and it remains to be explained why the name of either should be selected to screen a *cabaret d'eau-de-vie* at Toronto.

There is a copy of the Abbé Picquet's original journal in the Public Archives at Ottawa.   Here are the *ipsissima verba* of his visit to Toronto:

The 26th, I reached Fort Toronto sixty leagues or thereabouts from Fort Frontenac; I only stopped there to get provisions, being out of bread, I had got bad bread and bad lard at Fort Frontenac and only enough for a week, and it is twelve days since I left that place; I was very well received at Toronto and it is there that I ate the best bread and drank the best wine. There is no scarcity in this fort; everything is in abundance excellent and good, I should not be surprised if I were told that this post has done as much alone for him[1] as all the others together which have all lacked the necessities for the trade. I shall not make any reflections in this journal on this new establishment as I was not supposed even to stop here according to the intentions of the Governor-General and the Intendant.

On the 25th, I was ready to embark when the Mississagués all gathered to talk to me.   I told the commandant at first that the Governor and the Intendant had forbidden me to draw them to a mission; in spite of myself I had to listen to them.   They spoke at first of the happiness which their young people, their wives and children would enjoy if the King had the same blessings for them as he had for the Iroquois for whom he procures missionaries; that instead of building them a church, a brandy shop (*cabaret d'eau de vie*) had been placed among them.   I did not let them finish and told them that they had been treated according to their taste, that they had never shown the least zeal for religion, on the contrary they had been much opposed to it and that the Iroquois had done much to show their love for Christianity.   Being afraid that my zeal

1 It is not clear to whom Picquet refers.

would urge me to act contrary to the intentions of the Governor and the Intendant I set out at once and spent the night six leagues from this post.

In the middle of autumn we catch another glimpse of life at the fort. This time Du Chouquet, the storekeeper, writes to the commandant of either Frontenac or Niagara, for the address is missing:

Sir,
    I have the honour of writing to inform you that a canoe is leaving here to go for a man who died at your fort named Poutine. He belonged to M. de Bellestre's party. His grandfather here who is called "Miscouanquier" begs you to have pity on the mother of the said defunct; she goes to bring her son; and he asks you to have a coffin made to put the dead man in so that they can carry him more easily. He begs you too to have rations given them to bring them as far as this place. The old Miscouanquier is a good chief and deserving; he keeps the young people in order. There is nothing new here of importance.
        Sir, your humble and obedient servant,
                            LEFEBVRE DUCHOUQUET.
Fort Rouillé,
    October 12th, 1751.

Early in 1752 the Chevalier de Portneuf was succeeded as commandant at Toronto by Thomas Robutel de la Noue. M. Massicotte informs me that de la Noue was born at Montreal, December 21, 1702, and was the son of Zacharie Robutel de la Noue, seigneur of Chateauguay, who had married Catharine Le Moyne at Montreal in 1689. The second commandant at Toronto remained single and died at Montreal, April 3, 1754. The sources of our information for the year 1752 include a letter from de la Noue, two letters from the store-keeper at Fort Rouillé, Du Chouquet, who seems to have spent the winter at Toronto, and several references to the post in official despatches to France. We shall begin with the despatches. On April 21, 1752, M. de Longueuil[1] wrote to the Minister, M. de Rouillé:[2]

1 M. DE LONGUEUIL had assumed control on the death of M. de la Jonquière.
2 PARKMAN, Montcalm and Wolf, I, p. 88.

M. de Celeron had addressed these despatches to M. de la Valterie,[1] the Commandant at Niagara, who detached a soldier to convey them to Fort Rouillé, with orders to the store-keeper at that post to transmit them promptly to Montreal. It is not known what became of that soldier. About the same time a Mississague from Toronto arrived at Niagara, who informed M. de la Valterie that he had not seen that soldier at the fort, nor met him on the way. 'Tis to be feared that he has been killed by the Indians, and the despatches carried to the English. M. de la Valterie has not failed to recommend to this Indian to make every search on his way back to his village and to assure him, that should he find that soldier, and convey the despatches entrusted to him to the store-keeper of Toronto, he would be well rewarded.[2]

From another passage in the same despatch we obtain the following information:

The store-keeper at Toronto writes to M. de Verchères, commandant at Fort Frontenac, that some trustworthy Indians have assured him that the Saulteux (Missisaugas) who killed our Frenchman some years ago, have dispersed themselves along the head of Lake Ontario; and seeing himself surrounded by them, he doubts not but they have some evil design on his Fort. There is no doubt but 'tis the English who are inducing the Indians to destroy the French, and that they would give a good deal to get the Savages to destroy Fort Toronto, on account of the essential injury it does their trade at Chouéguen.

And again in October of the same year, de Longueuil writes of various outrages committed on Frenchmen by the Indians in the south-west, on the Wabash and the Illinois rivers: "You are fully informed, my Lord, by the details that I have just had the honour to submit to you:—"(here he enumerates the perils which threatened the French, of which the eighth and ninth alone concern the present record). "8th. That we are menaced with a general conspiracy. 9th. That we must fear even for Toronto."[3]

The three letters from Fort Rouillé dating from this year, recently discovered by M. Massicotte in the Baby collection and

---

1 For de la Valterie consult *Bulletin des Recherches Historiques*, Vol. 23, p. 71.
2 *New York Colonial Documents*, Vol. X, p. 246.
3 Ibid., Vol. IX, p. 250.

now published for the first time, all refer to the disappearance of the soldier and the loss of despatches to which M. de Longueuil refers in his report to M. de Rouillé. The incident was apparently serious enough to be reported to the Minister. In February the store-keeper, Du Chouquet, wrote from Fort Toronto to the commandant at Fort Niagara (the address is missing):

Sir,

I have received the honour of your letter of the 14th of February informing me of the annoying accident to your soldier. I have not had any news. You tell me to try and get some. You can be sure, Sir, that I will do all I can to find out what has become of him. For this purpose I sent three savages to go and look for the said soldier. The said tribes of this post are not at all satisfied with this news. They say they will know what has become of this man. I reckon that he has been killed, for there are bad men in the country round the head of the lake who have killed Frenchmen in Lake Huron. I hope soon to have news of your soldier, for the three men I sent to look for him are very faithful, and he who bears the said letter is very deserving for his devotion to the good of the service, so are the men of his band who are searching for the poor soldier.

I have had the honour to receive a letter from Monsr. Celoron by the couriers coming from Detroit in which he informs me of the massacre of our poor French and asks me to be sure to see that your letters reach you at any cost. And it is so important that you receive them that I have made the said occasion as much for your letter as for the soldier.

I kept the couriers a day knowing that the savage who was coming from you had letters for Montreal so I gave them to them; they went the 24th of this month.

The man who carries your letter asks as his pay the value of ten beaver skins in goods; I ask you, sir, to have this given him and to do your best to see that he is satisfied, he is a man loyal to the French.

My wife takes the liberty of sending her respects and I who am with deep respect sir

Your humble and obedient servant

LEFEBVRE DUCHOUQUET.

Fort Rouillé
February 27th, 1752.

In April Du Chouquet wrote again about the same matter:

Sir,

According to your letter I have sent three times savages to search for the man nam ed La Lime and the last time they found him, without his coat; his waistcoat was not pierced, all his head was there, not a wound remained on what was left of his body, but the arm and the left side were carried away. I am telling you what they told me.

The savages have also reported to me that the English were building in a river between Niagara and Chouéguen; I think perhaps at Gascouchagon.[1]

You will make, Sir, whatever use you like of this information I am only warning you on the report of the savages.

I address myself to you, sir, and I have written to M. Sermet to get a cooper for us. A cooper is of infinite importance here for the trade. M. le Commissaire has this matter much at heart and if you do not procure us this advantage we shall not be able to pour out brandy not having any kegs and lots of savages.

My wife presents her respects and I beg you to believe that no one is with more respect than I,

Sir,

Your humble and obedient servant,

LEFEBVRE DUCHOUQUET.

Fort Rouillé
April 23rd, 1752.

A letter from the commandant, de la Noue, was written on the same day and was also addressed to the commandant at Niagara; the address is lacking:

Sir,

M. de Verchères acting on the orders of M. de Longueuil having detached me to come and take command in this post I left Fort Frontenac on the tenth of April and arrived here on the 19th of the same month.

I am sending you M. Vaucouret to carry your letters. I should have detached him immediately after my arrival according to the intention of these gentlemen if it had been possible for me to find canoes.

1 The Genessee River.

I beg you, Sir, to be so good as to give orders to send us a cooper from your fort. The store-keeper has shown me a letter in which M. le Commissaire instructs him to ask you for one and as for the store-keeper he seems to have this matter very much at heart; we are almost out of kegs and consequently almost out of business.

I have been informed by the savages that the body of La Lime has been found all the left side carried away, without other wounds, and that the English were building in a river between Chouéguen and Niagara.

I shall have the honour, Sir, to inform you of any news here. All is very quiet, and I beg you to be persuaded that no one is with more respect than I, Sir,

Your humble and obedient servant,

ROBUTELLE (DE LA NOUE).

Fort Rouillé
April 23rd, 1752.

If your orders do not retain M. de Vaucauret I beg you to send him back as soon as possible as we need the men.

It is plain that the encroachments of the English into the lake region and into the valley of the Ohio had shaken the loyalty of the Indians, and that events were rapidly drifting towards the final struggle. Meantime the inhabitants of the isolated posts in the interior led anxious lives; the French government could send them little assistance, they were menaced by the disaffection of the savages who still came to trade, and the trade itself was debauched by the corruption of the Intendant Bigot and his satellites. There is one more reference to Toronto this year. A French military expedition on its way from Quebec to the Ohio paused at Toronto. We gather this from the narrative of Stephen Coffin, a captive from New England, who accompanied the troops as a volunteer. "They stopped," he says, "on their way a couple of days at Cadaraghqui Fort, also at Taranto (*sic*) on the north side of Lake Ontario; then at Niagara fifteen days."[1]

1 *New York Colonial Documents*, Vol. VI, p. 855.

Between 1752 and 1756,[1] when the Seven Years War broke out in earnest, there are scanty materials for the history of Fort Toronto.[2] When it becomes possible to write the annals of the fort for these years the record will probably be found to consist of furtive attacks upon Chouéguen and the efforts of the English to lure the Missisaugas from the French. An official report of the lake posts for 1754 reveals the fact that the garrison at Toronto at that time consisted of one officer, two sergeants, four soldiers and a store-keeper; eight men constituted the entire military establishment. Some Canadians, labourers or boatmen, lived in or near the fort.[3] In the same year an expedition under Captain Contrecoeur left Quebec on January 15th and Montreal on February 3rd. Following the north shore of Lake Ontario, there were long stretches where many of the soldiers skated in single file "drawing seven or eight sledges one after the other with men on them, making in this way as much as twenty leagues." In this way the hardy troops entered Toronto Bay, thence they crossed by *bateaux* to Fort Niagara, which they reached on February 25th. A member of this party, J. C. Bonnefons, afterwards secretary to Captain Pouchot, kept a

1 M.E.-Z. MASSICOTTE has sent me a copy of an unpublished document dated 22nd of February, 1756, and drawn by notary G. Hodiesne, in which it is stated that Basile Gagnier, blacksmith, of the Fort of Toronto, entrusts to his father (also a Montreal blacksmith) and his mother the sum of 1810 *livres* 10 sols, and that he will resume possession on demand. Two years later, on the 19th of February, 1758, Basile Gagnier, then in Montreal and residing in the "faubourg St. Laurent" (a suburb of north Craig Street) declares that his mother (widow of Pierre Gagnier) has given him back the amount mentioned. Basile Gagnier was born in Laprairie, near Montreal, in 1725, and married in Montreal in 1757 Marie Amable Perras. He must have been thrifty to be able to put aside so large a sum at the age of 31. He may have been at Toronto two or three years before 1756.

2 At the New York Council which opened December 12, 1755, Governor Shirley asserted, "That could the French be dislodged from Frontenac, and the little fort at Fronto (*sic*) and their entrance into Lake Ontario obstructed, all their other forts and settlements on the Ohio and the western lakes were deprived of their support from Canada and must ere long be evacuated."

3 At Fort Niagara there were five officers—one of them usually attached to Little Niagara above the Falls, and residing there—two sergeants, a drummer, twenty-four soldiers, a storekeeper, surgeon and chaplain, the last named being expected occasionally to visit Toronto and any other isolated white men in the region. Five canoes came up from below annually, with supplies for Toronto, ten were sent to Niagara and (in 1754) seventeen others with goods for Detroit and its dependencies." SEVERANCE, *An Old Frontier of France*, Vol. II, p. 90.

journal of this and other experiences in Canada between 1751 and 1761 which was published at Quebec by the Abbé Casgrain in 1887.

The time had now come for the long-delayed attack upon the hated Chouéguen. M. Massicotte has supplied me with four hitherto unpublished letters from the Baby collection written by the commandant at Fort Rouillé, M. de Noyelle,[1] and addressed to the commandant at Fort Frontenac in the winter and spring of this year. In February, M. de Noyelle wrote:

Sir,

I had the honour to inform you of what news there is here by two Frenchmen who came from Detroit about whom I am very much disturbed, Mr. de Lorimier not having met them and three days after they left their dog came back here.

The Missisakés of this post and of the *fond du lac* have received several belts of wampum which the English have sent by a renegade Montagné (Onondaga); Mr. Duplessis has got back one of them and some strings of wampum. I have got back two, four strings and a shell.

The Governor-General instructs me to send bands of savages continually to harrass the English at Chou8akin; I have brought the Missisaké of this post to this decision: they are preparing to set out as soon as navigation opens.

I shall continue, Sir, to have the honour of informing you of all that comes to my knowledge.

I am with deep respect
Sir,
Your humble and obedient servant
Noyelle.[2]

Fort Rouillé
February 15th, 1756.

1 "In November, 1756, De Noyelle, with ten men, was assigned to Toronto." Severance, *An Old Frontier of France,* Vol. II, p. 188.

2 M. Aegidius Fauteux informs me that the commandant at Toronto in 1756 was Charles Joseph de Noyelle, one of the three sons, all officers, of Nicolas Joseph de Noyelle, mayor of Three Rivers and later "lieutenant du roy."

In March he wrote again to the commandant at Fort Frontenac:

Sir,

Here is a courrier from the Illinois charged with despatches from *Mr. Le gouverneur de La Louisiane* and *Mr. Le Commandant des Illinois* for the Governor-General. Not being able to find a guide to show him the way to you he has been obliged to stay here eight days. I was waiting for Chaurette with impatience being sure that the companion you had been so good as to give him would have gone back to Frontenac with this courrier; but my anxiety for this Chaurette increases; it is twenty-seven days since he left; something must have happened to him. He is however one of the most capable mariners for refitting the barque. In case he is still at Frontenac I beg you, Sir, to have the goodness to send him back with this savage whom I am giving for guide to the man named Mercier.

There is no news at all here worthy of your attention. I am always with much respect
  Sir,
    Your humble and obedient servant
         NOYELLE.
Fort Rouillé
 March 15th, 1756.

By the middle of April the war-parties from Fort Rouillé were ready to set out and de Noyelle wrote to the commandant at Fort Frontenac:

Sir,

I have the honour to direct to you this war party of ten savages from this post which I have raised in accordance with the instructions of the Governor-General, to go and strike at Chou8akin. As there are two parties which I am embarking for the same place and at the same time, one has decided to go by your post and the other I shall send by Niagara.

I beg you, Sir, to be so kind as to be ready to have them supplied with provisions to pursue their way. This fort, as I have had the honour to inform you, is so absolutely stripped I have been able to give them only enough ammunition for hunting till they reach you, as I am doing for the party which is to pass M. Duplessis's fort, from whom I am expecting relief every day, for we haven't more than two quarts of flour.

130 TORONTO DURING THE FRENCH RÉGIME

There is however some reason to suppose that the barques are at Niagara, we heard three days ago twenty-seven cannon-shots. I am with deep respect

Your very humble and obedient servant

NOYELLE.

Fort Rouillé
April 19th, 1756.

In May, Vaudreuil sent Coulon de Villiers, with eleven hundred soldiers, Canadians and Indians, to harass Oswego and cut its communications with Albany. The following letter from de Noyelle to the commandant at Fort Frontenac indicates that Toronto furnished its quota for this expedition:

Sir,

I received from Chabot who arrived this morning and set out at the end of an hour, your honoured communication of the ninth of the month.

The Governor-General instructs me, as you do me the honour to inform me, to send thirty Missisakés to Mr. de Villiers.

I have seven here who are setting out to-morrow morning for Pimidaichekontayny (Port-Hope?) to enlist there seven others of their people, and to embark there for your post. They assure me that there will be at least fourteen and probably twenty. But that I may be sure of their numbers they are to send and let me know at the moment of their departure how many they will be so that I can carry out to the letter the Governor's order. Most of these savages have just left their winter encampment; ten leagues from here they say there is still snow and ice on the ground and that that is the reason of their tardiness in setting out this spring. The scarcity of provisions also with which this fort was supplied has also been in part the cause, for if I had been in a position to support their families some of them would have gone in the month of February.

I am sending off those here in great haste and even without being able to give them provisions. Several of them have no guns or tomahawks. It is impossible to give them guns, as for tomahawks I should have had some made for them if I had not made them set out so quickly. They have asked me to beg you to supply their needs. The Governor instructs me to tell them that if they are afraid that their wives cannot live in their absence, to bring them to your post to live there till their return.

I shall do everything, Sir, to despatch as quickly as possible these thirty savages; but the scarcity of provisions where I am is a great obstacle. However we have heard several cannon-shots from Niagara which makes us hope that the barques reached there to-day.

Accept my humble thanks for charging yourself with the letter which I wrote to my wife.

I am with deep respect, Sir,
> Your humble and obedient servant,
> > NOYELLE.

Fort Rouillé
May 18th, 1756.

In July, Vaudreuil and Montcalm[1] had completed their preparations for the attack upon Oswego (Chouéguen). The troops assembled at Montreal and were joined by Indians from the far west; among them were Menominees from beyond Lake Michigan. These warriors, "naked, painted, plumed, greased, stamping, uttering short yelps, shaking feathered lances, brandishing tomahawks, danced the war-dance before the Governor, to the thumping of the Indian drum."[2] The Governor commended them for their zeal in spite of the ravages of smallpox, praised their valour in their recent campaign with M. de Villiers, and rewarded the most distinguished among them. He then proceeded to urge them to accompany M. de Rigaud,[3] his brother, in the expedition against Chouéguen, reminding them that it would not take them out of their path on their way back to Toronto. He begged them not to listen to the words of any evil persons who should attempt to seduce them from obedience to the voice of their father. The orator

1 "Du 3 juin 1756—On a eu des nouvelles du 27 avril, des forts Duquesne, Rouillé, Machault, la Presqu'île, Toronto. Il parvit par les diverses lettres que les sauvages d'En-Haut son bien disposés et font de fréquents courses chez les Anglois, où nous avons toujours la supériorité par les prisonniers que l'on amène. Nous avons perdu trois Mississagués et un enseigne des troupes de la colonie appelé M. Douville. Dans ces divers postes, on se plaint du retard pour les subsistances." *Journal du Marquis de Montcalm,* p. 68. (The M. Douville mentioned was a son of the Sieur de la Saussaye.)

2 PARKMAN, *Montcalm and Wolf,* I, p. 421.

3 *"Official Report on French Posts,"* Michigan Historical Magazine, *Winter Number,* 1932, p. 73.

of the Menominees rose; he thanked the governor for the presents, accepted the wampum belts and promised that they would all follow M. de Rigaud on the expedition, with the exception of the sick and wounded. He asked for some new canoes, and for provisions to take them as far as Toronto, and from there to the bay,[1] as usual. His request was granted.[2] It will not be necessary to follow these warriors to Oswego, whose walls collapsed so suddenly before the attack of the French; what we are concerned with is to observe that the road from Montreal to the west lay across the Toronto Carrying-Place and that many other fantastic savages probably passed that way during the years of struggle which ended in the defeat of the French.

Another brief mention of Toronto occurs in the account of the arrival at the rendezvous at Fort Frontenac of a part of the regiment of Béarn from Niagara:

Niagara, du 31 Juillet-Ier Août. Béarn est arrivé à 3h. La cause de son retard a été des gros vents qui l'ont obligé de relâcher à Toronto et de retourner à Niagara dont il est parti hier matin. Le navigation du lac Ontario est assez périlleuse et fort pénible. Le moindre vent le rend clapoteux; les lames y sont courtes et frequentes et dans les gros temps on y est plus fatigué qu'en pleine mer.[3] (The men of Béarn arrived at three o'clock. The cause of their delay was the strong winds which compelled them to put in at Toronto and to return to Niagara from which they had set out yesterday morning. Navigation is quite dangerous and very unpleasant on Lake Ontario. The least wind renders it choppy; the waves are short and frequent and in bad weather one is more fatigued than on the ocean.)

There is an allusion to the same incident in the diary of Malartic. The Count de Maurès de Malartic, a brigade major in the regiment of Béarn, was stationed with his regiment at

1 La Baye (Green Bay, Wisconsin), a post established upon the Baye des Puants. This post was worth in three years to Messrs. Rigaud and Morin, 312,000 *livres*. *Le Bulletin des Recherches Historiques*, July, 1931, and article by Hon. Mr. Justice Riddell, *Michigan Historical Magazine*, Vol. 16, No. 1, p. 72.

2 *Rapport de l'Archiviste de la Province de Québec*, 1923-1924, p. 209.

3 Ibid., 1923-1924, p. 215.

Fort Frontenac in August, 1755; his diary, published at Dijon in 1890, contains many vivid glimpses of life at Cataraqui and of the traffic on Lake Ontario. On August 27, 1755, ten Indians from Niagara reached Frontenac and spread out the plunder they had taken at the defeat of Braddock. One wonders how many Missisaugas from Toronto[1] shared in that bloody triumph. Next year the regiment of Béarn was at Niagara, and the diary contains several allusions to Toronto. On the seventh of June, 1756, while still stationed at Frontenac and waiting for transport for Niagara, he remarks, "The *bateau*, *Victor*, which had anchored at Toronto to load furs there, came into the bay, discharged her cargo and took on stores." This *bateau* was one of four armed ships on Lake Ontario commanded at this time by the Sieur La Force;[2] the corvette, *Marquise de Vaudreuil*, of twenty cannon, the corvette, *Hurault*, of fourteen, the schooner, *Louise*, of eight, and the *bateau*, *Victor*, or, as Montcalm's *Journal* calls her, the *Saint-Victor*,[3] which carried four small cannon. Probably all these ships were familiar with the anchorage at Toronto, which, as Walter Butler's *Journal* informs us, was not opposite the fort but "a few miles below the fort down the bay."[4]

On June the 14th the regiment of Béarn embarked at Cataraqui on the *Marquise de Vaudreuil;* but even in June the weather could be stormy, and it was two weeks before they reached Niagara. On the twentieth Malartic records, "The wind rose in the south-west, freshened a good deal, piling up seas on which we tossed till sunset, when the wind dropped. At ten o'clock the wind rose in the north-north-east and we were off again. The moon was bright and we could see the Rivière

1 In the list of Indians in Montcalm's army, July 28, 1757, there were "35 Mississagués de Toronto" under the command of M. de la Corne et de Saint Luc. *Journal du Marquis de Montcalm*, p. 265.

2 VAUDREUIL's letter dated Montreal, April 22, 1756, to the commandant at Fort Frontenac announces the appointment of La Force and defines his duties. The Governor enclosed a letter to M. de Noyelle at Toronto. The original of Vaudreuil's letter is in the Baby Collection.

3 See page 121.

4 See page 157.

au Boeuf to the south, and to the north the Great Bluffs
(Scarborough Heights) and lands of Toronto." Again, on the
twenty-first, he remarks: "The wind veered to the south-
south-west; we saw land often. We came in sight again of the
Great Bluffs and their river (the Rouge). After noon we kept
to the north to gain the anchorage at Toronto, but night kept
us from making it." Two days later the storm-tossed regiment
reached Niagara, where the soldiers were set to work on the
fortifications. The entry for the sixth and seventh of July
contains the following: "Work as usual; the demi-bastion
towards the lake has been finished; a boat sent to Toronto with
fresh provisions returned; the man in charge said he had seen
three prisoners and nine scalps taken by the savages from an
English boat crossing (Lake Ontario) at the Gallop Islands
(near Sackett's Harbour). The Mississagues brought us
roebuck." Again, on the thirteenth: "A dull sound was heard
in the distance; we supposed it came from the guns[1] of Toronto,
the workers along the shore thought of protecting the boats.
Three Mississagues brought us a buck and told us they had
met their companions who had left us yesterday." On the
twenty-third:

The regiment embarked at 8 o'clock in the four corvettes
or barks. The boats set sail before nine from the river with
the wind south-south-west; at noon the wind veered to the
north and forced us to put back to Toronto where we anchored
at four o'clock. On the 24th, the wind being still in the north-
east, we lay at anchor. I landed and went into the fort, which
I found like the others in the country, in bad condition and
built of wood; it is situated on the north, twelve leagues from
the head of the lake and one league from the river from which it
takes its name. The 25th, the commander of the fleet, fearing
that we could not leave Toronto if the wind changed, signalled
to all the ships to weigh anchor. We sailed at 8 o'clock and
made several tacks. The wind remaining in the north, we
steered for Niagara and entered the river at eight in the evening.

1 The fort at Toronto mounted four small cannon. These were probably
only *boîtes à pierriers* which were loaded with stones. Malartic speaks of the
boetes of Toronto. See also SNIDER, *The Glorious Shannon's Old Blue Duster*,
p. 45.

THE TORONTO RIVER; THE SECOND BEND
Looking down from Riverside Drive.

Next day the regiment sailed again, and this time the wind favoured them, for in twenty-seven hours they disembarked at Cataraqui, where Montcalm, who was on the eve of his attack upon Oswego, awaited them. On the thirteenth of December, Malartic records that the envoys of the Five Nations "begged Ononthio to see that the store-houses at Frontenac, Toronto and Niagara should be supplied with goods so that they would not feel the loss of Chouéguen." In the beginning of 1759, the diary has a brief entry recording the fact that an artillery officer, travelling with two officers from Fort Duquesne, had lost his way between Toronto and Frontenac, and that there was no news of him; this was on the tenth. On the eighteenth, the diary records that the lost officer arrived at Frontenac on the eleventh day after his departure from Toronto; he had been obliged to return there to pick up his direction.

During the winter of 1756 and 1757, which was severe, all the posts suffered from a shortage of supplies. Hordes of savages came to Niagara to live on the bounty of the fort. The soldiers there were employed on the fortifications during the winter, and to amuse their leisure Pouchot permitted amateur theatricals. Montcalm remarks in the *Journal:* "The bad weather not allowing the soldiers at Niagara to work on the fortifications, M. Pouchot has allowed them to present a comedy. Someone has even composed a little piece called 'The Old Man Duped.'" One wonders if any of M. de Noyelle's garrison of ten men at Toronto were present on the occasion of this, the first dramatic presentation in the west.

In 1757 Montcalm held a great council with the Indians at Montreal. More than a thousand Indians had gathered from the lakes, from Wisconsin, from the Illinois and from the banks of the Des Moines. His success at Oswego had given him a great ascendancy over the tribes, and it appears from Pouchot's narrative[1] that a contingent of Missisauga Indians to the number of ninety had gathered at Toronto with the intention of proceeding to Montreal. Before doing so, however, they

1 Vol. I, p. 82.

conceived the idea of pillaging the fort as they passed, in spite of the fact that it belonged to friends whom they were about to assist. It is supposed that the supply of brandy stored in the fort proved too great a temptation for their loyalty. The following is Dr. Scadding's account of the incident as drawn from Pouchot's narrative:

The only persons within the fort at the time were M. Varren, the store-keeper, and ten men under M. de Noyelle.[1] The latter had been secretly apprised of the plot by a French domestic. A canoe with two men was instantly despatched, unobserved by the conspirators, to Fort Niagara across the lake. Capt. Pouchot, in command there, on hearing the story, lost no time in sending two officers, Capt. de la Ferté and M. de Pinsun, with sixty-one men in two *bateaux*, each armed with a swivel gun at the bow. They reached Toronto at four o'clock in the afternoon of the next day. They found the Missisaugas still encamped near the fort; and passing in front of them the boats saluted the wigwams with "artillery and musket balls," directed, however, into the air, as Capt. Pouchot had given orders. The Indians were immediately summoned to attend a council. They were greatly astonished at the adventure, Capt. Pouchot tells us, and confessed everything; they had false news delivered to them, they said, to the effect that the English had beaten the French. But the true reason of their action, Pouchot adds, was that they felt themselves in force, and could get plenty of brandy for nothing.[2]

It was in this year that the terms of the contract executed on October 26, 1756, at Quebec, between the Intendant Bigot and the contractors, Cadet[3] and Martel, for supplying the posts

1 *Journal du Marquis de Montcalm*, p. 82.

2 "Les novelles du 4 (juin 1757) de Niagara parlent de la tranquillité du fort de Toronto; des Mississagués ivres d'eau-de-vie, avaient fait les insolents et menacèrent de détruire le fort. M. Pouchot, commandant de Niagara, qui a reçu un collier, y fit marcher M. de la Ferté, capitaine au régiment de la Saire, avec cinquante hommes. Tout etoit déjà assez tranquille. Les Poutéotamies nos alliés, qui avoient passé l'hiver à Montréal avoient calmé les esprits." *Journal du Marquis de Montcalm*, p. 213.

3 M.E.-Z. MASSICOTTE has sent me a copy of the engagement of the Sieur Bonnaventure Augé by the notorious Joseph Cadet, commissary-general, as head clerk at Fort Toronto; this document is dated 8th of June, 1757.

in the west with food and other necessaries, went into effect; in accordance with this contract, Cadet agreed to furnish rations and necessary supplies to Toronto from July 1, 1757, to June 30, 1766. Under this agreement neither the common soldier nor his officers were to fare too sumptuously, either in garrison or on the march. The daily ration of the soldier, regular or Canadian militia, and of the employed Indian, was two pounds of coarse bread, half a pound of pork and four ounces of peas. The officers received the same ration as the men, save that their bread was finer, and they were allowed a gill of brandy. One of the swindles which was early employed was that the soldiers' bread was made of a mixture of wheat and oats. More notorious was the favouritism in behalf of the officers, for whom the contractor sent into the Niagara wilderness, at the King's expense, many a cask of wine and other luxury not hinted at in the prescribed ration.[1] Cadet and his associates made all they could out of the contract for supplying the Ontario, Niagara and Ohio posts, but at the conclusion of the war he and the store-keepers who pillaged the King's treasury so greedily were impeached and committed to the Bastille. Douville, of Toronto, was among the number. Montcalm, in protesting against the carnival of greed and graft amid which the power of France in the west went down to destruction, remarks: "I forgot to say that this very day, in spite of the demands of dire peril, in place of making the convoys consist of articles requisite for the defence of the frontier, the great Company, more powerful than the governor-general, gives the preference in transmitting goods to Niagara and Toronto to the goods necessary for their commerce. Everyone sees this; everyone knows it; the outcry is general. What does it matter to these agents, who dispute authority. Separated from the throne by an interval of 1,500 leagues, assured for the present of impunity, because they had ventured to secure accomplices in the inner circle of supreme power, they

1 SEVERANCE, *An Old Frontier of France*, II, p. 404.

have accustomed trade, private persons, the people to see all, to suffer all, to be the instrument of their fortune."[1]

But the downfall of the corrupt Bigot and his associates was at hand; it involved the downfall of Niagara and Toronto. The next year—in 1758—the English made a sudden descent upon Fort Frontenac and captured and destroyed the place. The Governor-General, de Vaudreuil, writes to inform the Minister, M. de Messiac, in Paris: "Should the English make their appearance at Toronto, I have given orders to burn it and to fall back on Niagara."[2] And in 1759, when the attack upon Niagara was apprehended, the governor states in his despatch that he has summoned troops from the Illinois and from Detroit, with instructions to rendezvous at Presqu'Ile on Lake Erie, and adds: "As these forces will proceed to the relief of Niagara, should the enemy besiege it, I have in like manner sent orders to Toronto to collect the Mississagués and other natives, to forward them to Niagara."[3]

The threatened siege of Niagara did not last long; it began on the sixth of July, 1759, and the fort capitulated on the twenty-fifth. Early in the siege, Captain Douville from his post at Toronto sent a canoe across the lake to ascertain the progress of events; and again on the twentieth we catch a glimpse of the French schooner, *Iroquoise*, commanded by Captain La Force, one of three armed ships maintained by the French on the lake at this time, hovering at a safe distance off Fort Niagara and waiting for despatches. Two canoes from the beleaguered garrison brave the fire of the besiegers and reach the schooner,

1 *Journal du Marquis de Montcalm*, pp. 460-461, "M. de Montigny ne songeait qu'aux moyens de s'enricher. Il avait des intérêts à Niagara. Ce fut le motif qui l'engagea le plus à se faire nommer pour commander le parti qui devait y aller. Il fit charger ses canots de vivres et de marchandises sans oublier les barils de vin et d'eau-de-vie, qu'il vendit fort bien en route à son détachement et aux sauvages, Il se rendit en douze jours à Niagara, quoiqu'il eût été obligé de passer par Toronto, de s'y arrêter pour ses affaires, et d'y prendre sous prétexte de rafraichessements pour sa troupe, des vivres et de l'eau-de-vie." *Rapport de l'Archiviste de la Province de Québec*, 1925, pp. 143-144. (The fall of Fort Frontenac was not known on M. de Montigny's arrival at Niagara.) *Rapport de l'Archiviste de la Province de Québec*, 1923-1924, p. 367.

2 *New York Colonial Documents*, Vol. X, p. 824.

3 Ibid., Vol X, p. 932.

which sails at once with messages for Toronto and Montreal. This is our last distant glimpse of the fort. Dr. Scadding remarks:[1]

About this time watchers on the ramparts of Fort Niagara would see ascending from a point on the far horizon to the north-west across the lake, a dark column of smoke—sure indication that the orders of de Vaudreuil were being executed, and that in a few hours all that the English or any one else, on approaching Toronto, would discover of the once flourishing trading-post would be five heaps of charred timbers and planks, with a low chimney-stack of coarse brick and a shattered flooring at its foot, made of flag-stones from the adjoining beach, the whole surrounded on the inland side by three lines of cedar pickets more or less broken down and scathed by the fire.

Malartic records in his diary that the garrison made good their escape: "Le capitaine Douville réussit à conduire ses quinze soldats a Montreal." On October 30th de Vaudreuil wrote to the Minister, "M. Douville has burnt his fort at Toronto." This is the last reference to Toronto from a French source.[2]

Sir William Johnson, now in possession of Niagara, lost no time in despatching a party across the lake. He writes in his journal:[3] "The evening of the 27th, I sent three whale-boats with a party of above thirty men to reconnoitre Fort Toronto, and on their return propose to send to destroy it." On the 30th, he writes: "At night Lieutenant Francis returned from Toronto, and reported that the enemy had burned and abandoned that post, and destroyed many things which they could not carry along, viz., working utensils, arms, etc. A Chippeway chief came with Mr. Francis, in order to speak with me."

Of the four commandants at Toronto, Pierre Robineau, Chevalier de Portneuf; Thomas Robutel de la Noue; Charles Joseph de Noyelle, and Captain Alexandre Douville, the latter

1 SCADDING, *History of Old French Fort and its Monuments*, p. 22; ROBERTSON, *Landmarks*, Vol. I, Chap. XXXI; Vol. II, Chap. CCXV.
2 *Publications of the Canadian Archives*, 1899, p. 180
3 *Champlain Society Publications*, Vol. III, p. 189.

deserves a more extended notice on account of his long connection with Toronto. Thirty years before, one of the Douvilles in 1720 had built the first French post at Toronto. It is possible that the builder of the 1720 post and the commandant in 1759 who burned his fort and retired to Montreal are identical. Alexandre Dagneau Douville was born in 1698 and was the second son of the Sieur Michel Dagneau Douville and an elder brother of the Sieur Philippe Dagneau de la Saussaye, who obtained a lease of the post at Toronto in 1727. It was to Alexandre that Philippe delegated his authority at Toronto while employed as *garde-magasin* at Niagara. After 1730 we find Alexandre at Green Bay with his father-in-law, Coulon de Villiers. The elder de Villiers had married in 1705 or 1706 Angélique Jarret de Verchères, a sister of Madeleine de Verchères, so that the first wife of Captain Douville, the last defender of Fort Toronto, was a niece of that heroine of Canadian history. He was also a brother-in-law of that Jumonville whose death in 1754 at the hands of the party commanded by the young Washington is described as the immediate cause of the Seven Years War; he was also a brother-in-law of the de Villiers who avenged him. Alexandre Douville obtained his commission as ensign in 1735.[1] His name appears among the fifty-five persons accused of misconduct in Canada, twenty-two only of whom were actually under arrest.[2] Douville was fined twenty francs and banished from Paris for three years. It does not appear that he ever actually returned to France. He was living at Verchères in 1763,[3] and died in Montreal about 1773.

NOTE. In the absence of indications on the maps of the period it is difficult to determine the direction of the trails to the French Fort, Toronto. There is a tradition that Indian Road was one of these. As it is in a line with the street known as Weston Road, which diverges from the Carrying-Place at Weston, it is probable that this was one of several routes followed by the tribes from the north when visiting the fort during its brief existence. There was also a well-known trail along the shore, and there are maps which at a later date show a path connected with Dundas St. Bouchette's map shows the site of the blacksmith shop erected after 1788 for the use of the Indians about half a mile to the west of the Fort.

1 *Publication of the Canadian Archives,* 1904, p. 212.
2 SEVERANCE, *An Old Frontier of France,* Vol. II, p. 412.
3 *Rapport de l'Archiviste de la Province de Québec,* 1924, p. 235.

VII

FROM THE FALL OF NIAGARA TO THE END OF THE CONSPIRACY OF PONTIAC: 1759-1764

AS far back as 1729 the President of the Navy Board had written to M. Hocquart that the post at Toronto had been carried on for all time for the king as a dependency of Niagara; and now the fall of the strongest fort in the west had involved the fall of Toronto and of all the weaker posts in the interior. Sir William Johnson was for the moment the most powerful man in America. Disappointed in an early love affair, he had come to America at the age of nineteen, where he speedily consoled himself by an alliance with a Dutch maiden, and after her death by an alliance with Molly Brant, the sister of the great Mohawk chief. Johnson acquired large estates in New York, exercised a dominating influence over the Indians and was made a baronet by the British government. He continued to be a person of great importance long after the fall of Niagara, and as Superintendent of Indian Affairs he was the mediator between the British government and the Indian tribes, including the Indians of the west and north as well as the Iroquois of New York; his jurisdiction extended over all the northern colonies, and from the fall of Niagara till his death in 1774 this brilliant Irishman was the virtual ruler of a region which included the present Province of Ontario. On the outbreak of the Revolutionary War, distracted between his loyalty to the Crown and his reluctance to lead his Indian allies against his old friends in New York, Johnson fell ill, and in the midst of his agony of indecision he died, possibly by his own hand.

After the surrender of Fort Niagara, with characteristic French *esprit*, Pouchot entertained Johnson at dinner. It was a dramatic and historic occasion, for, with the fort, what is now Ontario passed from the French to the English, with all the memories of a century and a half. The interview between Sir

141

William and the Missisauga chief from Toronto, which took place on August the 2nd, contained something of the same dramatic importance. Tequakareigh is given as the name of this sachem, and in his person the tribes north of the lake submitted to the British Crown. Sir William in his *Journal* describes the interview at some length:

With a string and two belts of wampum I bid him welcome, and shook him by the hand. By the second, which was a black belt, I took the hatchet out of the hands of his and all the surrounding nations; recommended hunting and trade to them, which would be more to their interest than quarrelling with the English, who have ever been their friends, and supplied them at the cheapest rates with the necessaries of life, and would do it again, both here (Niagara) and at Oswego, provided they quitted the French interest. This I desired he would acquaint all the surrounding nations with. A black belt, the third and last, was to invite his and all other nations living near them, to repair early next spring to this place and Oswego, where there should be a large assortment of all kinds of goods fit for their use; also recommended it to them to send some of their young men here to hunt and fish for the garrison, for which they would be paid, and kindly treated. Told them at the same time that I would send some of my interpreters, etc., with him on the lake to the next town of the Mississagas, with whom I desired he would use his best endeavours to convince them that it would be in their interest to live in friendship with the English, and that we had no ill intentions against them, if they did not oblige us to it. To which he (Tequakareigh) answered, and said it gave him great pleasure to hear our good words, and was certain it would be extremely agreeable to all the nations with whom he was acquainted, who, with his, were wheedled and led on to strike the English, which he now confessed he was sorry for, and assured they never would again; and that should the French, according to custom, ask them to do so any more, they would turn them out of the country. He, at the same time, begged earnestly, that a plenty of goods might be brought here and to Oswego; and there they, as well as all the other nations around, would come to trade; and their young men should hunt for their brothers, whom they now took fast hold of by the hand, and called upon the Six Nations, who were present, to bear witness to what he had promised. He also desired I would send some person to the Mississaga town, near where Toronto stood, to hear what he would say to their nation, and to see that he would deliver my belts and message honestly. . . . I clothed him very well, and gave him a handsome present to carry home; then took from about his neck a large French medal, and gave him an English one, and a gorget of silver, desiring, whenever he looked at them, he would remember the engagement he now made.

On the third, the *Journal* contains a brief entry: "I gave Lieut. Nellus and de Couange[1] orders to go over the lake with the Chippeway (Missisauga) chief, and call the Mississagays, and speak with the commanding officers of Niagara and Oswego; also to trade with and hunt for their brethren the English." And on Sunday, the nineteenth of August, Johnson, who was now as Oswego, notes in his *Journal* that he had news that two sachems of the Missisaugas would be at Oswego in four or five days, and that they had a great many furs and skins to trade, and that they hoped there would be plenty of goods for that purpose. A little later he remarks: "By letters from thence (Niagara) I learn that the Mississageys came there on my invitation, and have made peace with us, as by Colonel Farquharson's letter, and Lieutenant Nellar's (Nellus's) will appear which letters must be entered in the Indian Records." And on Monday, the 24th of September, "the Mississagays, of whom there came about one hundred and fifty, to Niagara, brought and delivered up two of our men taken at Belle Famille in the battle of the twenty-fourth."

These extracts from the *Journal* of Sir William Johnson describe the alliance now formed between the Missisaugas and the English. The French had lost their allies. All that was now left of their former power on Lake Ontario was the two insignificant schooners, the *Iroquoise* and the *Outaouaise*, which continued to cruise about the lake during the summer of 1760. The *Iroquoise*, which we have seen flitting between Niagara and Toronto with despatches, was the last to disappear.[2]

1 He was retained by Johnson as interpreter after the fall of Niagara.
2 SEVERANCE, *An Old Frontier of France*, Vol. II, p. 386.

It was after the destruction of these last vestiges of French power on the lake that Major Robert Rogers set out from Montreal on September 13, 1760, with two hundred Rangers in fifteen whale-boats to take formal possession for the British of the forts in the west vacated by the French. Rogers was a native of New Hampshire and his exploits in the war with the French made him famous; his subsequent career was not so glorious; six years after this expedition he was tried for treason, and passed into the service of the Dey of Algiers; returning to America at the outbreak of the War of Independence, he was suspected of acting the part of a spy; he finally declared openly for the British, but ended his life in obscurity. In the summer after the fall of Niagara we find him at Toronto. He records in his *Journal* that they had left the ruins of Fort Frontenac on the twenty-fifth of September, and on the thirtieth the *Journal* proceeds:

We embarked at the first dawn of day, and, with the assistance of sails and oars, made great way in a south-west course; and in the evening reached the river Toronto, having run seventy miles. Many points extending far into the water occasioned a frequent alteration of our course. We passed a bank twenty miles in length, but the land behind it seemed to be level, well timbered with large oaks, hickories, maples and some poplars. No mountains appeared in sight. Round the place where formerly the French had a fort, that was called Fort Toronto, there was a tract of about 300 acres of cleared ground. The soil here is principally clay. The deer are extremely plentiful in this country. Some Indians were hunting at the mouth of the river, who ran into the woods at our approach, very much frightened. They came in, however, in the morning, and testified their joy at the news of our success against the French. They told us that we could easily accomplish our journey from thence to Detroit in eight days; that when the French traded at that place (Toronto) the Indians used to come with their peltry from Michilimackina down the river Toronto; that the portage was but twenty miles from that to a river falling into Lake Huron, which had some falls, but none very considerable; they added that there was a carrying-place of fifteen miles from some westerly part of Lake Erie to a river running without falls through several Indian towns into Lake St. Clair. I think Toronto a most convenient place for a factory, and that from thence we may easily settle the north side of Lake Erie.

After leaving Toronto, Rogers proceeded to Niagara and then by way of Lake Erie to Detroit, which passed into the hands of the British on the twenty-ninth of November. Michilimackinac and some of the remoter posts in the west remained in the possession of the French till the following year, when they, too, surrendered to the British. Hardly had the English asserted their authority when the conspiracy of Pontiac broke out, gravely imperilling the lives of the isolated garrisons in the wilderness. The Indians did not readily submit to their new masters, who treated them with less consideration than the French. On March 19, 1762, Governor Burton of Montreal found it necessary to issue a warning to treat the Indians with humanity. In the summer of 1761, the year after Rogers' visit to Toronto, a general plot had been formed to attack Detroit, Niagara, Fort Pitt and other posts garrisoned by the British; and on June 17th, Captain Campbell, commanding at Detroit, wrote to Major Walters, in command at Niagara, to warn him of the impending danger. "I hope," he said, "this will Come time Enough to put You on Your Guard and to send to Oswego, and all the Posts on that communication they Expect to be joined by the Nations that are come from the North by Toronto." From this letter it is learned that the Missisaugas had wavered in their new fidelity to the English and had been employed by the Six Nations to carry wampum belts to the northern nations inciting them to war. Although the attack upon Niagara did not develop at this time, we may imagine that there was much coming and going across the Toronto Carrying-Place, which formed so easy a method of communication with the tribes in the north and with Michilimackinac.

On April 1, 1762, General Gage at Montreal issued a proclamation declaring the fur trade free to all, but forbidding the export of peltries to France.   The rivalry between Montreal and Albany for the control of the trade flared up again.   This time the French in Quebec found powerful allies in British trading interests in Montreal and in England.   It was largely, as Professor McArthur has shown, this trade rivalry between the mother country and the American colonies which determined a little later the boundary provisions of the Quebec Act.

In the summer of 1762, three years after the French had abandoned Toronto, there was again trading at that place; a certain Monsieur Baby and others were operating on passes granted by Gage himself.   The Babys of Detroit had been engaged in the fur trade in the lake region, especially with the Mohicans and the Chaouenons, long before the conquest. After a stout defence of the French cause, they had shown themselves equally loyal to the British.   Jacques Duperon Baby, the friend of Pontiac and of the British, is the best known of the four brothers engaged in the trade at Detroit, which he resumed again under British auspices.   At a later date, Baby became superintendent of Indians and died at Sandwich, Ontario, in 1789.   It is of interest to note that his more distinguished son, the Hon. James Baby, established himself on the site of the old Seneca village of Teiaiagon on the Humber, which was so near the scene of these trading operations of 1762.

Under date of July 2nd, Major Walters, commandant at Niagara, had written to Amherst in New York that he had seized fifteen barrels of brandy of eight gallons each (presumably at Toronto); and on the twenty-fifth of the same month, Amherst wrote from New York to Major Wilkins, the new commandant:

As I conclude Major Walters will be set out before this reaches Niagara (I am writing to you). . . . He had seized fifteen barrels of brandy belonging to a Monsieur Baby who had Governor Gage's pass. . . Walters transmitted (to me) copies of Gage's passes permitting traders to carry rum for the use of Indians at Toronto. . . . you will keep the brandy till I write Gage."

On the seventh of October, Gage himself wrote from Montreal to Wilkins:

Complaints have been made here from Michilimackinac that the traders of Toronto debauch all the Indians from those quarters by selling them rum, I suppose you have a detachment at Toronto as I am told no traders are permitted to go where there are no troops.

Gage also wrote to Amherst, and the latter wrote to Johnson, enclosing an extract from Gage's letter. From the *Johnson Papers*[1] we learn the names of the offending traders, Schuyler, Stevenson, Everart, Wendel and Company, all of them Albany people. They had summoned the Indians from Michilimackinac, had taken all their skins in return for rum, and had left them destitute. This sinister incident throws a light upon the savage fury of the Indians at Michilimackinac during the conspiracy of Pontiac.

On the twenty-fourth General Amherst wrote from New York to Wilkins; he had written to Gage about the passes. "I believe," he writes, "that he (Gage) will allow no rum carried .... but I fear the traders fall upon very unfair means of getting up that pernicious liquor even by altering passes." Amherst had given a pass to Steadman,[2] a sutler to the Niagara garrison, and he remarks, "One of his partners, Mitchell, had the assurance to present it to me ... in the old pass he was permitted to carry wines but no rum. The words 'but no' were scratched out and the following substituted in their room, 'he is permitted to carry wines, spirits and rum.'"

On the eighth, Wilkins informed Amherst that the Indian interpreter, de Couange, a Frenchman whom Johnson had retained after the capture of Niagara, had written to him a letter of complaints made to him by the Indians from and about Toronto that they had been cheated and very ill-used by the traders at that place, and that they begged for redress from the commandant at Niagara.

1 1 Vol. III, p. 943.
2 The lessee of the Niagara Portage.

On the twenty-first of November, Amherst wrote again to Wilkins from New York:

> What you mention of the distressful situation of the Indians occasioned with their being supplied with that pernicious liquor at Toronto fully proves that the traders fall upon very unfair means to get it up. . . and as that place is near your post I desire you will send parties thither whenever you think it necessary and seize every drop of rum or spirituous liquor. . . in the traders' stores.

Gage from Montreal wrote again to Wilkins on the second of December in a very peremptory manner:

> If Toronto was a little nearer Fort William Augustus, I should soon put an end to their rum-selling and had I been acquainted with your unwillingness to go thither without particular orders, I should most undoubtedly beat up their quarters. For the future if you see a gill of spirits in any of my passes you may conclude it put in clandestinely. I shall not grant a single drop to any soul and shall secure every pass the moment the waters are navigable in the spring.

At the same time, Sir William Johnson, writing from Johnson Hall on the twenty-second of December, repeated Amherst's desire for Wilkins to send parties to Toronto.

Apparently the situation was now critical; Amherst, Gage and Johnson would hardly have combined to focus their attention upon a mere trifle at an obscure outpost; possibly defection was feared.

To all this pressure, Wilkins responded slowly; the Babys were still powerful persons in the wilderness; he waited till the spring of 1763.[1] On May the tenth, he reported to Amherst:

> I have sent a lieutenant, one sergeant, two corporals and twenty men on a visit to Toronto and they are returned with one Knaggs, a trader, and one servant and all his goods which are very considerable and are lodged in a house with the traders of this place. When the party arrived at Toronto he had left

1 On the 4th of March, 1763, "Joseph Dubois, marchand-voyageur" of Montreal, engaged "J.-B. Senecal, pour transporter des marchandises à Toronto, en canot." Senecal would be a "milieu," i.e., a man hired to paddle in the middle of the canoe who would be paid less. E.-Z.M.

only about ten gallons of rum which he gave to the party at a gill a man a day. But Knaggs says he was in daily expectation of his partners with another pass and goods from Montreal to trade at Cataraqui . . . No other trader was found there on this visit. I shall send parties on the same occasion as often as possible, though it is above 100 miles by the coast and not prudent to venture across in an open boat. . . The Indians at Toronto made no objection to the party's bringing Knaggs away but assisted them in repairing their boats etc. Since the above, many Indians are come here to complain of the treatment received from other traders lately arrived at Toronto . . . local traders complain about others getting passes to trade at Toronto and places where there are no troops (they want the same permission).[1]

From another source we learn that the Missisauga chief at Toronto, Wabecommegat, engaged to allow no further trade at that place. With the outbreak of the conspiracy of Pontiac, Gage forbade all trade with the Indians. In 1764, so far as Quebec was concerned, the trade was restricted to Carillon on the Ottawa and the Cedars on the St. Lawrence; the Indians were compelled to bring their peltries to these places, and traders were to refrain from penetrating into the interior.

Already, however, the English traders, who had followed in the wake of the army into Quebec, had begun to take an active part in the fur trade; and these adventurous spirits were as difficult to control as the *coureurs-de-bois*. Alexander Henry, the most adventurous of them all, was at Mackinac in 1763 when that place was captured by the allies of Pontiac; he escaped the massacre, but was made prisoner by the Missisaugas, who brought him with them in 1764 when they came to Johnson's great council at Niagara. The route which the Missisaugas followed with their prisoner was the familiar route by the eastern shore of the Georgian Bay, Lake Simcoe and the Toronto Carrying-Place. Henry recounts his experi-

1 For the details of this incident I am indebted to Professor W. B. Kerr, of the University of Buffalo, who has placed at my disposal material drawn from the Amherst correspondence in the Public Records Office, London, England.

ences in his *Travels and Adventures*. He remarks, after
describing the trip down the Georgian Bay:

The next day was calm, and we arrived at the entrance of
the navigation which leads to Lake aux Claies. We presently
passed two short carrying-places at each of which were several
lodges of Indians, containing only women and children, the
men being gone to the Council at Niagara. From this, as from
a former instance, my companions derived fresh courage. On
the 18th of June, we crossed Lake aux Claies,[1] which appeared
to be upwards of twenty miles in length. At its farther end we
came to the carrying-place of Toranto. Here the Indians
obliged me to carry a burden of more than a hundred pounds
weight. The day was very hot, and the woods and marshes
abounded with mosquitoes; but, the Indians walked at a quick
pace, and I could by no means see myself left behind. The
whole country was a thick forest, through which our only road
was a foot-path, or such as, in America, is exclusively termed
an Indian path. Next morning, at ten o'clock, we reached the
shore of Lake Ontario. Here we were employed two days in
making canoes, out of the bark of the elm-tree, in which we were
to transport ourselves to Niagara. For this purpose the
Indians first cut down a tree; then stripped off the bark, in one
entire sheet, of about eighteen feet in length, the incision
being length-wise. The canoe was now complete, as to its
top, bottom and sides. Its ends were next closed, by sewing
the bark together; and a few ribs and bars being introduced,
the architecture was finished. In this manner, we made two
canoes; of which one carried eight men, the other, nine. On
the 21st, we embarked at Toranto, and encamped, in the
evening, four miles short of Fort Niagara, which the Indians
would not approach till morning.[2]

Some conception of the rapidity of the movements of the
Indians can be formed from the fact that, according to Henry,
the Missisaugas crossed Lake Simcoe on the eighteenth and
were at the mouth of the Humber on the morning of the nineteenth at ten o'clock; and of the vigour of Henry himself, who
carried a load of a hundred pounds on his back twenty-nine
miles in so short a time.

1 Lake Toronto has now become Lac aux Claies. Consult Hunter, *A History of Simcoe County*, Vol. I, p. 11.
2 *Travels and Adventures*, Alexander Henry, edited by Dr. James Bain; p. XIX, note. Ibid., pp. 170-172.

VIII

FROM THE CONSPIRACY OF PONTIAC TO THE QUEBEC ACT: 1764-1774

THE first act of the British government after the signing of the Treaty of Paris was to define by proclamation the boundaries of the new Province of Quebec. Its western limits were determined by a line running from the St. Lawrence River, at the intersection of the forty-fifth parallel, to the south-east corner of Lake Nipissing. Ontario and all the western country was thus outside the new Province, and although the governors of Quebec passed regulations with regard to the Indian territory, and issued licenses to those who went there to trade, this vast region was somewhat loosely governed. The original intention of placing the whole of the western country under one general control and government by Act of Parliament was not carried out. The New England colonies regarded the regions south of the lakes as their natural area for expansion. The traders from Albany lost no time in appropriating as much as they could of the fur trade of their conquered French rivals in Quebec on both sides of the lakes. Sir William Johnson, while admitting the authority of Sir Guy Carleton, continued to divert the fur trade to New England, and through his great influence with the tribes, and his authority as Indian Agent, controlled great portions of the new territory.

It is not likely that much trading went on at the mouth of the Humber for some years after the conspiracy of Pontiac.[1] Both sides of the lake were now under one crown, but the trade rivalries continued, and for the moment the furs passed down the Mohawk to Albany. Toronto, however, was a post too valuable to be neglected. In a report on the value of the trade at the three posts on Lake Ontario, submitted to the French

1 "It was not till 1771 that the western fur trade recovered from the conspiracy of Pontiac." Atcheson, *Origin and Progress of the North-West Company of Canada*, 1811, p. 5.

government in 1757, it is stated that a hundred and fifty bales of peltries might be collected at Toronto in a year,[1] two hundred and fifty to three hundred at Niagara, while at Fort Frontenac, which seems to have sunk into insignificance, only twenty or thirty were to be expected. After the fall of Chouéguen, Toronto for a short time appeared as the rival of Niagara. Johnson made every effort to control this trade in the interests of the merchants of Albany, but not always with success. In the beginning of 1767 we find him writing to General Gage, at Montreal:

Capt. Browne writes me that he has, at the request of Commissary Roberts, caused two traders to be apprehended at Toronto, where they were trading contrary to authority. I hope Lieut.-Gov. Carleton will, agreeable to the declaration in one of his letters, have them prosecuted and punished as an example to the rest. I am informed that there are several more from Canada trading with the Indians on the north side of Lake Ontario, and up along the rivers in that quarter, which, if not prevented, must entirely ruin the fair trader.[2]

Later in the summer, Wabecommegat, the chief of the Missisaugas at Toronto, visited Niagara; he had an interview with Norman M'Leod, the Indian Agent at that place, who writes in his journal:

July 17th (1767). Arrived Wabecommegat, chief of the Mississagas. July 18th.—This day Wabecommegat came to speak to me, but was so drunk that no one could understand him.—July 19th. Had a small conference with Wabecommegat. Present—Norman M'Leod, Esq.; Mr. Neil MacLean, Commissary of Provisions; Jean Baptiste de Couange, interpreter. Wabecommegat spoke first, and, after the usual compliments, told that as soon as he had heard of my arrival, he and his

1 "Toronto, situé au nord du lac Ontario vis-a-vis de Niagara, établi pour empêcher les sauvages du nord d'aller commercier à Chouéguen n'existant plus, ce poste devient inutile. Le roi en fait le commerce, les effets y montent des batteaux conduits par des miliciens commandés pour cela; les sauvages qui y traitent sont les Mississagués et les Salteux. Il en peut sortir cent cinquante paquets de pelleteries." "Mémoire sur l'état de la Nouvelle France, 1757," *Rapport de l'Archiviste de la Province de Québec*, 1923-1924, p. 49.

2 *Publication of the Canadian Archives*, 1890, State Papers, p. 31, Q 5-1; Ibid., p. 24, Johnson to Carleton, p. 25, Carleton to Johnson.

young men came to see me.   He then asked me if I had any news, and desired I should tell all I had.   Then he gave four strings of wampum.   I then told them: "Children, I am glad to see you.   I am sent by your father, Sir William Johnson, to take care of your trade, and to prevent abuses therein.— Children, I am sorry to hear you have permitted people to trade at Toronto.   I hope you will prevent it for the future.   All of you know the reason of this belt of wampum being left in this place.   (I then showed them a large belt left here five or six years ago by Wabecommegat, by which belt he was under promise not to allow anybody whatever to carry on trade at Toronto.)   Now, children, I have no more to say, but desire you to remember and keep close to all the promises you have made to your English father.   You must not listen to any bad news.   When you hear any, good or bad, come to me with it. You may depend upon it I shall always tell you the truth." (I gave four strings of wampum.)

Wabecommegat replied: "Father, we have heard you with attention.—We will allow no more trade to be carried on at Toronto.   As for myself, it is well known I don't approve of it, as I went with the interpreter to bring in those who were trading at that place.   We go away this day, and hope our father will give us some provisions, rum, powder and shot, and we will bring you venison when we return."   I replied, it was not in my power to give them much, but as it was the first time I had the pleasure of speaking to them, they should have a little of what they wanted.

It is plain from these two incidents that Sir William was having a good deal of trouble in excluding traders from Quebec from the regions north of the lake, and especially from the foot of the Toronto Carrying-Place.   Later in the year he made up his mind that a new system was necessary, and we find him writing to the Earl of Selbourne under the date of December 3rd, advising that exclusive rights to trade should be given to approved persons at certain posts in the wilderness, and selecting Toronto to illustrate his point.   He remarks:

On the other hand, every step our Traders take beyond the Posts is attended at least with some *risque*, and a very heavy expence, which the Indians must feel as heavily on the purchase of their commodities, all which considered, is it not reasonable to suppose that they would rather employ their Idle time in quest of a cheep Market, than sit down with such slender returns as they must receive in their own Villages; as a proof of which I shall give one instance concerning Toronto on the North shore of Lake Ontario formerly dependant on Niagara, which notwithstanding the assertion of Major Rogers "that even a single trader would not think it worth attention to supply a dependant Post" yet I have heard traders of long experience and good circumstances affirm that for the exclusive trade of that place for one season they would willingly pay £1000, so certain were they of a quiet Market from the cheapness at which they could afford their goods their, and I am certain that a handsome Fund would arise from farming out the places of Trade to Merchants of Fortune and Character, they giving security to be answerable for the misconduct of the Factors, which could not be more than we find at present.[1]

Apparently Sir William had been no more successful than the French in coping with the evils of the trade, drunkenness among the Indians, illicit trading and the bad conduct of store-keepers and garrisons.

Three years after this, a Frenchman from Montreal, St. Jean Rousseau, established himself at the mouth of the Humber and, in 1774, with the passing of the Quebec Act, the whole of the "Old North-West," which included the territory north and south of the lakes to the Ohio and the Mississippi, was annexed to Quebec. Under the leadership of a group of Scotch and French fur-traders, who afterwards grew into the North-West Company, Montreal recaptured the ascendancy. We shall find that the North-Westers immediately turned their eyes to Toronto.

1 *New York Colonial Documents,* Vol. VI, p. 1000.

IX

FROM THE QUEBEC ACT TO THE FOUNDING OF YORK: 1774-1793

T HE Quebec Act of 1774, which restored to the French their language and religion, restored also that rich and fertile region lying between the Ohio and the Mississippi to its original owners. It is said that English statesmen, discerning the growing independence of the American colonies, intended the Act as a salutary warning; but that the colonies, gravely displeased with the liberties, civil and religious, accorded to the conquered French, and aghast at the alienation of territory which they had come to regard as their natural area of expansion, saw themselves shut in on the north and the west, and menaced by feudalism more deeply entrenched than before, and that the Quebec Act proved to be not the least of the causes of the American Revolution.

In the following year the war broke out and a veil descends upon events in the peninsula of Ontario[1] until the coming of the Loyalists in 1784. The colonies, after their first unsuccessful attempt to seize Quebec, seem to have been content that the Canadians should remain neutral. They did little to provoke the *habitants* in the St. Lawrence Valley, and since both sides tacitly agreed not to bring the Indians into the quarrel,[2] the latter, with the exception of the Iroquois, remained for the most part passive spectators, ready to declare for the victors. On August 14, 1775, however, when Montgomery's invasion was imminent, Carleton wrote to Dartmouth, "The Indians on the St. Lawrence have promised their assistance and with some Missisaugas from north of Lake Ontario (possibly from the mouth of the Toronto river) have done duty with the troops at St. John's since the

1 "Neither boat nor individual could leave or enter the region without a permit, not even Mme. Langlade." McIlwraith, *Life of Haldimand*, p. 164.
2 BRADLEY, *The Making of Canada*, p. 119.

155

18th of June."[1]   And on September 21st of the same year
Cramahé wrote to Dartmouth, "The rebels have been beaten
back near St. John's; the Indians behaved with great spirit,
and had they remained firm the Province would have been
saved this year, but finding the Canadians averse to taking up
arms in defence of their country, they withdrew." And on the
same date Carleton wrote from Montreal, "The Indians have
left and will do nothing, unless the Canadians exert themselves
also." As the war progressed, the Indians of the lake region
adopted the apathetic attitude of the *habitants* of Quebec.[2]
In 1778 there was only a single British regiment between
Montreal and Michilimackinac,[3] and between the posts on the
lakes and New Orleans there was not in that year a single fort
or garrison to check the encroachments of the French and
Spanish from the Mississippi Valley and the American revolutionaries from Virginia. Niagara, Detroit, Michilimackinac
were not seriously menaced during the war which left the
peninsula of Ontario untouched.

In March, 1779, we catch one brief, vivid glimpse of
abandoned Toronto. Captain Walter Butler,[4] eldest son of
Lieut.-Col. John Butler of Butler's Rangers, had been stationed
at Niagara during the preceding autumn and winter; as he did
not reach Niagara till the end of July, he had consequently no
part in the destruction of Wyoming; but owing to his father's
illness, he commanded in person the raid into Cherry Valley
which took place in November, where the Indians again got out
of hand. In the spring of 1779 Walter Butler was despatched

---

1 *Publication of the Canadian Archives,* 1890, State Papers, p. 63, Carleton
to Dartmouth.

2 "That aromatic root (ginseng) which the old Jesuits used to ship to
China, where it brought five dollars a pound, proved a sore temptation to the
Mississagas on the northern shore of Lake Ontario. They were faithful and
well-disposed to their neighbours of Carleton Island, but always clamouring
for goods and rum, which they often found could be more quickly gained in
the ginseng trade than by going to war." McIlwraith, *Life of Haldimand,*
p. 164.   Chabert on the Niagara portage had made a fortune from ginseng

3 "Lieutenant-Governor Sinclair tried to find a shorter route from his
post (Michilimackinac) to Niagara by way of Lake Huron and Lake Simcoe,
portaging thence to Toronto." McIlwraith, *Life of Haldimand,* p. 163.

4 Memoir by General Ernest Cruikshank, *Transactions Canadian Institute,* 1892-1893, p. 284; *Publication of the Canadian Archives,* 1886, B 105,
p. 70.

to Quebec with the pay-lists and accounts of his regiment. He left Niagara on the eighth of March, reached the head of the lake on the eleventh, and next day camped on the shore below Scarborough Heights. He records in his diary:[1]

March 12th.—Set off at seven o'clock this morning; the wind at N.W.; too much off shore to sail; rowed till 11 o'clock; put into the river called the Credit, 17 miles from the last station. The shore in general good for boats to land; the land low and a good beach, except the points, which are bluff. Two Missassaugas came to me and informed me a number of them lived up this river. Gave them bread and put off at 12; rowed to the bay above Toronto; hoisted sail: found the wind too high to go round the long point forming the basin or bay below Toronto. Continuing sailing down the bay to the camping place, unloaded the boat, hauled her over and loaded again in an hour and a half; rowed from this to the beginning of the high lands, encamped on the beach and secured the boat. Toronto was built on a level spot of ground nearly opposite a long neck or point of land running seven or eight miles into the lake, forming a noble bay of eight or nine miles deep, two or three miles from the bottom of which, on the north side, ships can ride in safety. It's strange the French built the fort where they did, and not where their shipping were wont to lay, which was a few miles below the fort down the bay.[2] The bay of Toronto was filled with all kinds of wild fowl. Saw on the north side of the bay several wigwams and canoes turned up on the shore. The land about Toronto appears very good for cultivation. From Toronto to the river *du Credit* it is 12 miles across the bay, but better than 20 along shore, which is the way boats must take except the weather is very calm or a light breeze in your favour. From Toronto to the beginning of the high lands is nine or ten miles down the basin, but nearly double round the point.[3]

1 Memoir by General Ernest Cruikshank, *Transactions Canadian Institute,* 1892-1893, p. 280.

2 Probably at the mouth of the Humber.

3 (a) On September 14, 1780, Major Bolton wrote to Haldimand from Niagara, "You have, Sir, a journal of the party I sent to Lake Huron by way of Toronto." This document has not yet been discovered. Ibid., p. 304.

(b) On September 13, 1782, Col. H. Dundas wrote to Major R. Matthews, "Mr. Thompson, a merchant here (Niagara) has applied to me for leave to send a person to Toronto, opposite this, to trade with the Indians. I told him I could not grant his request until His Excellency's pleasure on that head was known. I must observe that Mr. Thompson is a very moderate man and has suffered much from the rebels on the Mohawk river." Ibid., p. 305.

Meantime, though Ontario remained untouched by the war, away to the south-west, near the junction of the Ohio and the Mississippi, events were transpiring in the country of the Illinois which might have had a profound effect upon the future destiny of the city of Toronto had the intentions of Lord Dorchester been carried out; and since the details of the story are comparatively unknown, it may be of interest to recount at greater length how nearly the capital of the Upper Province began its career under French auspices; for as we shall presently see, Dorchester intended, and perhaps with justice, to reward the loyal devotion of three French-Canadians to himself and to the British Crown with extensive grants of land in the neighbourhood of the proposed capital.

Kaskaskia,[1] on the east bank of the Mississippi, halfway between the modern cities of St. Louis and Cairo, had been a French trading-post and a mission of the Jesuits since the beginning of the eighteenth century. Indeed, the connection of the French with the Kaskaskies had begun with the explorations of Marquette. The Kaskaskies had been the allies of the French in many of their wars with the English, and had shared with the Abenakies the reputation of being the best Catholics and the most devoted allies of the French among all the tribes in America. Their chief at the time of the British conquest had declared that not one of the Kaskaskies would submit to the English. "Not a single Englishman shall come here," they said, "so long as the red men live. Our hearts are with the French; we detest the English and we should like to kill them all."[2] Under the tutelage of the missionaries, they had made good progress in agriculture; their wheat was as good as that grown in France; they had their vegetable gardens and their orchards, and there were three mills near their village to grind their grain; they had a large church with a clock in the steeple, and the manners of the people had become so far refined that the French were not unwilling to espouse their daughters.

1 Kaskaskia has disappeared, swept away by floods of the Mississippi.
2 ROCHEMONTEIX, Les Jésuites et la Nouvelle France, Tome III, p. 546.

Kaskaskia, renamed Fort Gage, was held for the English at the time of the Revolutionary War by Philippe François de Rastel, Sieur de Rocheblave,[1] who had won the confidence of Sir Guy Carleton and had succeeded in reconciling the inhabitants to the new régime. On August 13, 1777, Sir Guy Carleton wrote to Lord Sackville, Secretary for the Colonies: "Mr. de Rocheblave is a Canadian gentleman, formerly in the French service, whom I have employed to have an eye on the Spaniards and the management of the Indians on that side." At this time de Rocheblave had been in charge for three years at Fort Gage, and had rendered such valuable services to the English that it was proposed to make him Governor of New Orleans,[2] or at least to encourage him with the hope of that office should the British acquire that city. His position was a difficult one; the intrigues of the Spanish, who were in possession of the west bank of the Mississippi, ceded to them by France in 1662, threatened the loyalty of the Indians, and on July 4, 1778, de Rocheblave wrote urgently to Haldimand for troops, adding that he would struggle as long as possible to maintain the post. Almost immediately, Illinois was overrun by the revolutionaries, and Kaskaskia was surprised at night and de Rocheblave was taken prisoner in his bed, put in irons, flung into a pig-stye and eventually consigned to a prison in Virginia, from which he managed to escape in 1780 and to find his way back to Canada. De Rocheblave had lost all his property in Kaskaskia and had suffered in a Virginia prison for his devotion to the British cause; accordingly at the conclusion of the war, he lost no time in claiming what he conceived to be just compensation for his sufferings and his losses; he asked for the site of the future city of Toronto.

It was in 1785 that de Rocheblave first discussed this matter with Lieutenant-Governor Hamilton.[3] There were

1 "Philippe François de Rastel de Rocheblave," par Francis Audet et l'honorable Édouard Fabre Surveyer. *La Presse*, Montreal, December 10, 1927.
2 Consult McIlwraith's *Life of Haldimand*, pp. 77, 78, 80-81.
3 BRADLEY, *Life of Dorchester*, p. 158.

already others who had cast their eyes upon the abandoned trading-post and carrying-place at Toronto. The exclusion of American traders from British territory as a result of the war had given an immense impetus to the Canadian trade, and as early as 1783 the merchants of Montreal, under the leadership of the two Frobishers and others, had united to form the North-West Company, which was destined to control the fur trade for so many years and to explore the unknown west. Their first task at the conclusion of the war was to search for a passage from Lake Superior to the Winnipeg River, where their communications would be secure from interruption on the part of the Americans, and their second task was to discover some other approach to Lake Huron and the Sault than the road by the Ottawa River and Lake Nipissing.

In April, 1784, Benjamin Frobisher, one of the most active partners of the new North-West Company, wrote to a member of the Executive Council asking for definite information respecting the international boundary, westward from Lake Superior, as he suspected that the Grand Portage was included by the treaty within the United States, as actually proved to be the case. At the same time he requested a passport for twenty-eight long canoes, valued with their cargoes at £20,000, which the company intended to despatch to the North-West in May.

This large supply, added to the property the Company already have in that country, demands their utmost attention. They do not know how soon they may be deprived of the immediate, and at present the only, communication from Lake Superior, and on that account they intend at their own expense, unless Government prefer to undertake it, to discover, if possible, another passage that will in all events fall within the British line, of which they may avail themselves in case of need. Such an undertaking must prove an arduous one and be attended with great expense, while their success will remain very uncertain, on which account the Company are induced to hope that if it is discovered it will be granted to them in full right for a certain term of years, not less than seven, as a reward for their public spirit and the advantages that will result to this province from its discovery.

Frobisher also advised the establishment of a small military post to command the entrance into Lake Superior.

These proposals were favourably received by the government and Captain Robertson was immediately instructed to examine the coast and report without delay.   He selected the bay at Tessalon as the most suitable site for a fort, and reported among other matters that "he had obtained some intelligence from white men and Indians of a very fertile and advantageous tract of land between Lakes Huron and Ontario, and by communication that way the trade with Canada must be carried on to put us on a footing with our neighbors from the colonies."

In July, Frobisher and McTavish arrived at Mackinac, and Robertson again wrote to the Governor:

With them I have had several conferences with regard to the future communication to this country so as to enable them or others to trade in those parts on a footing with the Americans, and after inquiry, that between Lakes Ontario and Huron is the only one to be attempted, and that very practicable, by shortening the road greatly and avoiding the Niagara carrying-place and any interference with our neighbors.

Robertson then declared his intention of returning that way (i.e. by the Toronto Carrying-Place) to Quebec when relieved of his command.[1]   In the same year Captain Robertson, along with Frobisher, McTavish and others, applied for a grant of a tract of land along the route between the Georgian Bay and Lake Ontario in order to carry on the North-West trade.[2]

Frobisher and his associates were not long in discovering a route from Lake Superior to the Winnipeg River which would lie within British territory, and in the spring of the next year we find him urging upon the government the claims of the Toronto Carrying-Place as a substitute for the Ottawa route which he described in a letter under the date of May 2, 1785, to

1 GENERAL ERNEST CRUIKSHANK, "The Fur Trade, 1763-1787," *Transactions Canadian Institute*, 1894-1895, pp. 75-76.

2 *Publication of the Canadian Archives*, 1888.   Note E.   "Robertson to Haldimand, Michilimackinac, July 10, 1784." *Ontario Public Archives*, 1890, p. 371 ; "Carleton to Collins, May 2, 1785."

the Hon. Henry Hamilton, "as most eminently dangerous for the Transport of Goods from the number of Cataracts, and the length and rapidity of the river, not to mention the Carrying-Places, which from hence to Lake Huron, are upwards of Forty in number." Hamilton, apparently, had instructed Frobisher to inquire into the merits of the Trent Valley route from Cataraqui to Lac aux Claies, which turned out to be impracticable and, in fact, longer than the Carrying-Place. Frobisher expresses himself strongly in favour of the latter route.

In the letter from which quotation has already been made, he remarks:

Since I had the Honour to receive your letter of the 10th of March, I have made every inquiry in my power, Not only in Town but in different Parts of the Country, respecting the practicability of a communication from Lake Ontario to Lake Huron, and I am sorry to say, all my endeavours to acquire knowledge of it are far from being satisfactory. I have seen several persons who have gone from hence to Lake Huron by the carrying place of Torronto, but have only met with one who has set out from the Bay of Kentie, and that so far back as the year 1761, and the knowledge he seems to have of the country he travelled through I consider as very imperfect. I have however laid it down in the inclosed sketch, more to show that there is such a Road, than any opinion I have of its being Correct. I am told the Lands from the Bay of Kentie to Lake La Clie abound with good Wood and are generally fit for Cultivation; there are several villages of the Mississagues on different parts of that Road who raise Indian Corn and other grains, and whose friendship it will be necessary to Cultivate, if upon survey it should be found practicable, but if I may rely on information, there is very little probability of establishing in that quarter a Communication for Boats or Large Canoes on account of the Water being generally very shallow between the different Lakes, except in the Spring, and even then it is described to me as being insufficient for large Canoes, not to mention the Carrying Places which are Six or Seven in Number to reach Lake La Clie, and I am told three of them are near three leagues in length; I am, however, informed that to the distance of the Rice, or the *folle avoine* lake, from the Bay of Kentie, there is plenty of water for Boats of any Burthen. From all these circumstances as related to me, I judge a Communication that way without paying any regard to Carrying places, to be from the want of water totally impracticable; however as I believe there is no man in the country capable of giving any certain information about it, I think a Project that holds out so many advantages to the Province at large ought not to be relinquished until it is found upon Survey, to be as represented really impracticable, and should that be the case, the next object that offers to Introduce a Communication between the two Lakes is the Carrying place of Torronto, which from the Ontario side to Lake Huron in a direct line, is no more than 100 miles, and by water it does not exceed 160—That is, Torronto (*sic*), 45 miles, Lake La Clie, 37, thence to Lake Huron over Land, 18; or by the River as laid down in the enclosed sketch about 70.—These, Sir are my sentiments, until we are better informed of the nature of the Communication from the Bay of Kentie to Lake La Clie, and let what will be the Event of that Survey, I conceive there is a necessity for Establishing the Carrying place of Torronto as speedily as possible—On the other hand we must also consider the advantages that would arrise from so ready a Communication with Lake Huron, which while it extends, and adds strength and Security to our Frontier (if I may be allowed the expression) will with the other settlements afford effectual Protection to the Natives between the Two Lakes, who are Mississagues and some Tribes of the Chippawas, from whence I conceive there will be no difficulty in making the purchase, more especially as I believe their best hunting Lands are at some distance from the Tract that would be chosen for the purpose of establishing an intercourse of Transport between the two Lakes.[1]

No steps were taken immediately to secure from the Indians the tract which Frobisher considered necessary for establishing communication across the Toronto Carrying-Place. The Hon. Henry Hamilton, to whom he had addressed himself, had been appointed Lieutenant-Governor on the departure of Haldimand in 1784; he has been described as an energetic soldier and popular both with his men and with the Indians, but as an incautious

---

1 *Publication of the Canadian Archives*, 1890, pp. 54-56 ; Ibid., p. 48, Hamilton to Sydney, June 6, 1785. "The enclosed plan No. 1 shows the communication from Lake Ontario to Lake Huron." Ibid., Q. CCLXXX, Pt. II (1794), Q. CCLXXXI, Pt. I (1795), passim and Q. CCXIV.

and tactless politician; he had been appointed as a reward for his activity in frontier wars and his sufferings after Vincennes and at the hands of his Virginian gaolers.   It is he who had forwarded to Haldimand, from Detroit, on August 11, 1778, the news of the capture of de Rocheblave by the rebels at Kaskaskia, a fate which he was to share himself in the next year when the important post of Vincennes fell to the revolutionaries.   Hamilton's term in office was brief; he was recalled and succeeded by Hope, who, in turn, was presently to give place to Carleton, who returned to Quebec in October, 1786, for his second term of office.

For two years de Rocheblave had done nothing; but with the return of Carleton, to whom he was known personally, he proceeded to press his claim for the Toronto lands with great energy.   On January 16, 1787, he presented a memorial to Lord Dorchester, in which he stated that, two years before, he had proposed to His Honour Lieutenant-Governor Hamilton[1] that for reasons of public utility the route followed in communicating with the upper countries should be changed, and that he himself should be given the preference of the Portage of Toronto with a tract of land at that place.   On the twentieth of May, he reiterated his appeal, adding that he wished to make provision for his family and for his old age.   On the twenty-fifth of the same month, in a third memorial, he defined the boundaries of the piece of land which he wished to obtain at Toronto, and petitioned the government to grant him:

a thousand acres on Toronto Bay to commence at the river which falls into Lake Ontario above the bluffs to the north-east of the said Toronto and extending to the old settlement at the said place of Toronto, and to grant him in the same way without deduction from the said amount, a small island lying between the said old settlement and the said river in the same Bay on which to keep some animals; and that His Lordship should grant and concede in the name of the Government to his wife three sons and a daughter the usual amount of land adjoining those for which he petitioned.

1 *Publication of the Canadian Archives,* 1890, Q. 24—1.242, p. 149, "Hamilton to Sydney, March 10, 1785."

It would be interesting to learn on what occasion de Rocheblave became so intimately acquainted with the configuration of the site of the present city of Toronto; possibly in 1786 when he received a permit to trade at Michilimackinac. He must have had previous knowledge of the value of the district and now, with the loss of the territory south of the lakes, the Carrying-Place was about to assume a new importance as the approach to the great area north-west of Lake Superior. De Rocheblave supported his request for land at Toronto by the statement that he had been the first to recommend the change of route, and to point out the advantage of the Carrying-Place. We shall presently see how the Governor and his council dealt with his application. In the meantime, acting either on de Rocheblave's petition or on Frobisher's advice, steps were taken to secure from the Indians the land afterwards known as "The Toronto Purchase." *

On the twenty-third of September in the same year, 1787, a meeting took place at the Carrying-Place on the Bay of Quinte, between Deputy Surveyor-General Collins from Quebec, acting on behalf of the Crown, and three chiefs of the Missisauga Indians, who expressed their willingness to convey to the white men the desired land. On this occasion the exact limits of the property transferred were not defined. The price paid to the Indians for an area which embraces about one-third of the county of York was the sum of £1,700 in cash and goods, of which it is not now possible to ascertain how much was paid to the Indians in cash. The boundaries of the tract were defined and certain defects in the original purchase rectified, in a subsequent agreement made with the Missisaugas in 1805. The second meeting took place at the River Credit. The Carrying-Place on the Bay of Quinte, which spanned the peninsula connecting Prince Edward County with the mainland, provided an historic setting for the original transfer: near at hand was the site of the Iroquois village of Kenté, the scene of the missionary efforts of the Sulpicians and of the Récollets; far to the east lay the ruins of Fort Frontenac, with its memories

of La Salle; Hay Bay and Ameliasburg were already occupied by the Loyalists; it was an historic region, rendered still more memorable at a later period by the fervours of early Methodism and the conflicts of the War of 1812. Wabukanyne, the chief sachem of the Missisaugas, whose name occurs on other Indian treaties of the period, was the first to attach his signature; Neace and Pakquan are the names of the other chiefs who transferred to the Crown the land which included the Carrying-Place at Toronto and the site of the present city; in addition to
* John Collins, Louis Protle and Nathaniel Lines, witnessed the document.[1]

On July 7, 1788, Deputy Surveyor-General Collins instructed Alexander Aitkin to commence a survey of the land purchased at Toronto from the Indians in the preceding year. On September 15, 1788, Aitkin wrote from Kingston, describing his experiences:

Sir, Agreeable to your instructions of the 7th of July last which I received the 25th of the same month, I hired a party with all possible despatch and embarked on board the *Seneca*[2] for Toronto where I landed the 1st of August. For two or three days after our landing we were employed in building a kind of store house to preserve the Indian presents as well as my own provisions from the rain and bad weather. I then desired Mr. Lines, the Interpreter, to signify to the Indian Chief then on the spot my intention of beginning to survey the land purchased from them last year by Sir John Johnson and pointed out to him where I was to begin. I requested of him to go with me to the spot along with Mr. Lines, which he did, but instead of going to the lower end of the Beach which forms the Harbour he brought me to the river called on the Plan Nechengquakekonk which is upwards of three miles nearer the Old Fort than the place you mention in your instructions: he insisted that they had sold the land no further, so that to prevent disputes I had to put it off for some days longer untill a few more of the Chiefs came in, when Mr. Lines settled with them that I was to

---

1 *Ontario Public Archives*, 1905, p. 379, "Dorchester to Collins"; Robertson, *Landmarks*, fifth series, Chap. XXXIV.

2 Described as "a snow of 18 guns built at Oswegatchie, 1777, by Captain La Force." See also Snider, *The Glorious Shannon's Old Blue Duster*, p. 254.

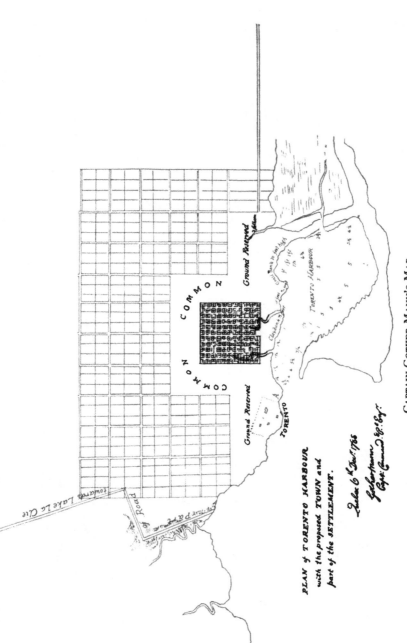

CAPTAIN GOTHER MANN'S MAP
Proposed Plan of Toronto, 1788.

begin my Survey at the west end of the High Lands which I did
on the 11th of August having lost a week of the finest weather we
had during my stay at Toronto.

Matters being settled with the Indians I continued my
Survey westward untill I came to the Toronto River which the
Indians looked upon to be the west boundary of the purchase
untill Col. Butler got them prevailed upon to give up to the
River Tobicoak but no further nor would they on any account
suffer me to cross the River with ye Bound[y]. line between
them and Government altho I had them brought twice to the
spot they told us they did not look upon a straight line as a
proper Bound[y]. the creek they said was a Boundary that
could not be altered or moved but that a line in a few years
unless always cut open and frequented would soon grow up with
Brush and trees.

Having finished the Survey of the Front I then began the
West Boundary line afore mentioned which I ran back perpendicular to the Front about two miles and three quarters
untill I fell in with the creek which I found with the course I
then run I would cross and have considerably to the Right.   I
then was obliged to stop rather than run the risk of having any
disputes with the Indian Chief from whom the land was purchased and who was that morning along the line and had
cautioned me against crossing it openly as Col. Butler & Mr.
Lines were both gone and I left without any one to settle any
disputes that might arise between me and the Indians.

The duplicate of my instructions enclosing the Plan of the
Town I only received when on my way back from Toronto,
however I have laid it out in what I thought the most advantageous Situation and opposite the middle of the Harbour.
I would have laid it out nearer the old Fort, but then it would
have been too near the Point I have marked in the Plan cal-
culated for building a fort upon, rather than half a mile below
the Old Fort.

The lands in general below the Old Fort down to the High
lands are a light sandy soil and the timber mostly Oak and
Pine for upwards of a mile above the Fort and the land has a
clay bottom & from thence up to Toronto River it is very
broken interspersed with sandy hills, Swamps and Ponds of
water the land near the Tobicoak is generally pretty good, as
for the Peninsula which forms the Harbour it is not fit for any
kind of cultivation or improvement.   The Survey I believe you

will find to be pretty accurate & I hope my proceedings may meet with your and His Lordship's approbation.— with great respect   I have the Honour to be
                Sir   Your most obedient
                                        Humble Servant
                                ALEXR. AITKIN D^Y. P.SY.

P.S. After the land was purchased from the Indians from Toronto[1] to Pemitescutiang I thought it would be unnecessary to run the East Boundary. The extra expenses of a surveying party amount to £29. 4-Curry. A.A.[2]

Hon^{bl} John Collins Esq.
D^y. Surveyor-General.

This account of Aitkin's survey at Toronto five years before Simcoe founded the town of York, recently came to light in the Ontario Archives, and is now published for the first time. I have not discovered any account of Col. Butler's negotiations with the Indians for the purchase of the land to the east of the Toronto Purchase along the north shore of Lake Ontario. These negotiations took place at Toronto during the summer of 1788, and the presents mentioned by Surveyor Aitkin were no doubt part of the price paid. This newly-discovered document raises the interesting question whether Simcoe or Dorchester is to be considered the founder of Toronto.

Let us now return to Quebec and observe the progress Philippe François de Rastel de Rocheblave, the former Governor of Illinois, as he loved to style himself, was making in his efforts to obtain possession of so desirable a piece of property.

On Saturday, May 19, 1787, Lord Dorchester, who had returned to Canada in 1786 to fill for the second time the office of Governor-General, presided in the Council Chamber of the Bishop's Palace in Quebec over a meeting of the council, at which the Honourable the Lieutenant-Governor and all the other members of the council were present. The minutes of this meeting contain the following item: "Mr. Rocheblave: Read a

1 A council with the Indians was held at Toronto in 1788 for the purchase of lands between Toronto and the Bay of Quinte—*Ontario Archives Report,* 1905, p. 410, "Butler to Johnson."
2 Unpublished letter in Ontario Archives.

petition of Mr. Rocheblave's, praying a grant of the Carrying-Place, and lands at Toronto. Referred to the Committee for Lands."

I shall now give in their sequence the various entries in the minutes of the council relating to de Rocheblave's petition, as they have been transcribed from Land Books A and B of the Council Office at Quebec and reprinted in the *Seventeenth Report of the Ontario Archives* (1929). At the meeting of the council on Thursday, the thirty-first of May, no business relating to land transfers in the Upper Districts was transacted; but on June 25, 1787, the following entry is found:

Mr. Rocheblave prayed for lands at Toronto and for the Carrying Place there. The several petitions of Mr. Rocheblave read. Ordered by His Excellency by the advice of the Council that the Surveyor or Deputy Surveyor-General report the survey of a location of one thousand acres not interfering with the establishment of a township of thirty thousand acres in that vicinity. And that the several petitions be in the interim referred to Messieurs Fraser, Bellestre, De Longueuil, Sir John Johnson and Mr. Boucherville who are to report thereon for the further consideration of Government respecting the other objects of the petitions.

No more is heard of this matter till a meeting of the council on March 20, 1788, at which His Excellency Lord Dorchester was pleased to order the third, fourth and fifth reports of the Land Committee to be laid on the table for perusal. Among the extracts from the Third Report there is the following item:

Mr. Rocheblave: Mr. Rocheblave attended the Committee on the 15th of February, to pray that his application for lands at Toronto might be taken into immediate consideration, because the approach of spring presses for a decision on his request. He represents his case to merit as much attention as that of any suffering loyalist from the Colonies, now the States; that from his sincere attachment to the British Government and steady adherence to his loyalty he had been driven from his possessions at Kaskakias (Fort Gage); he lost his all and was afterwards imprisoned in a dungeon in Virginia from whence he contrived to make his escape. Lands were promised to him in this province, but he is yet without any, for which reason he prays the committee to report to Your Lordship on his application for a grant of the portage or carrying-place of Toronto. The Committee having considered Mr. Rochblave's request as a suffering loyalist are of opinion that if Your Excellency shall see proper to establish the projected carrying-place between Toronto and Lake Leclaie (28 miles over) in consideration of Mr. Rochblave's having been the first to point out the advantages that would accrue to the upper-country trade by opening that communication, he may, if it is Your Excellency's pleasure that it be put into the hands of an individual, be indulged with a lease of it for a limited time, provided he agrees to conform to all such regulations as may be established by Government for the transportation of goods across it. The Deputy-Surveyor informed the Committee that the lands petitioned for by Mr. Rochblave, in case he obtained a grant of the carrying-place, are in Your Lordship's gift, none having as yet been laid off in that part of the province. He asks for 1000 acres for himself; and in a separate grant of lands for his wife, three sons and a daughter, to join his lands in such quantity as it may please Your Lordship to grant. The Committee see no objection, if it is Your Excellency's pleasure, to grant the lands prayed for by Mr. Rochblave, provided the place he describes shall not be found to be the fittest scite for a town, in that case the lands Your Lordship may be pleased to grant to him may be set off at a convenient distance from the town.

On Friday, June 13, 1788, the council met and among the extracts read from the Tenth Report of the Land Committee meeting on Friday, May 2nd, there is the following item:

Mr. Rochblave. Toronto Carrying Place: Read Mons'r Rocheblave's representation of 23rd April concerning the portage of Toronto, wherin he states that it is thirty miles over and that the carrying place of Niagara is but nine; he therefore conceives that the price of carrying goods across ought to be increased in proportion to the distance carried as the expense of horses, carriages and servants will be three times greater at Toronto carrying-place than it is at Niagara; and if it shall be Lord Dorchester's pleasure to grant him an exclusive privilege of carrying goods across from Toronto to Lake La Claie, he will undertake it on the following terms:

He will carry merchants' goods across at 5/ cur'y pr. ct. w.t., and every pack of peltries and furs 5/ cur'y pr. ct. w.t. The charge for carrying across Niagara carrying-place is for merchandise pr. ct. w.t. 4/6 New York or 2/9¾ Quebec curr'y. for every pack of peltries 5/ New York or 3/1½ Quebec money.

Mr. Rocheblave will carry *bateaux* in the same proportion. He will carry His Majesty's effects for double the price now paid at Niagara, which will make six shillings pr. barrel of two hundred weight, Quebec money; provided Government will allow him equal advantages with those granted the present contractor for carrying across Niagara carrying-place: that is to say, twenty rations per day, and that all carriages, horses and oxen taken away or destroyed by the Indians, or lost or destroyed whilst employed in Carrying the King's effects, or in consequence of orders from Government, be paid for by His Majesty.[1]

The Committee conceive that it may be proper to learn the opinion of the merchants concerned in the Indian trade, relative to the advantages the commerce in the upper countries might reap from a carrying-place at Toronto, and likewise to lay before them the prices at which Mr. Rochblave proposes to carry merchandise across from Toronto to Lake La Claie, if it shall please Your Excellency to suffer a road to be cut there.

On reading the report of the committee relating to the petitions of Mr. Rocheblave concerning the portage at Toronto, it was ordered by His Lordship, with the advice of the Board, "that Messrs. Caldwell, Harrison and Baby and the gentlemen of the Council residing at Montreal communicate the report to the petitioner, receive his proposals, find ways and means to make the overture known to those concerned or interested in the Indian commerce, and then to report to His Lordship what may be expedient to be carried into execution."

There is no further allusion to Mr. Rocheblave's application till the meeting of the council on October 22nd, but apparently the opinion had gone abroad that he was likely to receive his grant, for at that meeting the Land Committee among other items reported as follows:

Frederick Rastoul, Louis March a terre, Francois Jaquette and J. B. Feré: The joint petition of Frederick Rastoul, a mason; Louis Marchatere, a shingler, François Jacquette, a

1 The younger Joncaire made a fortune on the Niagara portage.

potter, and J. B. Feré, a millwright and joiner, pray for lands for themselves and families at Toronto near Monsieur De Rochblave's tract, and representing that they are capable of work and faithful subjects who wish to settle at Toronto. If Your Lordship has not set apart those lands for loyalists from the States, the Committee do not perceive any objection to the prayer of those people.

Antoine Landriaux:—Antoine Landriaux states that his father served as a surgeon in the hospitals at Montreal gratis, and prays that he, his son, may obtain 400 acres of land at Toronto near Mons'r De Rochblave's tract. in reward for his father's services. The Committee can only remark on this petition that if your Excellency chooses to favour Mr. Landriaux with a grant, there's waste land appertaining to the Crown near Mr. Rochblave's tract at Toronto, where the petitioner wishes to settle.

Joseph Page: Joseph Page for four hundred acres there likewise. He does not state how many his family consists of, but if Your Lordship shall please to permit him to settle there the quantity of acres allotted may be proportioned to the number of persons in his family.

Elizabeth Lord and her brother: Elizabeth Lord and Joseph, her brother, were left a burden on Mr. De Rochblave. He has supported them from their infancy. They pray for lands at Toronto to make a settlement for themselves. The Committee are inclined to recommend a grant of the prayer of this petition to ease Mons'r De Rochblave of the burden he has long borne and to enable the petitioners to acquire the means of supporting themselves.

Jacob Weimer: Jacob Weimer (a poor German) states that he disposed of his effects in his native country to procure a passage to America, and that he might become a subject of His Britannic Majesty; he therefore prays for land at Toronto. The Committee do not apprehend that any inconvenience can attend the granting of the petitioner's prayer; if it is Your Lordship's will to allot the usual allowance.

Richard Beasely and Peter Smyth: Richard Beasely and Peter Smyth, loyalists, pray for land at Toronto and at Pemitiscutiank,[1] a place on the north side of Lake Ontario, having

---

1 At Ganaraske, later Port Hope, foot of Trail to Rice Lake. Consult also *Transactions Canadian Institute*, 1892-1893, p. 301, "Trading houses existed for some years between 1770 and 1780 at Pinewood Creek and Piminiscotyan Landing on the north shore of Lake Ontario."—General Ernest Cruikshank.

already built a house at each of those places, and they petition for as many acres around each as is the usual allowance made to loyalists.

As it is proposed by Your Lordship to lay out a town at Toronto, the Committee cannot recommend a grant of lands round the house which the petitioners have built there, lest that grant might interfere with the intended plan; but if it is Your Excellency's pleasure to settle the north side of Lake Ontario at present, the Committee perceive not any objection to the petitioners having land round the house they built at Pemiscutiank in such portion as Your Lordship may think fit to allow.

Widow Orillat: The Widow Orillat and her daughter pray for lands at Toronto near Mr. Rochblave's tract in common with the loyalists. She sets forth that her late husband performed services for Government and that he met with losses and suffered hardships at the time the Americans invaded this Province, in consequence of his loyalty to the King. The Committee can perceive no objection against granting the prayer of the Widow Orillat, if it is Your Excellency's pleasure to favour her with a lot in any of the new townships lately laid off between the upper and lower settlements.

Charles Réaume: Charles Réaume of Montreal petitions for 700 acres land at Toronto, near Mr. Rochblave's tract. The Committee see no objection to his obtaining the common allowance of 100 acres as master of a family with fifty for every person of which his family consists.[1]

The report which contained these items was dated Quebec, November 26, 1788, and the Report being read, His Lordship, with the advice of the Board, made the following orders, *viz.*:

Charles Réaume: That the Surveyor-General report a survey of two hundred acres to be granted to him.
And at a meeting of the Council on Tuesday, July 14, 1789, it was ordered by His Excellency the Governor, with the advice of the Board, that the Surveyor-General report the following surveys:
11) For Frederick Rastoul, Louis March a terre, François Jacquet and J. B. Ferré: Two hundred acres each at Toronto near Mr. Rochblave's tract.

1 TASSÉ, *Les Canadiens de l'Ouest*, Vol. I, pp. 123-135; *Ontario Archives Report*, 1931, p. 173. Réaume's name as interpreter is attached to the Lake Erie purchase of 1790.

12) For Antoine Landriaux, Joseph Page, Jacob Weimer, and the heirs of Orillat: Two hundred acres each at Toronto.
14) For Richard Beasely and Peter Smyth: Two hundred acres each, one at Toronto, the other at Pemistiscutiank, a place on the north of Lake Ontario, if in the gift of the Crown, and not interfering with any public arrangement.

It is of some interest historically to record the names of these persons, though so far as the records show none of them actually acquired lands in or near Toronto in consequence of the grants made to them by Lord Dorchester.   When their applications were made and granted the term Toronto meant the Toronto Purchase, that is, the piece of land roughly twenty-eight by fourteen miles within which lay the familiar Toronto Portage at the foot of which Fort Toronto had been built in 1750.   The applicants whose names are recorded in the Land Books might have been the pioneers and first settlers at Toronto.   They seem to have been, with the exception of Charles Réaume, rather obscure people.   We do not hear again of Jacob Weimer, a poor German, nor of the widow Orillat, who might, had fortune favoured them, have been the progenitors of opulent descendants; nor of Elizabeth and Joseph Lord, who had been a burden for so many years to de Rocheblave; nor of Louis Marchatere, the shingler, and François Jacquette, the potter, nor of Antoine Landriaux, the surgeon's son, nor of any of the other applicants with the exception of Monsieur de Rocheblave, who was the moving spirit in the enterprise.

   Monsieur de Rocheblave's application for the Toronto Carrying-Place had been one of the first to come before Lord Dorchester on his return to Canada in 1786.   It was followed within a few weeks by an application from the North-West Company for the possession and control of the Grand Portage from Lake Superior to Long Lake, a vital link in the communication with the great North-West.   It is not impossible that there was some connection between the two applications; the Toronto Portage had now become, with the cession of the territory south of the lakes, a communication of great value.

De Rocheblave's request was referred to the officials of the North-West Company, and both applications, de Rocheblave's for the Carrying-Place and the North-West Company's for the Grand Portage, were referred to the same committee of the council for consideration; this committee consisted of Messrs. Harrison, Caldwell and Baby; the latter, being a Frenchman from Detroit, knew the history and value of the route.

On July 19, 1787, Lord Dorchester wrote to John Collins, Deputy Surveyor-General, respecting surveys and settlements in the western country above Montreal as follows:

It being thought expedient to join the settlements of the Loyalists near to Niagara, to those west of Cataraqui Sir John Johnson has been directed to take such steps with the Indians concerned, as may be necessary to establish a free and amicable right for Government to the interjacent lands not yet purchased on the north of Lake Ontario, for that purpose, as well as to such parts of the country as may be necessary on both sides of the proposed communication from Toronto to Lake Huron.[1]

It was on June 13, 1787, that de Rocheblave's full plan for improving the portage and securing a monopoly of the carrying rights had come before His Excellency. Lord Dorchester, well aware of the importance of the site, chose Toronto for the future capital of Upper Canada, and it is to him, not to Simcoe, that Toronto is indebted for its selection as the capital of Ontario; for Simcoe, as is well known, although he wished to make the naval headquarters at Toronto, had selected London as the seat of government.

The choice of Toronto as the capital of Upper Canada was made long before steamboats and railways; Dorchester, in touch with the merchants of Quebec, wished the new capital to command the new route to the great west and the fur trade there.

From these extracts from the minutes of the Council it seems apparent that although no lease of the portage was granted, de Rocheblave was awarded his thousand acres, and that it was

1 *Ontario Archives Report*, 1905, p. 379.

generally assumed that there would be no further obstacle to his entering into possession; his land became immediately Mr. Rocheblave's tract at Toronto, and others flocked to share his good fortune. At this time, however, no surveys had been made within the Toronto Purchase and before anything was done the Canada Act was passed, and Upper Canada became in 1791 an independent Province with a land board of its own. The Land Board for the District of Nassau, in which Toronto was situated, had been constituted under the Quebec Act by a letter from Lord Dorchester of October 13, 1788. On June 10, 1791, Mr. John Collins, the Deputy Surveyor-General, wrote to Mr. Augustus Jones at Newark:

Sir:—His Excellency Lord Dorchester has been pleased to order one thousand acres to be laid out at Toronto for Mr. Rocheblave; and for Captain La Force and for Captain Bouchette seven hundred acres each, at the same place, which please to lay out accordingly and report the same to this office with all convenient speed. I am, Sir, Your most obt. Servt. John Collins, D.S.G.[1]

On June 15, 1792, a year later, we find Mr. Augustus Jones writing to the Honourable John Collins:

Your order of the 10th June, 1791, for land at Toronto in favour of Mr. Rocheblave and others I only received the other day, and as the members of the Land Board think their powers dissolved by our Governor's late Proclamation relative to granting of lands in Upper Canada they recommend it to me to postpone doing in respect of said order until I may receive some further instructions. I am your obt. Hl. Servant. Augustus Jones, D.P.S.[2]

This ended the affair so far as Monsieur de Rocheblave was concerned; but no doubt the incident added to the growing friction between Simcoe and Dorchester. Possibly the temper of the new administration was adverse to the intrusion of a group of Frenchmen into the best lands in the Province; the Loyalists,

1 *Ontario Archives Report*, 1905, p. 321.
2 Ibid., p. 329.

now numerically strong and beginning to take root in their adopted country, had chafed under the Quebec Act and were determined to create an English Canada. Simcoe himself was thoroughly in sympathy with these aspirations. With "the infelicitous mania for tautology of his generation," he proceeded to wipe out all the old French and Indian appellations; Toronto became York, and with the change vanished all memory of the Portage and its traditions. De Rocheblave, who had contributed so much to the selection of the site for the new capital, did not receive his land, nor did his associates, Captain La Force and Captain Bouchette, although Bouchette subsequently received grants of land in the neighbourhood of Toronto.

La Force and Bouchette deserve a more extended biographical notice. They had served the British Crown loyally on Lake Ontario during the Revolution. They missed their reward at Toronto, but their services should not be unrecorded. It was the navy on the lakes that saved the western country to the British during the American Revolution, and both these officers had a long connection not only with the British navy on the lakes but with other events of historic interest. La Force especially had been closely connected with Lake Ontario. He had had a long and varied career. Along with Pouchot and La Broquerie, who has left us a fine map of the lake, he was among the last to defend the French flag. He was among the first to come to the defence of the British. Thanks to the co-operation of Mr. F. Audet of the Public Archives, Ottawa, I am now able to present for the first time the story of his life. René-Hypolite La Force was the great-grandfather of Sir Hector Langevin and of Monseigneur Langevin, the first Bishop of Rimouski, and is the best known of the numerous children of Pierre Pepin *dit* La Force and his wife, Michelle Le Bert; he was born December 5, 1728, at La Prairie. Pierre La Force, his father, is said to have been a captain in the militia and to have been Royal Land Surveyor at Montreal; we find him in 1729, a year after the birth of his son, Hypolite, serving as *garde-magasin* at Niagara; he must have been a man of influence, as all appointments in the interior were regarded as sinecures and opportunities for personal emolument. The elder La Force retained his office at Niagara until the year 1738, when it was discovered that he was debtor to the king's account to the amount of 127,842 *chats* (the unit of exchange in estimating the price of peltries). The *garde-magasin* was imprisoned and brought to trial, and though it seems to have been proved that he was not really dishonest, but only negligent and embarrassed with the cares of a large family, he was dismissed from the king's service.

During the first ten years of René-Hypolite's life we may imagine him at Fort Niagara, leading what must have been an ideal existence to a stirring small boy. During these years the father probably imparted to the son the rudiments of the art of surveying, an art which in later years the boy was to place at the service of the British in surveying the shores of Lake Ontario. But there were more interesting lessons to be learnt from the Indians who came to barter their peltries at the fort; from them the young La Force learned woodcraft and that knowledge of the Iroquois language which made him, in later life, a valued interpreter and leader of war parties. There was shipping, too, on the lake, and on its stormy waters the boy got his first taste for the sea. We may surmise that he made many a trip across the lake to the trading-post at Toronto, and that he soon acquired a knowledge of the adjacent shores and harbours which was to stand him in good stead later on. Indeed, he was to use all that he learned at Niagara in one way or another; for he appears as a trader, an interpreter, an officer in the French navy on the lake, a sea captain trading in the West Indies, and finally again on Lake Ontario as commodore and builder of ships and surveyor.

On June 10, 1757, Hypolite La Force married, at Quebec, Madeleine, the daughter of Gaspar Richard Corbin; he is described at this time as a merchant or trader; but commerce can have been only one of several vocations. From 1756 to

1760 he was in command on Lake Ontario,[1] first of the corvette, *Marquise de Vaudreuil*, a vessel carrying twenty-four guns and a crew of eighty sailors and soldiers, and later of the *Iroquoise*, the last vessel to fly the French flag on the lake.[2] It will not be necessary to follow in detail the naval conflicts of the closing years of the war, in which La Force, though so young a man, played his part. He did not confine himself to the water, but turned with equal readiness to raiding with the Indians on land. In 1757 he served with the Abbé Picquet as interpreter at the siege of Fort William Henry;[3] and in the same year we find him raiding in the direction of Schenectady, and Vaudreuil writes: "Le Sieur La Force à la tête de 4 sauvages de La Présentation tua un anglois près de la rivière de Corlat a peu distance de la ville." His name appears in the description of the Indian forces under the command of La Corne, as interpreter of the Iroquois included in that body.

After the fall of Fort Lévis on the St. Lawrence and the conclusion of naval operations on the lake, La Force and others were sent to New York by way of Oswego as prisoners of war. Released on the conclusion of peace, he embarked on the ill-fated *Auguste* with so many of the other actors in the last act of the drama. The *Auguste* was wrecked on the coast of Cape Breton; La Force was one of eight persons to escape.

For a few years after the Peace of Paris we hear nothing of him; he seems, however, to have returned to his trading. In 1767, 1768 and 1772 he commanded the *Jazon* and made several voyages to Dominica; from 1769 to 1772 he was in command of *Le Vigilant*, and from 1774 to 1777 of the schooner *Providence*, the joint property of himself and Joseph Chabot, and in it made several trips to the West Indies.

In 1775 La Force received a commission as Captain of

1 VAUDREUIL's letter dated Montreal, April 22, 1756, to the commandant at Fort Frontenac, announces the appointment of La Force and defines his duties. The governor encloses a letter to M. de Noyelle at Toronto. The original of Vaudreuil's letter is in the Baby collection.

2 See La Force's journal in Knox's *Journals of the War*, Champlain Society.

3 *Journal du Marquis de Montcalm*, p. 264.

Artillery in the militia at Quebec and took part in the defence of that city against the forces of Montgomery. M. Roy writes:

Sa femme Madeleine Corbin n'a pas moins de patriotisme que lui. Si La Force, raconte un contemporain, accablé de fatigue succombe au sommeil, et qu'elle entend sonner l'alarme, elle l'eveille aussitôt, lui apporte ses armes en lui criant:— "Dépêche-toi, La Force, Quelle honte pour nous, si tu n'étais pas le premier rendu sur les remparts."[1]

In the same year La Force leased the *Providence* to the government for service on the lakes, and two years later he was appointed "*commodore de la flotte de tous les lacs et rivières de la province du Canada*," an office which he retained till June 30, 1786, when he retired on half-pay. The winter of 1777 and 1778 he seems to have spent at Oswegatchie, for in the spring he forwarded his account to Haldimand for the construction of the armed snow, *Seneca*, at that place. In the autumn of 1779 Haldimand wrote to Lieut.-Col. Bolton at Niagara that he had given permission to La Force and Bouchette, at the request of Schank, to winter in Canada (Upper Canada). In 1780 Haldimand, although he thought him too old for the task, appointed La Force commander of ships on Lake Ontario, and we find him about this time Superintendent of the Civil Department of the Dock Yard at Carleton Island.[2] In 1783 Holland was employing him at Cataraqui taking soundings in Kingston harbour; later in the year, with Kotte and Peachy, La Force surveyed the north shore of Lake Ontario and round to Niagara;[3] on which occasion he must have revisited the haunts of his

1 *Les Petites Choses de Notre Histoire*, troisième série, 1922, par Pierre-Georges Roy, pp. 224-225. It was not Hypolite La Force who escorted Washington from Venango to Le Boeuf in 1754, but his brother Michel.

2 One of the first acts of Haldimand was to establish a post at Carleton Island. Fortifications and a barracks were begun under Twiss of the engineers; while Schank (see *Dictionary National Biography*) of the navy was to superintend the building of gunboats on Lake Ontario. The construction of Fort Haldimand on Carleton Island began in 1788; £20,000 are said to have been spent. In 1783, Carleton Island had a garrison of 664 including sailors. It was a rendezvous for the raid which ended in the massacre of Wyoming.

3 *Ontario Public Archives*, 1905, pp. CXX and CXXI. There is a copy of La Force's map of Lake Ontario in the Toronto Public Library.

boyhood at Toronto and Niagara. From 1784 to 1786 he is again back at his trade with the West Indies and in command of the *Rose*. In 1788 there is an entry in the land book, Quebec, "that Lieut. Maxwell and Hypolite La Force have all the lands they are entitled too," an indication that La Force had already been rewarded for his services to the Crown. Next year he is again associated with Kotte preparing plans for a wharf at Kingston and surveying the east and south shores of Lake Ontario to Niagara.[1] In 1790 he and Bouchette were still in service at Kingston and occupied in the construction of vessels which were to be the foundations of the British navy on the lake. On June 10, 1791, as we have seen, Mr. Collins wrote to Augustus Jones at Newark informing him of Lord Dorchester's grant. It was a recognition of long and honourable services, but its value lay in the future, and the loss of it probably did not entail much disappointment at the moment. La Force continued to reside in Quebec. In 1794 he was one of the committee entrusted with the task of preparing the address to H.R.H. Prince Edward on his departure from the city. In 1800 he obtained a further grant from the government for military services, and patents were issued to his wife after his death for lands in Somerset and Nelson townships. He died on February 5, 1802, and is described in the register of Notre Dame de Québec as a "justice of the peace, lieutenant-colonel of the first battalion of the Canadian militia, formerly captain of the King's vessel, and a church warden of this parish"—a peaceful end for one who had raided with the Abbé Picquet and had lived through the Seven Years War and the American Revolution and had witnessed all the changes which these events had brought to Canada.

The Sieur Philippe de Rocheblave and Captain René-Hypolite La Force, by their devotion to the British Crown, had no doubt earned the reward which Dorchester proposed to give them when he set aside for their possession large tracts of land adjacent to the capital which he was about to establish for the new

1 *Publication of the Canadian Archives*, 1890, Q. 47.1, p. 266.

Province of Upper Canada. Captain Jean Baptist Bouchette had a special and more personal claim to compensation. M. Benjamin Sulte writes:[1]

J'ai vous à parler d'un simple marin qui, a servi de pivot, ou si vous voulez, de point tournant à l'histoire du Canada. Son case est rare. Il était seul et décidait du sort d'un pays. Avoir eu une heure semblable dans son existense, c'est assez pour vivre toujours.

What had Bouchette done? We see him at the founding of the new city playing a minor part as commander of the *Mississaga*, which conveyed the Governor's party from Newark to Toronto. But had there been no Bouchette, there might very well have been no Simcoe and no Upper Canada at all. Jean Baptist Bouchette in 1775 saved Governor Carleton from ignominious capture by Montgomery's forces and thereby saved Canada to the British.

Bouchette, who was born at Quebec in 1736, was twenty-three years of age at the taking of Quebec and must have served in the militia at that period; quite possibly he was present at the battle of the Plains of Abraham. Very little is known of his early life. In 1772 he married Angélique Duhamel of Quebec, a young lady of great personal beauty and charm; he is described at this time as the owner of his own brigantine and engaged in the fisheries in the Gulf of St. Lawrence. In 1774 his more famous son, Joseph, was born, to be known afterwards as one of the handsomest men of his time, a distinction which he must have inherited from his mother, inasmuch as his father was by no means a handsome gallant. In 1775 Bouchette commanded a brigantine, *le Gaspe*, which he perhaps owned, and we find him already known as *la Tourtre*, from the celerity of his voyages. It is at this point that he comes into history.

In the spring of 1775 Carleton arrived in Montreal to

1 "Jean-Baptiste Bouchette par M. Benjamin Sulte," *Transactions of the Royal Society of Canada*, 3rd series, Vol. II, p. 67.

organize the defence of that part of Canada against the threatened American invasion; on the twelfth of November the city capitulated to the enemy. Carleton had made his escape from Montreal the day before and with a number of vessels succeeded in reaching la Valtrie, seven leagues above Sorel, where he lay windbound and exposed to capture by the invaders, who by this time lined the banks of the river. M. Sulte suggests that the Governor up to this point had relied upon the advice and the services of his British officers, but seeing the imminent approach of calamity, he now confided himself to a Canadian. Captain Bouchette, "the wild pigeon," offered to conduct the Governor in an open boat through the narrow channels opposite Bertier and to bring him safe to Quebec.   The offer was accepted and Carleton entrusted his person and the future of Canada to the issue of the event. Muffling their oars, the five men who composed the party rowed as long as they dared; then sometimes paddling with their hands, and sometimes lying flat in the bottom of the boat and drifting with the current, which seemed menacingly slow, they passed the dangerous narrows where the challenge of the sentries could be distinctly heard and the water reflected the frequent watch-fires of the enemy. It was a bold adventure, but Bouchette succeeded. They reached Three Rivers and Carleton rested in a hostel with his head bowed on a table, asleep. The Americans were close at hand and had already sent officers in advance to arrange for quarters for the troops. They entered the hostel and Carleton, who fortunately was attired not in military uniform but in the dress of a *habitant*, escaped observation. Bouchette, now as ever equal to the occasion, shook him rudely by the shoulder and ordered him, as if he had been a common sailor, to get up and follow him to the boat. The ruse succeeded, and a second time Bouchette saved the Governor. On the nineteenth, the bells of Quebec rang to convoke a public assembly to arrange for the defence of the city, which in all likelihood would have fallen to Montgomery had it been deprived of the animating presence of Sir Guy Carleton.

As late as 1790 La Force and Bouchette[1] were still associated in the naval service at Kingston and occupied themselves with the construction of vessels. Bouchette seems to have succeeded La Force in command on the lake about 1784 and continued in command for about twenty years. He established a dock at Kingston in 1789, and made a substantial contribution to the growth of the British navy on the lake. He occupied with his family apartments in Fort Frederick at Kingston, where he died in 1804. He had attracted the attention of the Duke of Kent, who expressed a desire to secure for him as a reward for his services a decoration or a title. Bouchette's step-niece had married Surveyor-General Samuel Holland; the two brothers of this lady, Jean Joseph Rolet and Charles Frederic Rolet, distinguished themselves in the west and in the War of 1812; the latter, Charles Frederic Rolet, in turn had married the youngest daughter of Captain J. B. Bouchette.

Bouchette and La Force are examples of the loyalty with which many of the French in Canada rallied to the support of the British in the struggle with the seceding colonies. "*Le commodore Bouchette,*" writes the duc de la Rochefoucauld-Liancourt, in 1795, "*est un des plus grands détracteurs du projet de faire de York le centre de la marine du lac.*"

1 *Publication of the Canadian Archives*, 1886, p. 740.

X

The Founding of York and the Last Phase of The Carrying-Place: 1793

W̶E are now about to catch a last glimpse of the Toronto Carrying-Place before it finally vanishes beneath the ploughs of the settlers who even in 1793 were beginning to claim the rich lands of the County of York.

It was one of Simcoe's first duties, after his arrival in the summer of 1792, to select a permanent site for the capital of Upper Canada. Lord Dorchester, who had learned a good deal from Monsieur de Rocheblave and the directors of the North-West Company about the geography of the Toronto region and the possibilities of the Carrying-Place, favoured Toronto. In the spring of 1793 Simcoe visited Toronto; and in August of that year, with all the ceremony possible in the wilderness, he founded York, which did not actually become the capital till 1794. Some preliminary surveys had already been made.

In May, 1792, Lieutenant Bouchette,[1] son of *la Tourtre*, had been despatched from Newark with His Majesty's vessels, *Caldwell*[2] and *Buffalo*, with instructions to survey the harbour. In 1831 he writes:

I still distinctly recollect the untamed aspect which the country exhibited when first I entered the beautiful baisin, which thus became the scene of my early hydrographical operations. Dense and trackless forests lined the margin of the lake and reflected ther inverted images in its glassy surface. The wandering savage had constructed his ephemeral habitation beneath their luxuriant foliage—the group then consisting of two families of Mississagas,—and the bay and the neighbouring marshes were the hitherto uninvaded haunts of immense coveys of wild fowel. Indeed they were so abundant as in some measure to annoy us during the night.

1 Son of Captain J. B. Bouchette and successor of Holland as surveyor-general.
2 Described as a sloop of 37 tons built at Niagara in 1774, carrying a crew of 14 men and mounting 2 guns.

Between May and August very little change can have taken place in the primeval simplicity of the surroundings. Early in July, Parliament was prorogued at Newark and the Governor was free to combine inauguration ceremonies with a glorious picnic in the wilds. The Rangers were transported across the lake. A few twelve or eighteen pounders were brought from Oswegatchie or Carleton Islands. The famous canvas house, which had once belonged to Captain Cook, was erected east of what was afterwards the Old Fort, and by the end of July everything was ready. "On Monday evening (this would be Monday, the twenty-ninth of July)," says the *Gazette*, "his Excellency the Lieutenant-Governor left Navy Hall and embarked on board his Majesty's schooner, the *Mississaga*, which sailed immediately with a favourable gale for York, with the remainder of the Queen's Rangers." And from Mrs. Simcoe's diary we get further particulars:

Mon. 29th—We were prepared to sail for Toronto this morning, but the wind changed suddenly. We dined with the Chief Justice,[1] and were recalled from a walk at nine o'clock this evening, as the wind had become fair. We embarked on board the *Mississaga*, the band playing in the ship. It was dark and so I went to bed and slept until eight o'clock the next morning when I found myself in the harbour of Toronto. We had gone under an easy sail all night, for as no person on board had ever been at Toronto Mr. Bouchette was afraid to enter the harbour till daylight, when St. John Rousseau, an Indian trader who lives near, came in a boat to pilot us.

As the *Mississaga* slipped out from the mouth of the Niagara River under the glorious sky of that midsummer night in 1793, with the band playing, and the Governor no doubt dreaming of the future of the city he was about to found, the scene did not differ very much from that which meets the eye to-day as the shore recedes into the distance, except that the buildings were fewer and the forest to the west and east came down close to the water; the old "castle" of Fort Niagara, which Simcoe,

*   1 The Hon. Chief Justice Dummer Powell.

knowing that it would soon have to be relinquished to the Americans, could not bear to visit, reflected the lingering light, and venerable with memories of La Salle and his successors looked out across the lake to Toronto as it does to-day.

For the Simcoes the summer was full of the beating of drums and the crash of trees, of rides on the peninsula and rows to Scarborough and up the Don, of excursions to the old French fort, and visits from the Indians, besides a great deal of routine labour for the indefatigable Governor. On Wednesday, the twenty-fifth of September, accompanied by four officers and a dozen soldiers and some Indians, Simcoe set out to visit Lake Huron by way of the Carrying-Place and Lac aux Claies. The following extracts from Mrs. Simcoe's diary tell us something of this excursion:

Wed. Oct. 2nd,—The Governor's horses returned from the Mississaga Creek, now Holland's River, from whence he sent me some seeds. I received the outside garment sent from England by Mr. Davison. The ground mice are innumerable and most troublesome here. We want the edict published in Spain to excommunicate and banish them. I send you a bat remarkable for its size, and a beautiful black and yellow bird.

Fri. 25th.—I send a map to elucidate the Governor's journey, which was attended with danger as well as many pleasant circumstances. The western side of the lake is drawn from Mr. Pilkington's sketches, the eastern from former accounts. Mr. Pilkington who was one of the party, says the scenery was fit for pictures the whole way, and from his drawings I should suppose so. They rode 30 miles to the Miciaguean (sic) Creek, then passed a terrible bog of liquid mud. The Indians with some difficulty pushed the canoe the Governor was in through it. The Governor went to the habitation of Canise,[1] the Indian who held Francis in his arms during the firing when "York" was named. Canise and his eldest son were lately dead, and their widows and children were lamenting them. Young Canise gave the Governor a beaver blanket, and made speeches of excuse for not sooner having made his bed. The Governor went to see a very respectable Indian named "Old Sail" who lives on a branch of Holland's River. He advised

1 At DeGrassi Point.

him to return by the eastern branch of it to avoid the swamp.[1]
They proceeded about thirty miles across Lac aux Claies, now
named Simcoe, in which are many islands, which Coll. Simcoe
named after his father's friends and those gentlemen who
accompanied him. The river from thence to Matchedash Bay
afforded the most picturesque scenery, from the number of falls
and rapids upon it. Some of them were avoided by carrying
the canoe on shore; others they risked going down. In passing
a rapid an Indian in the Governor's canoe fell over, and the
canoe passed over him. He rose up on the other side and got
in again without seeming discomposure. On returning, one of
the soldiers cut his foot near Holland's River. Mr. Alexander
McDonnell and another gentleman stayed with him, as he was
unable to travel. The "Old Sail" received them hospitably,
and shot ducks for them. A small quantity of provisions
being left with them, and an Indian who carried a large cargo
quitting the party, reduced the stock so much that the Governor
set out with only two days' provisions and the expectation of
five days' march to bring them to York. The Indians lost their
way, and when they had provisions for one day only they knew
not where they were. The Governor had recourse to a compass,
and at the close of the day they came on a surveyor's line, and
next morning saw Lake Ontario. Its first appearance, Col.
Simcoe says, was the most delightful sight, at a time they were
in danger of starving, and about three miles from York they
breakfasted on the remaining provisions. Had they remained
in the woods another day it was feared that "Jack Snap"
would have been sacrificed to their hunger. He is a very fine
Newfoundland dog belonging to Mr. Sheehan, near Niagara,
but has lived at Navy Hall from the time of our coming there,
and walked to Detroit with Col. Simcoe. He has been troublesome enough on this excursion, as his size was very unsuitable
to a canoe, but he is a great favourite. Coll. Simcoe had the
satisfaction of finding Matchadash Bay such as gave him
reason to believe would be an excellent harbour for very large
ships. A bay near Prince William is called Penetanguishene,
a fine harbour. The fever at New York and Philadelphia
amounts almost to the plague. Sun. 27th.—A road for walking
is now opened up three miles on each side of the camp. I can

1 There was a trail running south from the east branch of the Holland
River to Bond Lake parallel to Yonge Street and about half a mile to the east.
This trail is shown on a map recently discovered, Y35, Drawer 38, Ontario
Archives.

THE TORONTO OR HUMBER RIVER

Canoes did not ascend the Toronto River above Teiaiagon.

therefore now take some exercise without going to the peninsula.
Mr. McDonell arrived with the soldiers from Holland's River.
He brought some wild ducks from Lake Simcoe which were
better than any I have ever tasted; these birds are so much
better than any in England from their feeding on wild rice.

Fortunately Mr. Macdonell, who brought the ducks from
Lake Simcoe, kept a diary of the expedition which was published
by one of his descendants in the *Transactions of the Canadian
Institute* for 1890, and we are able to follow the progress of the
party over the Carrying-Place and to identify many of the places
mentioned. The diary records:

1793, September 24th.—Lieutenant Pilkington of the R.E.,
Lieutenant Darling of the 5th Regiment, Lieutenant Givens of
the 2nd Rangers, and A. Aitken, D.P.S., with two Lake La
Claie and two Matchetache Bay Indians, embarked in a *bateau*,
and went that night to Mr. St. John's, on the Humber River.
25th.—Got up at daybreak to prepare matters for our journey.
His Excellency Lieutenant-General Simcoe joined us from
York. We shortly afterwards were ready and entered the
woods, keeping our course N.N.W., crossed a long pine ridge.
About one o'clock, dined upon a small river which empties itself
into the Humber, and, to make the loads lighter, took the bones
out of the pork. After dinner, re-loaded our horses and pursued
our journey. About four o'clock, it beginning to rain, we
encamped on the side of the Humber at the west extremity of the
3rd concession. We here got some wild grapes and a quantity
of cray-fish. 26th.—At eight o'clock continued our journey.
In the early part of the day went over a pine ridge; but from ten
till six in the evening, when we encamped, went through excellent
land for grain or grass, the trees uncommonly large and tall,
especially the pine. Crossed two small creeks which emptied
themselves into the Humber, on one of which (Drunken Creek)[1]
we dined, and encamped on the second. The land through
which we passed is chiefly wooded with maple, bass, beech,
pine and cedar. During this day's march we passed the
encampment of an Indian trader, who was on his way to his
wintering ground on Lake La Claie.[2] 27th.—Proceeded on

1 Duncan's Creek.
2 The map Y35, Drawer 38, Ontario Archives, shows a trader's house
at Roche's Point.

early in the morning. Shortly after leaving our fires went through a ridge of very fine pine, which appeared to be bounded by a deep ravine on the north. After crossing in an oblique direction the pine ridge, went over excellent land, black rich mould; timber, maple, beech, black birch, and bass. Crossed a ravine and ascended a small eminence of indifferent land. This height terminated in a point, and a gradual descent to the River Humber, which we crossed. We dined here, and remained two hours to refresh ourselves and horses. While at dinner two men with two horses, who left the end of the carrying place in the morning, met us. They were going to bring forward the trader which we passed the preceding day, and his goods. After dinner proceeded on. Went over very uneven ground, the soil in some places indifferent, but in general not bad land. Saw some very fine yellow pine and black birch. About six o'clock came to the end of the carrying place and encamped. Here we found Mr. Cuthbertson, Indian trader, and owner of hut we passed the day before, encamped. 28th.—After breakfast, Messrs. Givens and Aitken, with two Indians and two white men went up the river for three canoes which had been previously provided for the Governor, and I went with some rangers to erect a stage near the river to put the pork &c., on when brought down from the encampment. Having accomplished this, upon our return we cut a few trees to make a bridge upon a bad pass in the swamp. Returned to camp about two o'clock, and shortly afterwards to the stage with seven of the rangers, all with packs, which we put upon the stage. We here met Messrs. Givens and Aitken, having returned with the canoes. The whole then returned to camp, only me, who remained to take care of the baggage. In about two hours the whole camp came down, and we immediately embarked into five canoes, viz., the Governor, Mr. Aitken, and Indian, and two rangers in one; Messrs. Pilkington and Darling, with their two servants in the second; Mr. Givens and two Indians in a third; an Indian and two rangers with me in the fourth; and Mr. Aitken's surveying party in the fifth. We dragged our canoes till we came to the river, over a part of the swamp where it would be impossible to walk without their support, it being a quagmire, the skin or surface of which was very thin. Proceeded about a mile and a half or two miles along the river, which in this short distance has several turns. Went about a quarter of a mile up a smaller river which empties itself into the former and encamped. Soon after making our fires, the Great Sail and

his family (Messessagues), who were encamped further up the
river, came to visit their Great Father, the Governor, to whom
they presented a pair of ducks, some beaver's meat, and a
beaver's tail.   His Excellency gave them some rum and tobacco.

Next morning the party proceeded on their way, and as their
five canoes threaded the windings of the sinuous Holland River,
the vast marsh and wooded hills on either hand in all the glory
of early autumn must have charmed their eyes.   They passed
the village near De Grassi Point, where Chief Canise lay dying,
for there was a pestilence among the Indians; they coasted the
western shore of Lake Simcoe, bestowing a new nomenclature
on all the bays and islands, and so on to Matchedash Bay,
where they were entertained by Cowan,[1] the trader, the remains
of whose buildings are still visible opposite Fesserton.   They
were unable to enter the harbour of Penetanguishene on account
of one of those autumn gales with which the Georgian Bay is
familiar.   Simcoe, however, viewed the bay from a distance
and was so delighted with the prospect that land here was
purchased from the Indians in 1793.   Those familiar with the
northland in autumn, and the route which the party traversed,
will know that the country was at its best.

One at least of the travellers seems to have had an eye for
the picturesque: Mrs. Simcoe records in her diary, "Mr.
Pilkington says the scenery was fit for pictures the whole way,
and from his drawings I should suppose so."   Macdonell's
diary, too, is full of picturesque detail, but for the present
we are not concerned with that part which relates to their
adventures after they had traversed the Toronto Portage.
We left the party on the morning of the twenty-ninth, as they
embarked and paddled out of sight down the winding Holland
River.   Before they disappear, six of the members will deserve
some further description.   His Excellency the Governor,
the ardent, energetic, poetical Simcoe, is too well known and

---

1 His house is shown on Y35.   It stood opposite the trail from Lake
Simcoe to Matchedash Bay as Rousseau's at the south.   See also Hunter, *A
History of Simcoe County*, Vol. I, p. 21.

beloved to require any introduction. Alexander Macdonell, the author of the diary, was, next to the Governor, the most famous person in the party; born in 1762 in Scotland and a member of a well-known Canadian family, Alexander Macdonell had served during the Revolutionary War with Butler's Rangers. On the arrival of Simcoe he became a trusted member of the suite of the Governor, who appointed him Sheriff of Newark and York; at a later date he was for a time Speaker of the House. He was tall and commanding in figure and could converse fluently in Gaelic, French and Indian. In 1818 he erected a residence long prominent on the corner of John and Adelaide streets, and at his hospitable table most of the eminent men of the Province were at one time or another entertained; he died in 1842. Lieutenant Pilkington achieved the distinction of a notice in the *Dictionary of National Biography;* he returned to England in 1803, where he ultimately became inspector-general of fortifications, and died in 1830. The map which he made of the route followed by Simcoe on this occasion is familiar to all historians. Lieutenant, afterwards Colonel, James Givins had spent some years among the Indian tribes of the west and had acquired a knowledge of Indian languages which rendered him valuable to the Indian Department; he was subsequently appointed Superintendent of the Indian Department and held that office till his death in 1842. Of Lieutenant Darling little is known; he was an officer of the fifth regiment, which formed the garrison of Fort Niagara; the duc de la Rochefoucault-Liancourt remarks, "The officers of the fifth regiment, whom we have seen, were well-bred, polite, and excellent companions." Lieutenant Darling seems to have been fond of natural history; he made a collection of stuffed birds and animals at Niagara which Mrs. Simcoe found entertaining. Lieutenant Darling eventually became General Darling. Simcoe named an island in Lake Simcoe after him; it is now known as Snake Island. Mr. Alexander Aitkin, Deputy Provincial Surveyor, was much favoured by the Governor, and had the honour of making the first survey of Toronto and its

environs in 1788; during the latter years of his life he was a
resident of Kingston, where he died about 1830.   Of the rangers
and Indians who composed the rest of the party, little need be
said; the rangers were, no doubt, worthy fellows: according to
the duc de Liancourt and Isaac Weld, the Missisaugas, from
their habit of greasing their bodies to keep off mosquitoes, were
exceedingly malodorous.

The camping ground where Simcoe and his party spent the
night of the twenty-eighth can easily be identified from the
Macdonell diary and from the Pilkington map; it was on the
east side of the north branch of the Holland River.   It is a
spot well worth a visit, and can be reached most easily by the
road which runs through the village of Schomberg.   After
crossing the river north of the village—at this point reduced
to a mere runlet—the second turn to the east should be taken,
which will lead directly to the mouth of the north branch of the
Holland, a stream comparable in some respects to the lower
reaches of the Humber.   Looking across the channel, the
visitor will see the eminence on which Simcoe encamped on the
occasion of his first visit to the county which bears his name.
The sides of this eminence are bare of trees and have been so
in the memory of the oldest inhabitants.   To the north and
east are remnants of the forest, and from the crest of the hill
there is a noble view south over the marsh, now drained and
cultivated, towards the northern terminus of the Carrying-Place.
On the horizon is the height of land which is the watershed
between the Holland and the Humber; in the distance on the
marsh will be seen two small buildings which lie very close to
the spot where travellers formerly left the river to begin the
long portage.   The large house which overlooks the marsh so
picturesquely was built many years ago when it was supposed
that the Capreol ship-canal would follow the course of the
Holland to Schomberg and then down the Humber Valley, a
project which did not wholly expire till the eighties.

We now return to the mouth of the Humber to retrace in the
light of the diary and other sources of information the course

of the Toronto Carrying-Place. We have seen that the explorers gathered on the evening of the twenty-fourth of September at the house of the Indian trader, Rousseau, with whom we are familiar. Rousseau did not accompany the Governor into the wilderness. Both Givins and Macdonell had a good knowledge of the Indian language and an interpreter was not needed; the Indians who were with the party were to act as guides.

XI

Retracing the Trail

THE townships of York, Vaughan and King, within which the Toronto Carrying-Place lay, were surveyed and settled almost immediately, and it is not surprising that after the lapse of a century not a vestige of the original trail remains, except, possibly, as we shall presently see, at its northern terminus in the Holland River Marsh. And since there are now very few families who continue to occupy the farms which their ancestors carved out of the wilderness, it is not strange that no reliable tradition as to the course of the Carrying-Place has been preserved. In addition, there is a widespread misconception that the northern terminus of the trail was the village of Holland Landing. This misconception arose from the fact that Yonge St., which was built to replace the Carrying-Place, terminated at the Landing, and since that village, now so decayed and deserted, was at one time a busy and important little place, familiar to the early settlers as the point from which they plunged into the wilderness, it is not surprising that traditions should become attached to it, which belong elsewhere, so far as the seventeenth and eighteenth centuries are concerned. To add to this confusion, the Landing in the seventeenth century was itself the terminus of the eastern carrying-place to Ganatsekwyagon at the mouth of the Rouge, a trail which has a history of its own not to be confused with the history of the more important trail to the Humber mouth, known as the Toronto Carrying-Place.

In the absence, then, of definite remains of the trail and the failure of tradition, recourse must be had to early maps and surveys if the direction of the trail is to be recovered with any degree of certainty. And here, fortunately, sufficient evidence has been discovered to reconstruct the whole course of the Carrying-Place from the mouth of the Humber to a point on the Holland River which can be determined with precision.

195

Passing over for the moment the evidence of the early French maps which indicate the direction of the trail but are not sufficiently definite to be of assistance in determining its course with precision, the maps and documents which have been employed in this reconstruction are as follows:

(a) Collins' map of 1788.

(b) Gother Mann's map of 1788.

(c) Collins' map of the District of Nassau, 1790.

(d) Pilkington's map of 1793.

(e) Chewitt's map of 1805.

(f) Augustus Jones' survey of the northern boundary of the Toronto Purchase in 1817.

(g) Augustus Jones' notes of surveys in the township of York.

(h) Alexander Macdonell's diary of Governor Simcoe's trip over the Carrying-Place in 1793.

(i) Mrs. Simcoe's diary.

(j) The maps of the Department of Military Defence on the scale of one inch to the mile.

On the margin of Collins' map of 1788, the original of which is in the Toronto Public Library, is a note to the effect that it does not agree with the survey made by Lieut. Kotte in 1783, nor with that made by Bouchette in 1793. A comparison with these maps reveals the fact that Kotte and Bouchette delineate the coast line with great accuracy, whereas Collins has indicated the shore in a very sketchy fashion. Collins, however, gives about ten miles of the trail on the scale of two inches to the mile, and had his accuracy been equal to his draughtsmanship, the difficulties of the investigator would be over. There is reason, however, to suppose that the trail as indicated is on the scale of one inch instead of two to the mile, and that the angles are indications of direction, and that the distances between these turns or angles is not accurately delineated. This would, of course, be the only possible method of indicating the trail unless it was carefully chained or paced, and there is no proof on any of the existing maps that this was ever done. To establish this point, it may be observed that while the distance from the point near Bloor Street, where the trail turned north, as established by Jones' notes, to the point where it crossed the Black Creek, is given on the Collins' map as a little over a mile, the actual distance is about two miles. On this scale the first long reach of the trail would terminate about a mile beyond Weston on the bank of the Humber. In the same way an examination of the other two important maps of the trail, (c) and (e) in the above list, supports the view that these maps are correct only in indicating the various turns in the trail and the angle of each turn, but obviously inaccurate in the distances between the various turns. Had the existing maps been accurate in every detail, all that would have been necessary would have been to enlarge the outline to the scale of the modern maps and superimpose the enlargement, taking care to make the southern and northern ends coincide with known termini of the time. This method, however, has proved a failure, whereas the results obtained by regarding the angles as accurate and the distances between as rough approximations to be checked by the contours of the country has resulted in establishing a line which corresponds in every detail to the description of the route given in Alexander Macdonell's diary.

Collins spent some part of the summer of 1788 at Toronto; an interesting description of the harbour is included in his report to Lord Dorchester bearing the date of December 6, 1788.[1] Whether Collins' map of the southern portion of the trail (a) was made on this occasion, or whether it is a copy of an older map, it is not possible to determine. Lieut. Kotte had been instructed in 1785 to make a survey of the communication between the Bay of Quinte and Lake Huron by Lac aux Claies, and the Toronto portage may have been included in his commission. The inaccuracies in the shore line of Collins' map and the space assigned to the trail indicate that the chief purpose of this map was to delineate the Carrying-Place. If this is so, another sheet must be in existence somewhere showing the northern part of the trail and completing the map. When

1 Ont. Archives, 1905, p. 351.

Collins compiled his map of the District of Nassau in 1790 (c), he incorporated the 1788 map of the lower half of the trail in his delineation of the Carrying-Place.

Collins' 1790 map is the most detailed map of the Carrying-Place which has survived. The original of this map is to be found in the Ontario Department of Surveys. There is an inferior copy in the Dominion Archives. From the mouth of the Humber to the Holland River measures on this map thirteen and a quarter inches; the scale is two miles to the inch. The hills and streams crossed are indicated. The portages along the Trent Valley route and from Port Hope to Rice Lake are shown on the same scale and with equal detail, with manuscript notes as to their value as permanent communications. This map must have been prepared with the intention of determining once for all the question of the route to the great fur country of the north. The decision was given in favour of the Carrying-Place; the map shows conclusively that it was the shortest route. The letters P and Q refer to the Carrying-Place. "P.Q. Carrying Place from Toronto to a creek called Micicaguean that discharges itself into Lake Le Clie is twenty-nine miles and sixty chains at landing you ascend a high hill Eighty feet high which Continues half a mile it is almost perpendicular and two (*sic*) narrow for a Road, but it is not necessary to make use of the landing Place as the River Toronto has a sufficient depth of Water for large Canoes to where it intersects the road four miles from Toronto at R: from thence passes through excellent Country the whole of the way to a Creek at Q except in a Cedar Swamp of twenty Chains this road may be made fit for Carts or Waggons, for the sum of two hundred pounds Currency, should the Communication be made use of it will be Necessary to establish three Posts, one at each end of the road, and one in the Centre to forward the Transport." This map is of special value in indicating the extent of the Holland marsh traversed.

Gother Mann's map of 1788 and Pilkington's map of 1793 contribute very little to the solution of the problem but are important as contemporary documents.

Chewitt's map of 1805 was prepared for the ratification of the Toronto Purchase, which took place in that year at the Credit. The bargain concluded at Quinte in 1787 had been found to be imperfect; the Indians remained in doubt as to what they had transferred to the white men and there was no proper record of the proceedings. Chewitt's map repeats the peculiarities of the Collins' maps without their fullness of detail. It is the most familiar map of the Carrying-Place; it is reproduced in *Indian Treaties and Surrenders 1680-1890*. This map bears the totems of the chiefs who ratified the purchase in 1805 and the signature of J. B. Rousseau, who acted as interpreter.

There are thus two maps of the entire trail from the Humber mouth to the Holland River, and since these maps coincide in essential details, it would seem possible to recover the course of the Carrying-Place. Neither of these maps, however, indicates with sufficient accuracy the point at which the trail touched the Holland River. Fortunately we have the testimony of the Pilkington map, Alexander Macdonell's diary and the survey of the northern boundary of the Toronto Purchase made by Jones in 1817. From these sources of information, which will be considered in greater detail, it has been possible to determine with accuracy the point at which the Carrying-Place terminated. This has been confirmed by local tradition. Had it not been possible to determine the northern terminus of the trail it would have been difficult to interpret the existing maps.

Turning from the map-makers to the surveyors, very valuable information is contained in the field notes of Augustus Jones, who carefully indicated the position of the trail wherever he came across it. I am indebted to Mr. N. A. Burwash of the Surveys Department for the following items:

Jones' Notes, Index No. 294, page 95. South boundary, lot 40, concession 2, S 74 W, 18.40 chains to foot-path from St. John's to Lake La Clear (*sic*).—Line between 40 and 41 concession 1. South 16 east from rear of concession 1, 5.50 chains foot-path, 49.00 foot-path.—From front of concession 2 on west side lot 40 N. 16 W, 8.75 chains to foot-path.—Page

101.   From northwest corner, lot 40, concession 3, south 74 west, 13.50 chains to foot-path.—Page 103.   From north east corner lot 10 on the Humber, south 74 west, 20.30 chains to foot-path.

All these items refer to the footpath to what Jones calls "Lake La Clear." Mr. Burwash has determined for me the position of these various points on the streets of Toronto. The Carrying-Place crossed Eglinton Avenue, 20 chains thirty links west of Jane Street; St. Clair Avenue, 13 chains 50 links west of Jane Street; Jane Street 8 chains 75 links north of Bloor Street West; Bloor Street West, a short distance east of Jane Street (as Jones seems to have laid out these lots north and south, and as they were sold running east and west, this point has not been determined); Jane Street, south of Bloor Street, 5 chains 50 links, and again in the same line at 49 chains. This point brings us to the "hog's-back" on the east side of the Humber, and Jones adds the note, "near a pond of St. John's or Toronto Creek."

According to D. W. Smith's map of the east bank of the Humber from the mill south, St. John's house stood on the east bank of the stream about a quarter of a mile from the mouth; this map is dated January 31, 1798. There is another small map in the Ontario Archives which confirms this statement. Mrs. Simcoe in her diary tells us that, "There is a ridge of land extending beyond St. John's house 300 feet high and not more than three feet wide; the bank toward the river is of smooth turf.   There is a great deal of hemlock and spruce on this river; the banks are dry and very pleasant."   The Gother Mann map of 1788 indicates that the Carrying-Place ran along the crest of this ridge for some distance and then turned sharply to the east.

Many persons will remember the path along the east bank of the Humber.   It followed the crest of the ridge, descending to the level rather sharply at a point close to the site of the Rousseau house.   This path has been obliterated in recent years by the houses along Riverside Drive.   In the eighties of the last

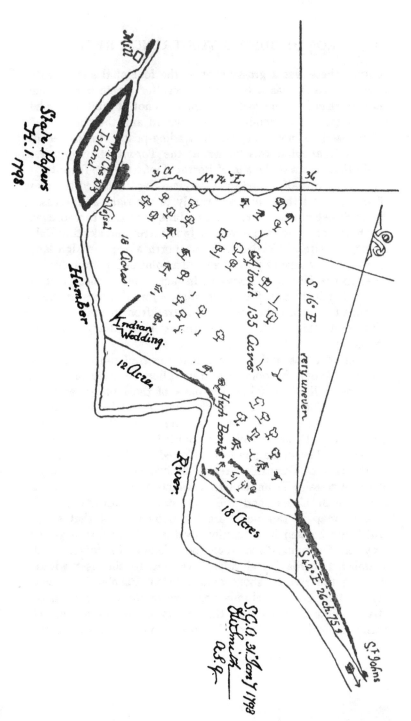

A MAP OF 1798 SHOWING THE SITE OF ST. JOHN'S (ROUSSEAU'S) HOUSE AT THE
MOUTH OF THE TORONTO RIVER

(The original is in the Public Archives, Ottawa.)

century there was a grassy spot at the foot of the hill, neatly terraced, which was a favourite resort for picnic parties; and there were still, if the writer's memory is not at fault, a number of fruit trees, the remains of the orchard and the cherry trees which used to bloom at the old trading-post. As Rousseau's house was at what was known as the Toronto Landing, it is likely that this was the site of Portneuf's first Fort Toronto.

For about half a mile the Carrying-Place followed the crest of the hill. It then turned abruptly to the right and, crossing Bloor Street not far to the east of Jane Street, it turned again north and crossing to the west of Jane Street and skirting Baby Point, the site of Teiaiagon, it ran north along the high land, never very far west of Jane Street, to a point on Eglinton Avenue close to the Humber, the point, in fact, where Simcoe and his party lunched and found crayfish. Jones' notes make it possible to indicate the course of the trail from the mouth of the Humber to this point. Beyond this, it is necessary to rely on the maps.

Collins' maps both indicate that the trail ran on for some distance beyond this point in a straight line. It may be assumed that the trail would follow the bank of the Humber as far as possible. The sharp turn on the map would be the point at which the trail turned away from the river. This point may be placed north-west of Weston, and it is a safe conjecture that the trail followed the line now followed by the C.P.R. railway to the east of Duncan's Creek. Macdonell's diary speaks of the trail crossing Drunken Creek, which, I assume, is a mistake for Duncan Creek, and the four streams indicated on the Collins' map at this point are the tributaries of that stream which are crossed in succession by the railway. In a general way the Carrying-Place would now follow the course of the Humber towards Woodbridge, swerving to the east without crossing the river. About a mile below Purpleville, a small stream falls into the Humber and where the trail crossed this stream Simcoe camped on the twenty-sixth. From here the trail ran north about four miles to the ford at the east branch

of the Humber, described rather minutely by Alexander Macdonell: "Crossed a ravine and ascended a small eminence of
indifferent land. This height terminated in a point with a
gradual descent to the Humber which we crossed." The
point of land is the area bounded by the stream as it sweeps
round the base of the hill in a wide loop. From the evidence
of the maps and from the contour of the land, it seems likely
that the trail crossed the east branch of the Humber close to
the spot where the road crosses it to-day at the little village of
King Creek.

To the north of this ford, the character of the country
changes. The trail enters a wilder region, and crosses the
height of land at a point some 1,150 feet above sea level; a region
which La Salle dignified with the name of mountain. When
the sixth concession road winds down the height of land, one
has the sensation of being on the old trail. Keeping slightly to
the east to avoid the sources of the numerous small streams
now flowing northward into the Holland, the trail ran north
a little east of the sixth concession road. The end of the
Carrying-Place, where Simcoe camped with his party on the
evening of the twenty-seventh, is to be found a quarter of a mile
south-west of the northern extremity of the sixth concession
road.

For the identification of the northern terminus of the trail
there are, as has already been remarked, three sources of
documentary evidence. The most important of these is the
map which is preserved in the Surveys Department in the
Ontario Parliament Buildings and known as the Map of the
Toronto Purchase, 1817, Q. 36, Indian Drawer No. 2. This is
the map of the survey made in 1817 by Augustus Jones of the
western, northern and eastern boundaries of the Purchase.
It establishes the fact that the Carrying-Place crossed the
northern boundary of the Purchase eight and a half miles east
of the north-west corner of the Purchase. As the western
boundary of the Purchase is identical with the western boundary
of the County of York, it is an easy matter to locate the north-

west corner of the Purchase. The Military Defence Department maps are on the scale of one inch to the mile, and by measuring twenty-eight inches from the mouth of the Etobicoke along the western boundary, the north-west corner can be determined. By measuring eight and a half inches towards the east and at right angles, we shall have the point at which the trail crossed the northern boundary of the Purchase. This point is indicated on Q. 36 by a dotted line with the legend, "Foot-path from the Humber to the Holland," and will be found to lie close to the sixth concession road in lot twenty-nine of King. About a mile to the north and adjacent to the northern terminus of the sixth concession, the Carrying-Place descended into the marsh at a point described by Macdonell as the "end of the Carrying-Place." It is the discovery of Q. 36 which removed all doubt as to the course of the Toronto Carrying-Place. It was on the evening of September 27, 1793, that Simcoe and his party arrived at the end of the Carrying-Place and camped there for the night. This spot would be about a quarter of a mile south-west from the corner of the road on the Dale farm, on which Indian relics have been found, showing that there was a village here or that articles had been dropped by travellers. Coins have been found on the adjoining Fox farm to the south.

It remains to trace the course of the Carrying-Place across the Holland Marsh to the point on the Holland River where the travellers took to the water. And here the evidence is complete and convincing. Owing to the draining of the Holland Marsh, it is now possible to explore a region hitherto inaccessible except in winter. An area which is roughly about eight miles long by a mile and a half wide has been drained, and a region of great fertility has been reclaimed. Collins' map (c) has this note about the Micicaguean Creek, as he calls the Holland River. "This Creek is thirty feet wide and six feet deep where the road intersects it and encreases (sic) in width and depth to where it falls into Lake le Cle where it is eighty feet wide and twenty deep." The bed of the river is now dry and its water has been diverted to two canals which diverge at a point about three miles east of Schomberg to unite again at the Bradford bridge, embracing in an elongated ellipse about twelve square miles of very valuable land.   The river, which was formerly the haunt of giant muskellunge, is now an empty channel, scarcely discernible by reason of the dense forest of reeds and rushes which choke its course.   The marshes, once vocal with so many waterfowl, are now under cultivation.   Research is still further facilitated by the accurate surveys embodied in the Military Defence Maps.   With the map of the district before him and guided by Alexander Macdonell's diary, it is easy for any one to arrive at conclusions which a visit to the locality will speedily confirm.

The diary remarks: "Proceeded about a mile and a half or two miles along the river, which in this short distance has several turns.   Went about a quarter of a mile up a smaller river which empties itself into the former and encamped."   Lieutenant Pilkington's map, though not very useful elsewhere, proves useful here.   He indicates Simcoe's camp on the night of the twenty-eighth, at a point on the east bank of the north branch of the Holland River about which there can be no uncertainty, for the north branch is the only stream of any magnitude on the north side.   A measurement on the Military Defence map shows that the distance from the main stream of the Holland to the point where the north branch issues from the escarpment is exactly a quarter of a mile.   There can be no doubt, then, that Simcoe encamped on rising ground known locally as "The Indian Burying-Ground," which, then as now, was in all probability bare of trees, as it has always been within the memory of old inhabitants.   It is an ideal camping-ground and commands a magnificent view of the surrounding country. It is directly opposite and in full view of the spot where the Toronto Carrying-Place comes to an end on the south side of the marsh, and of the King Ridges which form the watershed between the Holland and the Humber.   The traditional site of the "Great Sail's" encampment was further up the north branch at Lot 7, Concession 3, West Gwillimbury.   Indian relics are still turned up by the plough in the adjoining fields and there are many indications that this part of the county of Simcoe was a favourite resort of the aborigines. One old map bears the legend, "Indian Fields," at this point. The north branch of the Holland is the natural and, indeed, the only practicable outlet of the region, and inasmuch as it is only a short distance across country to the valley of the Nottawasaga, which was the main artery of the Petun country and a gateway to the Georgian Bay, it is an obvious conjecture that the north branch was an important link in the trail system of the aborigines, and that the fact that the Toronto Carrying-Place begins across the marsh immediately south of the *embouchure* of this stream was not accidental.

Let us again follow Alexander Macdonell's diary and make another measurement on the map. He tells us that Simcoe's party proceeded about a mile and a half or two miles along the river till they came to the entrance of the north branch. Allowing for the winding of the river, this measurement of a mile and a half or thereabouts will bring us back to an elbow in the river channel three-quarters of a mile north-west from the northern terminus of the sixth concession. At this point the distance across the marsh to high ground is less than at any other point in the locality, and the traveller would have had less mud and muskeg and thicket to traverse than either to the west or the east.

We have already, by means of the Collins map of 1790, and the survey map of 1817, known as Q. 36, traced the course of the Carrying-Place from the mouth of the Humber to a point just north-west of the corner of concession six and the sixth line of King; obviously the trail followed the easiest course from this point north three-quarters of a mile to the edge of the marsh, and at this point a quarter of a mile south-west from the northern end of the sixth concession road we have placed the end of the Carrying-Place, a conjecture which is confirmed by local tradition. From a point slightly west of the corner and extending across the marsh in the direction of the southern elbow of the Holland River, already identified as the spot at which travellers took to the water, there once existed a causeway of logs or poles laid down lengthways across the wet ground for the convenience of those who wished to fish for lunge in the river. These poles are said to have been placed there by the Indians before the coming of the white men; a section of about fifty feet of these tamarack poles is still (1933) in position, very much decayed and scarcely visible. Secondly, extending from the point already selected as the obvious terminus of the Carrying-Place, there used to be a path or trail through the dense bush and across the marsh to the same elbow of the river. My informant is a lifelong resident of the locality, Mr. Joseph Wilson, of lot 34, concession 5 of the township of King, who has known and used this path for more than fifty years, having hunted and trapped over the Holland Marsh all his life. Mr. Wilson described this path as sunk about a foot below the surface and well defined and running from a point south-west of the end of the sixth concession about a quarter of a mile across the fields, and from thence in a northerly direction to the river; he pointed out a dead tree from which, according to his recollection, the path began. This path, he said, ran down to a little pond not more than forty rods from the river and connected with it. It was in this pond, he thought, that they launched their canoes. This path has now been obliterated by the drainage canals, but standing on the road 125 rods to the west of the north-west corner of the sixth concession, Mr. Wilson pointed out to me the spot where it used to run, and remarked that in the bush to the south of where we were standing, the path crossed a small creek where there was a "run of logs," a causeway extending about ten rods. (This would be the "bad spot in the swamp," mentioned by Alexander Macdonell.) I observed that Mr. Wilson used the term "creek" to describe a mere runlet, formerly known as "Duck Pond Creek," which would, however, have been sufficient in such marshy ground to make a bad bog. This spot is indicated in Collins' map. In July, 1933, guided by Mr. Wilson, I visited the site of the northern terminus of the Carrying-Place.   Pushing through the rough undergrowth and pausing now and then to admire the lovely orchids, we came to the bed of the pond which, though quite dry, was marked by a dense growth of bulrushes.

As both Mr. Wilson's path and the causeway of tamarack logs, known locally as "the poles," converged on the same point on the river, it is probable that both were links in the original portage.   At any rate, the evidence of Alexander Macdonell's diary, the maps already cited, and the existing remains in the locality, combine to prove that the point on the river where travellers embarked is the elbow adjacent to the small buildings erected there by those now engaged in market gardening.   I mention this for the sake of those who may care to visit the spot but may not be inclined to go out on the marsh.

THE NORTHERN END

The Carrying-Place descended the hill on the horizon before crossing the marsh.

CROSSING THE MARSH

Until recent years a trail ran through the woods to the west of the northern
end of the sixth concession of King.

XII

JEAN BAPTISTE ROUSSEAU

IT was, as we have seen, from the house of Jean Baptiste
Rousseau,[1] at the foot of the Toronto Carrying-Place on the
east bank of the Humber, that Simcoe and his party set out
on the morning of September 25, 1793, on an exploring trip
to Matchedash Bay.   Rousseau has a rather important place
in any account of the early history of Toronto; he was the last
of those adventurous *coureurs-de-bois* and fur-traders, who for a
century and a half bartered for peltries at the mouth of the
Toronto River; he was the last citizen of the old French Toronto
and the first of the new English York.   At the time of the
founding of York the Rousseaus had been established, at one
time or another, for nearly twenty-five years at the mouth of
the Toronto River, and had fallen heirs to the trade which
Sir William Johnson had valued so highly in 1767.   The Toronto
River had even taken their name and was known as "St. John's
River."   The Rousseau house on the Humber must have
entertained many interesting visitors during these years, and
could never have been a dull or lonely place in summer with
so much coming and going between the lower and upper lakes;
how many of the French pioneers of Wisconsin passed this
way we cannot now say, but Langlade and Réaume, La Force

1 Ancestry of J. B. Rousseau (Tanguay and other sources):

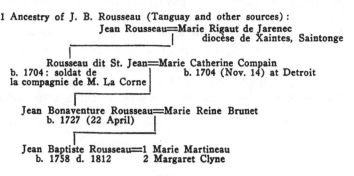

Jean Rousseau=Marie Rigaut de Jarenec
diocèse de Xaintes, Saintonge

Rousseau dit St. Jean=Marie Catherine Compain
b. 1704: soldat de   b. 1704 (Nov. 14) at Detroit
la compagnie de M. La Corne

Jean Bonaventure Rousseau=Marie Reine Brunet
b. 1727 (22 April)

Jean Baptiste Rousseau=1 Marie Martineau
b. 1758 d. 1812   2 Margaret Clyne

209

and Bouchette, Frobisher and the North-West fur-traders, the great Chief Brant and the early surveyors knew the place well; it served as an inn for wanderers in that wide wilderness. And it was Jean Baptiste Rousseau who had the honour on the official occasion of the founding of York of piloting the *Mississaga* with Governor Simcoe and his party on board into the harbour. St. John's Road in the city of Toronto commemorates the "laird" or "chief factor" of the Humber.

On September 13, 1770, at Quebec, under the hand and seal of the Honourable Hector Cramahé, President of His Majesty's Council, a license was issued to St. Jean Rousseau, with permission for one year "to pass unmolested with one canoe and six men from Montreal to Toronto, with liberty to dispose of his goods and effects as he should occasionally find a market in his passage." The merchandise itemized in this document included: eighty gallons of rum and brandy, sixteen gallons of wine, four fusils, three hundred pounds of gunpowder, sixteen hundredweight of shot and balls, in all amounting to three hundred pounds of lawful money of the same Province or thereabouts. Rousseau was required to take the Oath of Allegiance and to promise not to stir up strife or mischief among the Indians, "but as far as in me lies to promote Peace and Union among His Majesty's Old and New Subjects and the Savage Nations." His bond declared that he, "St. Jean Rousseau, of the city of Montreal, Merchant, was bound in the full sum of six hundred pounds for his license to trade with the Indian Nations living under His Majesty's Protection at Toronto, and from thence to any markets or parts which he should find advantageous for the sale of his merchandise."[1]

It is a fair assumption that the St. John Rousseau to whom this license was issued in 1770 was the father of Jean Baptiste Rousseau, who served as Simcoe's pilot on the historic occasion

---

1 M. GUSTAVE LANCTOT, of the Dominion Archives, has sent me a photostat of Rousseau's license. Rousseau had with him on his trip to Toronto the following *voyageurs:* Augustin Lefevre, Châteauguay; Jean Batiste Etien, Terrebonne; Fabian Coté, François Coté, Rivière Criane; Joseph Leberge, Châteauguay, and Joseph Sampson.

RELICS OF COLONEL J. B. ROUSSEAU, THE LAST OF THE FRENCH TRADERS AT TORONTO

Including powder-horn presented to him by Joseph Brant, scales for weighing coins of various denominations, military commissions, account-book and trunk belonging to his wife, Margaret Clyne. These relics are in the possession of Miss Muriel Rousseau, Hamilton.

of the founding of York in 1793. It is known that the latter was born in 1758 and that he was the son of Jean Bonaventure Rousseau (*dit* St. Jean), born 1727, who in turn was the son of a St. Jean Rousseau born in 1704 and a soldier in the company of La Corne. And we may also assume that the St. John Rousseau trading at the Humber in 1770 is the same person as the interpreter spoken of in 1772 as attached to the Indian Department. In August of that year Colonel Daniel Claus mentions that he had despatched the interpreter, Rousseau, with a message to the Indians above Carillon but that Rousseau had been unexpectedly seized with an attack of measles: "Last Monday," writes Claus to Governor Haldimand, "finding him able to go with said message, I despatched him accordingly."

It is quite possible, though it would be a point difficult to establish,[1] that the St. Jean mentioned in Montcalm's diary as attached to La Corne's Indian brigade as interpreter to the Ottawas in 1758 was the Toronto trader of 1770; this interpreter may also have been the grandfather, born in 1707. There is a tradition in the Rousseau family of an ancestor who was present at the siege of Quebec.

The Rousseau of Simcoe's time, according to his own statement, did not begin his connection with the Indian Department till the year 1775, when he would have been still only seventeen years old.[2] The evidence, however, in the Rousseau family points in the direction of long connection with the fur trade and the Indians, and it is probable that knowledge of the Indian language passed from father to son through several generations; it appears certain that two and possibly three of them served as official interpreters under the French and English régimes.

At the age of seventeen we find Jean Baptiste Rousseau serving as an interpreter, and since he continued in this capacity during the Revolutionary War, it is probable that he served

1 M. E-Z. MASSICOTTE informs me that over fifty families in Quebec adopted the name St. John.

2 For Simcoe's opinion of Rousseau, whom he regarded as indispensable, see *The Simcoe Papers*, Vol. I, p. 396.

under La Corne in the inglorious campaign which led to the surrender of Burgoyne at Saratoga; he may also have been present with the Missisaugas from the north of Lake Ontario, who made a faint-hearted attempt to save St. John from the Americans, and with Brant and the Mohawks in the Wyoming tragedy.

On July 14, 1780, Jean Baptiste Rousseau was united in marriage to Marie Martineau, of the parish of St. Michel, now a part of Montreal. The terms of the marriage contract add something to our information. This quaint document begins:

Jean Baptiste Rousseau, merchant, living near this town, son of Jean Bonaventure Rousseau and of Marie Reine Brunet, living at her said son's, stipulating for and in his name, of the one part, and Marie Martineau, daughter of deceased Mathurin Martineau and of Marie Josette David living at St. Michel, stipulating also for her and in her name, and of the other part: Which parties met together with the advice of their parents and friends, KNOW, on the part of the said Jean Baptiste Rousseau, Marie Reine Brunet, his mother, François and Louis Brunet, his uncles, Louis Tuiller, his step-father, Marie and Margaret Rousseau, his sisters, St. Denis La Ronde and Francis Billard, his friends—and on the other part of the said Marie Martineau, Jean Baptiste David, her uncle, François and Jean Martineau, her brothers, Marie Angrave, her aunt, Louis David, first cousin, all relatives and friends of the parties who have agreed together and made the agreements and marriage contracts which follow—that the said Jean Baptiste Rousseau and the said Marie Martineau, have promised and do promise to take for husband and wife (by name and law of marriage)—to be celebrated before the Apostolic and Roman Church—and as soon as it will be advised and celebrated between them.

Unfortunately, in spite of this formidable document, of which only a small portion is quoted above, the marriage did not prove a happy one. Domestic infelicities were notorious in the families of the *coureurs-de-bois*, where husband and wife were often long separated from one another, and the union of Marie Martineau and Jean Baptiste Rousseau proved no exception. About 1783 they seem to have settled in Cataraqui, for we find Rousseau's name among the inhabitants of that place in 1785.[1] Rousseau no doubt passed his summers trading at Toronto and elsewhere and serving as interpreter and returned to his wife during the winter. On June 23, 1786, an agreement of separation was drawn at Cataraqui and signed by Marie Martineau; it is a rather pathetic document:

To whom it may concern, know that I Marie Martineau, having had frequent difficulties with my husband, Jean Baptiste Rousseau, and seeing that we can no longer live together in harmony, have agreed by these presents to mutual and reciprocal separation and to no longer depend one upon the other, and by the said presents have agreed and promised never to trouble or injure my husband Rousseau in any manner whatsoever and in consequence declare him entirely free and independent of me, and by these presents promise to pay to Jean Baptiste Rousseau the sum of 500 L. money of the Province of Quebec if I should fail in the same condition.

In presence of   (Signed)
  J. Symington and   MARIE MARTINEAU.
  J. Ferguson.[2]

Shortly after this, Rousseau made a will which throws some light upon this unhappy transaction. In this document, which is undated, he makes the usual formal statements and declares himself a member of the Holy Catholic and Roman Church. In later life Rousseau became a mason and a member of Masonic Lodge No. 10 in the township of Barton, known to-day as Barton Lodge No. 6, Hamilton.[3] The land for St. John's Anglican Church, Ancaster, was the gift of the Rousseau family to that community, and the tradition still maintained among his descendants is that Rousseau was a French Protestant; possibly the Rousseau family were a remnant of the earlier Huguenot traders. However that may be, Rousseau's statement in his will is explicit. He proceeds to

1 *Ontario Public Archives*, 1905, p. 472; *Parish Register, St. George's,. Kingston*, edited by Prof. A. H. Young, p. 75.

2 Married to a daughter of Sir William Johnson and Mollie Brant.

3 The "Bro. Saint John" whose name appears in the minutes of Barton Lodge, Hamilton, January 31, 1796, was undoubtedly Brother Saint John Baptiste Rousseau. *History of Barton Lodge*, p. 183.

censure his wife for marrying again, and the fourth paragraph of this strange document reads as follows:

Although I ignore even the existence of my wife, I yet regard her as my wife, I recommend her to my universal legatee if she survives me. I beg him to do his utmost to lead her back to virtue and to make her during her life from my wealth an annual pension income for life as a proof that I forgive her, and again as I on my side, have need of being pardoned for the wrongs I have done her.

In those somewhat primitive times marriage and divorce were largely a matter of agreement; in the absence of clergymen and magistrates it was not always possible to obtain legal sanction. The wording of Rousseau's will is an indication that he had suffered deeply; but, alas, how often is a tragedy of the emotions a prelude to a sentimental consolation! Rousseau married again. Rousseau's second wife, Margaret Clyne, was the ward or adopted daughter of the great Brant; it is possible that Brant performed the ceremony, which must have taken place some time in 1787. However that may be, after one shipwreck on the matrimonial sea, Rousseau made assurance doubly and triply sure; his marriage to Margaret Clyne was more formally celebrated on the Mohawk reserve at the Grand River on October 15, 1795, by the Rev. Robert Addison of Niagara, and again, after the death of Marie Martineau, Rousseau and Margaret Clyne were married a third time by the same Rev. Robert Addison on June 30, 1807, at Niagara; in the certificate of this marriage, issued by the Rev. Robert Addison, Rousseau is described as a widower, and his wife, Margaret Clyne, as a spinster!

Margaret Clyne, the second wife of Jean Baptiste Rousseau, had had a romantic history. Somewhere in the State of New York[1] or Pennsylvania the Indians had attacked her father's house and had beaten him to death with the ramrods of their muskets and had dashed an older brother's brains out against a tree; her mother, overcome by horror, had expired on the

1 Margaret Clyne died in 1823 and was said to be in her 64th year.

spot. Fortunately, a squaw had taken a fancy to the helpless infant, still in the arms of an older sister; the lives of the two children were spared, and shortly after, Brant discovered them with the Indians and adopted them himself. At the conclusion of the War of Independence, the Mohawks migrated to the Grand River in Upper Canada, and Margaret Clyne and her sister accompanied them. The daughters of Molly Brant, the Indian wife of Sir William Johnson, were at this time married and living in Cataraqui, which had sprung to life again with the coming of the Loyalists. Mollie Brant had a house at Carleton Island. It is said, too, that Margaret Clyne had had news of relatives of her own, now resident in Cataraqui. Brant's wife possessed a somewhat difficult disposition, and Margaret sought and obtained permission to go to Cataraqui. The Indians accompanied her to the end of the lake, where the city of Hamilton now stands, placed her in her own canoe, and Margaret, as expert in managing a canoe as any Indian woman, paddled the length of Lake Ontario by herself, sleeping at night alone on shore in her blanket. Soon after this she must have met and married Rousseau; their eldest child was baptized by the Rev. Dr. Stewart in Cataraqui on July 29, 1788 (there were apparently no children by the first marriage); their second child was named Joseph Brant, in honour of the great Mohawk chief. Margaret Clyne survived her husband and administered his estate. The little case in which she kept her marriage lines is treasured by her descendants.

An agreement, drawn in Montreal and still extant, reveals the fact that, in 1787, Rousseau was associated with another trader, named McLean, and that they were engaged in the trade "in the Bay of Quinté and the regions thereabout." This would, no doubt, include the Toronto district. Probably Rousseau made the mouth of the Toronto River his headquarters during the summer and retired to less lonely Cataraqui during the winter; he describes himself as late as 1803 as a resident of Cataraqui. But when the first surveyors began in 1791 to survey the north shore of the lake, they found him at Toronto, and Mr. St. John of St. John's Creek became the host of all the early surveying parties.

Here, with his wife and young family, including a week-old infant, Jean Baptiste Rousseau was to be found on that eventful midsummer morning in 1793 when the *Mississaga*, with the Governor and his lady on board, waited to be piloted into the bay where the new capital was to be founded. The last Frenchman of Toronto was to welcome a governor who proceeded at once to wipe out all the traditions of the French régime.

Rousseau remained at York for some years, comfortably established in his house on the Humber among the cherry trees which are said to have supplied cuttings for numerous pioneer orchards.[1] A surveyor's map of the year 1798, of the Humber from the Old Mill to the mouth of the river, makes it possible to identify with precision the site of this house. Immediately to the north of the dance-hall known as the "Silver Slipper," there is a sheltered garden sloping down to the river; fruit trees, perhaps the descendants of Rousseau's own orchard, still flourish there; on the margin of the stream is a building much too modern to merit attention, but erected on the very spot where travellers drew up their canoes for centuries before Rousseau came to the Toronto River; there is no other spot on the east bank of the river where a landing could be made; the bank immediately to the north becomes high and precipitous, and the maps indicate that it was at this point that the Toronto Carrying-Place began. Here, too, or on the eminence occupied by the "Silver Slipper," may have stood the magazine erected by the French about the year 1720; and if Denonville in 1688 carried out his intention of a fortification at Toronto, this is a possible spot.

Rousseau was not successful in obtaining land in the immediate neighbourhood of Toronto. The Council, however, recommended that a part of lot 34 be granted him, and the map of the lots distributed at this time seems to indicate that this property was on the Humber; it was found to be very far to the

1 There were gardens and orchards at Niagara and Oswego.

east of the house on the river bank, and Rousseau does not seem to have converted that into a freehold. In 1794 we find him applying for two thousand acres on the ground that he had served as interpreter between the years 1775 and 1786; he states that he has only received five hundred acres; the petition was dismissed.[1]

In 1795 Rousseau established himself in Ancaster, where he built the first grist and sawmill on the site of the present village. He opened a general store and continued to trade with the Indians on the Grand River. Old account books show that Brant was one of his chief customers. In 1803 he obtained a grant of three hundred acres in Ancaster[2] and four hundred in the township of Oxford. We find him also in association with Richard Beasley and Willison, involved in a purchase of lands from the Six Nations[3] and giving security in the form of a mortgage for £8,887. It is clear from these transactions that Rousseau was a wealthy man; he owned, in fact, at the time of his death, a piece of property which would have made his descendants many times millionaires had it remained in their possession, being that part of the city of Hamilton which extends from the west side of Brant Street to the east side of Lock Street.

Rousseau's knowledge of the Indian languages and his familiarity with the country made him a valuable officer in the militia. A commission as Ensign in the militia forces of the county of Lincoln is dated June 24, 1797. A commission as Captain in the West Riding militia forces of York is dated July 15, 1799, and signed by T. Ridout. A commission as Lieutenant-Colonel in the 2nd Regiment of York Militia is dated May 16, 1811, and signed by Governor Gore. This was on the eve of the outbreak of the War of 1812, when everything was being done to prepare the Province for the struggle forced upon her. Unfortunately, Col. Rousseau died of pleurisy on

1 See also *Ontario Public Archives*, 1931, p. 32.
2 SMITH, *Canada, Past Present and Future*, Vol. I, p. 170.
3 Ibid., Vol. I, p. 229.

November 16, 1812, while on a visit to Niagara.   A letter from W. Johnson Chew to Mrs. Margaret Rousseau, notifying her of his decease, is preserved by her descendants; the letter concludes, "I have lost my best friend." Rousseau was buried in the churchyard of St. Marks at Niagara.

A tradition in the Rousseau family narrates that Jean Baptiste Rousseau's daughter, Margaret, happened to be visiting relatives in Niagara on the eve of the Battle of Queenston Heights, and that General Brock, who was quartered in the same house, took a ring from his finger on the morning of the battle with the remark, "Here, Peggy, here is my ring, and if I do not come back you may keep it."

As has been already stated, the original purchase of land, which includes the site of the city of Toronto, from the Missisauga Indians, was made at Quinte in 1787 and was found to be imperfect and had to be rectified at a council at the Credit River in 1805.   On this occasion, when Toronto finally acquired its title from the aborigines, Jean Baptiste Rousseau acted as interpreter, and his name is attached to the deed.   Among the Rousseau papers is a receipt which evidently refers to this transaction: "River Credit, 3rd August, 1805.   Col. Claus to Thomas Ingerston Dr. for Expences for himself and gentlemen attending a Council with the Indians for my account Hlfx Cy. £6,5,0.   Received payment in full.   Thos. Ingersoll." Rousseau's name appears also on the treaties negotiated with the Indians for the purchase of the lands west of Toronto to the head of the lake, and for the region of which Hamilton is the centre.   He seems to have possessed much influence with the Indians; he also attended important councils on the American side of the frontier.   His connection by marriage with Brant, and the long connection of his family with the Indian trade, must have made him a valued ally at a time when the Indians were still powerful.   A magnificent powder-horn, the gift of Brant to Rousseau, remains in the possession of his descendants.

Our regional history has now been extended far beyond the
fall of New France and has reached the limit imposed by
events. With the burning of Fort Toronto in 1758 the flag of
France disappeared from Ontario, but it was not till that
midsummer morning, when Rousseau piloted Governor Simcoe
and the *Mississaga* into the *Baye de Toronto*, crystal clear,
haunted by wild fowl and edged by the forest, that French
influence and the French régime in the Toronto region came to
an end. The flag of England was raised, the band of the
Queen's Rangers played, the drums rolled, cannon from Oswegatchie or Carleton Island were fired, and all that was
French began to fade from the landscape.

From Brûlé to Péré and Joliet, to Hennepin and La Salle
and Tonti of the Iron Hand, to Denonville and the Senecas and
the Missisaugas, to the Sieur Douville and the Sieur de la
Saussaye and the *magasin royal*, to Fort Toronto and Baby and
Rogers, Aitkin and Butler and Rousseau, the record is scarcely
broken, and runs back three centuries to the arrival of the white
man in Canada.   But so completely has Simcoe's ideal of a new
England in Upper Canada been realized that Toronto, the
citadel of British sentiment in America, and Ontario, the most
British of all the Provinces, retain in place-name or recording
tablet scarcely a vestige of all that happened before the coming
of that most loyal of all loyal governors.

Now that British traditions are immovably established in a
Province possessing such variety of lovely landscape and such
wealth of material prosperity, the lack of historic background
is often regretted.   With the passing of the years, as we strike
our roots deeper and deeper into the soil from which we spring,
this lack will be made good.   Meantime only the most stubborn
and insular patriotism would reject the rich legacy of romance
bequeathed by the pioneers of New France.   Hills stand more
majestic, streams murmur more melodiously, the splendours
of the setting sun are more magnificent, starry skies more
mysterious, where human associations enrich the scene.

We began with the Riverside Drive and the Humber and

their historic memories. Our narrative has carried us far afield; to Michilimackinac, to the valley of the Ohio, even to the banks of the Mississippi, but chiefly to Fort Frontenac, to Oswego, to Niagara and the shores of that great inland sea of which the Humber is only a humble tributary.

Lake Ontario remains, as it seemed to the Chevalier de Courcelles, *une pleine mer sans aucunes limites*. Its angry waves can still toss with a roar like the sea, as Malartic describes them. Could Frontenac or Denonville or Vaudreuil return to its borders the "beautiful lake" of the Iroquois would lie before them with the same charm as before. And Lake Ontario still has lonely beaches and desolate shores where when ripples lisp in the moonlight or waves thunder in the storm, romantic youth or meditative age may recall in imagination those formidable Iroquois, the most formidable of all savages, and those French soldiers and *voyageurs*, the most picturesque of all adventurers.

APPENDIX I

THE ETYMOLOGY OF "TORONTO"

The word *Toronto*[1] as a place-name occurs for the first time in any document or map on a large manuscript map somewhat more than four feet long and about two and a half wide which is preserved in the Library of the *Service Hydrographique de la Marine*, Paris. This map is No. 43 in the volume B 4044 (*Amérique Septentrionale, Canada*); it bears no signature and no date, but has been assigned by Parkman to the year 1673, and cannot in any case be later than 1674, as it bears no evidence of the discoveries of Marquette and Joliet. De la Roncière, in the *Catalogue Général des Manuscrits des Bibliothèques Publiques de France, Bibliothèque de la Marine*, Paris, 1907, p. 237, ascribes this map to Joliet. It seems more likely, however, that this map was prepared under the supervision of La Salle, since it contains exactly the information which La Salle alone could have possessed at that time; it differs also in important particulars from the Joliet maps of this period. The apparent purpose of the map is to justify the establishment of Fort Frontenac, and Frontenac himself in his letter to Colbert, bearing the date November 13, 1673, seems to make reference to the legends on this map and mentions a map of Lake Ontario which had been sent to him by La Salle. The cession of New Holland to the English impelled the French to make good their claims to Lake Ontario, if they were not to be confined to the country east of the Ottawa.

This important map is far in advance of the Galinée map of 1670 in the accurate knowledge displayed of the lake district. On it the name *Toronto* under the form *Taronto* is attached to Lake Simcoe, which is called *Lac de Taronto*. There is good reason to suppose that this was the original spelling of the word, and that Margry in making La Salle in 1680 speak of *Lac Toronto*, giving the word its familiar spelling, may have been in error in transcribing his document. For a hundred years after La Salle the makers of maps continued to attach the name to the lake and generally with the spelling, "Taronto." This is the first map to show the correct position of Teiaiagon and to indicate Toronto Island. Since it gives the eastern arm of the Carrying-Place and not the western, it is a fair inference that the latter began to be used by the Iroquois after the establishment of Fort Frontenac, and that they began to follow the route along the south shore to Teiaiagon when they found their passage to Ganatsekwyagon barred. Toronto thus became at this time "a place of meeting" between Iroquois traders and the Ottawas from the north.

Other facts must be considered before proceeding to a study of the etymology of the word. Lahontan, who gained his first knowledge of the lakes when serving with Denonville in 1687 in the raid on the Senecas, speaks of the Georgian Bay as the *Baye de Toronto*, and places the Torontogueronons on the north shore of Lake Simcoe; he also describes the Severn River as the Toronto River. The Humber, as early as 1725, is spoken of as the Toronto River. In 1746 the name *Taronto* is found attached to a river flowing from Rice Lake into the Severn, and in 1755, on the Danville map of that date,

1 CANNIFF in his *Historical Atlas of York County* gives the following variants of Toronto: *Tormaonto, Toronton, Taranton, Torinlog, Tarento, Taronthe, Atouronton, Otoronto*. To which may be added *Garoqua*, quoted in SEVERANCE, *An Old Frontier of France*, Vol. II, p. 294.

Rice Lake is called *L. Taronto*. Smith's Gazetteer is authority for the statement that the waterway from Lake Simcoe to the Bay of Quinte was also known as the Toronto River. This, I believe, is an error due to the Danville map. Whether the name is Huron or Iroquois, whether it originated in the Georgian Bay and gradually worked its way south, or began at the south and was afterwards applied to all parts of the *passage de Toronto*, historical testimony and the evidence of the majority of the maps favours the theory that the name originated as an appellation of Lake Simcoe. It is important to bear these facts in mind in considering the various theories as to its etymology.

Dr. Scadding, writing in 1891, remarks:

"There has been a long continued tradition in these parts of two interpretations of the Indian word *Toronto:* how or when these interpretations began to circulate among us I cannot recall. I certainly heard of them from the earliest moment of my residence here. They were generally understood to be meanings given by Indian interpreters of a former period, and certain reasons were usually assigned for the explanation of the word in the two several meanings given to it. 'Place of Meeting' was supposed to refer to certain gatherings of the Indian bands or tribes at this spot periodically for purposes of traffic, or for hunting expeditions, or it may be for hostile excursions. 'Trees in the water,'[1] on the other hand, was imagined with considerable plausibility to be a reference to certain trees which aforetime used to appear here and there along the whole length of our island or peninsula, as it then really was, which trees must have been notable landmarks for canoes, or other small craft then coasting about the edges of our lakes. Indians, we know, everywhere make use of landmarks of this sort from a kind of necessity."

Dr. Scadding then proceeds to present the arguments in support of the meaning "Place of Meeting," and derives the word Toronto from the Huron word *otoronton* or *toronton*, which is to be found in Sagard's Huron lectionary with the meaning *beaucoup*, much or many. Sagard gives several examples of the use of this word, and remarks in one passage that *toronton* means not only "much" but "place where there are many people." Dr. Scadding does not seem to have observed this last passage, which adds considerable weight to his contention. For the Huron country, and especially the district surrounding the outlet of Lake Simcoe, was very populous when the French first visited the country; it is here that Lahonton places his Torontogueronons, a term which he seems to have invented himself to describe the Hurons who lived in the vicinity of Lake Toronto (the word is not found elsewhere). The neighbourhood of Orillia was the region where the Hurons came in contact with the Algonquin tribes of the north and traded with them. It is a plausible conjecture that the term *Toronto*, in the sense "place of meeting" as Dr. Scadding suggests, may have been applied to this region either by the Hurons themselves or by the French. This theory is based upon the discovery of the word *otoronton* in the lectionaries of Sagard and Lahontan; the latter gives a list of only forty-nine Huron words, and the word *atoronton* in the sense "very much" is included.

Additional information about the use of this apparently common word may be obtained from Potier's *Radices Huronicae*.[2] The word *atonronton* may be used either of things or of persons, either "there are a great many" alluding to things, or "there are a great many," alluding to persons; e.g.

---

[1] MRS. H. A. BRANT, of Deseronto, herself a descendant of the great chief, informs me that the Mohawks on that reserve give the word the meaning "trees in the water."

[2] P. 40.

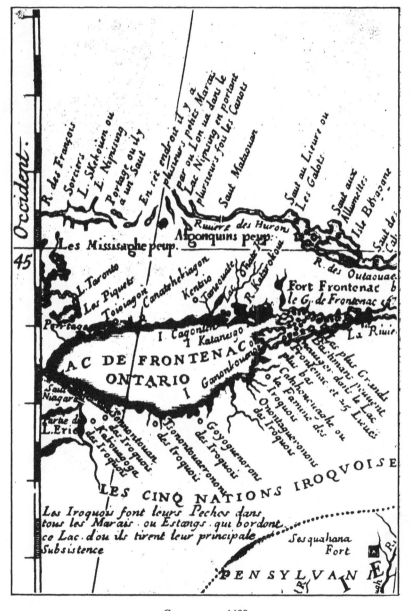

CORONELLI—1689

This very inaccurate map contains the words *Les Piquets* under *L. Taronto*.

Otonronton atiaondi means "in truth there are a lot of them"; *Onouatonronton*, "there are a lot of us"; *skouatonronton*, "you are a large company"; *hondatonronto*, "there are a lot of men"; *ondatonronton*, "there are a lot of women"; *aotonronton*, "there are a lot of them"; *sonouatonronton*, "we are scarcely any"; *conouatonronton*, "we shall be a good many"; *aionouatonronton*, "we should be a good many," etc.; (NOTE: although the future affirmative is paradigm S., still *eouatonronton* is used impersonally in paradigm C. to indicate "that will increase, there will be a lot of them," the same as *eiouannha*.); *kouatonronton*, *onk*, *on*, *onde*, C. personally "to take a lot of trouble with something," "to tire out," "to do as much as a lot of people"; *akatonronton atiaondi ahehetsaron*, "I have taken a lot of trouble to accomplish it," "I have done all I can," "I have put all I have into it," "I have employed every means."

W. E. Connelly, in the *Ontario Archaeological Report* for 1899, states that the Wyandots, or their progenitors, the Tionnontates, once had a settlement at Toronto from which they were forced to flee by the Senecas, and that the Wyandots called their settlement at Toronto *Toh-roohn-tohnk*, which means in the Wyandot language, "plenty," and that they employed this term because they had found food in abundance at Toronto,[1] it was a land of plenty. This legend which Connelly claims to have obtained from the Wyandots, may be regarded as an argument in favour of Dr. Scadding's theory, or it may be an outgrowth of the phonetic similarity of Toronto and *otoronton*.

If, on the other hand, the explanation that Toronto means "tree in the water" be accepted, then it may be that the term was employed by Indians crossing the lake, who saw the trees on the north shore miraged in the water and gave the name Toronto to the shore opposite Niagara. Or, again, the name may have been first employed to indicate the trees or branches fixed in the water at the Narrows near Orillia; Champlain describes these fish weirs, and some of the stakes were still to be seen under the water within recent years in the neighbourhood of the railway bridge. The French name for Lake Simcoe, *Lac aux Claies*, "fish-weir lake,"[2] might then be regarded as a translation of "trees in the water." The French name certainly refers to these fish-weirs, and on the Coronelli map of 1688, underneath the name L. Taronto is written *Les Piquets*, "the stakes," an obvious allusion to the fish-weirs. The Ojibways still speak of the Narrows as *Michekun*, which means "fence" or "the place fenced or staked off."

The explanation "trees in the water" is quite as old as Dr. Scadding's "place of meeting"; it is given in Lossing's *Field Book of the War of 1812* on the authority of a Mohawk interpreter; it has the support of the Jesuit missionary, Father Jacques Bruyas, and of Father J. A. Cuoq in his *Lexique de la langue Iroquoise*. Potier, in his *Radices Huronicae*,[3] gives *garonto,—une arbre dans l'eau qui sert de pont pour passer un rivière,—un pont*. Professor Louis Allen, of the University of Toronto, informs me that the change from g to t at the beginning of the word is due to the prefixing of a prefix expressing distance, the word Toronto meaning "tree in the water there"; he also informs me that *tgarondo* is the name which the Mohawks to-day apply to Toronto and that they give it this explanation.

1 See *Transactions and Papers of the Ontario Historical Society*, Vol. VIII, p. 35.

2 In a manuscript dictionary of the Onondaga language of about 1700 in the Mazarin Library, Paris, *Gaya-ouenta-ha* is given as the equivalent of the French word *claye*. *Gah-a-yeh* is given by Rev. Asher Wright as "fence" in Seneca. *Gaya-ouenta-ha* would, then, mean literally "fish fence"; cp. Huron *ahouenta*, "a small fish."

3 P. 241.

Before Dr. Scadding had decided in favour of the meaning "place of meeting," and of the derivation from *otoronton*, he had suggested that possibly the word *Toronto* might be the remnant of the word *Oentaron* which appears in Sanson's map of 1656 as the name of Lake Simcoe. Du Creux (1660), who prints all the names on his map with Latin terminations, writes *Lacus Ouentaronius*. Down to 1746 Lake Simcoe often appears on the maps as *lake Taronto* or *Toronto;* the name *Oentaronk* then appears in Danville's map of that date and continued to appear till Delamarche's map of 1785, where it is spelled *Oentaronck*. The name *Oentaronk* looks very like the last part of the appellation *Attiouendaronk*, one of the many names given to the Hurons and the Neutrals. On Du Creux's map, Lake Cayuga appears as *Lacus Oiogoenronius*, and it is tempting to explain the termination *-ronius* in his *Lacus Ouentaronius* as the equivalent of the Huron termination *-ronnon*, meaning "people," on the analogy of *Oigoenronius* and other names on the map ending in *-ronius* which are obviously tribal names which would end in *-ronnon* in the Huron language. If this is possible, the first part of the word would be the familiar *ouendat* or *ouentat*, which was the Hurons' own name for themselves, and hence *lacus ouentaronius* would mean "lake of the Wentats or Hurons." Some support is lent to this theory by the fact that small lakes in the State of New York still bear the tribal names, e.g. Seneca Lake, Oneida Lake, Cayuga Lake. Father Jones, however, in his *Huronia*, derives the name *Oentaron* from *ahouenta*, a small fish, and *aroni*, to pierce, so that the meaning would be "fish-spearing lake."[1] In regard to the form *Oentaronk*, introduced by Danville in his map of 1746, it is worth noting that this is only one of a number of interesting facts about his map; he is the first to lay down with accuracy the position of Fort Ste. Marie; the mission region and the southern Georgian Bay are delineated with more than usual precision, while the north shore of Lake Ontario is even more than usually inaccurate. Possibly Danville may have had before him the map which Lalemant made in 1639, which has never been found, and the form *oentaronk* may be the correct and original form of the name. Toronto may be, as Dr. Scadding at first suggested, the remnant of this Huron appellation. Another theory of the etymology of the word Toronto must now be considered. General John S. Clark, of Auburn, New York, in the *Ontario Archaeological Report* for 1899, suggests that the origin of the word is the same as that of Irondequoit Bay, the entrance to the Seneca country on the south side of the lake.

"It is an interesting fact that wherever the name Toronto has appeared as combined with other words, or in its evidently contracted form, it has always from the beginning been on an important thoroughfare of communication. The fact that it has appeared in several positions with several hundred miles intervening, is proof conclusive that the name is not based on any fact incident to any locality.—There is no question whatever in my opinion as to a common origin of *Caniederi Guaruntie* as applied to Lake Champlain, the *Gania Toronto Gouat* of De Lamberville as the name of Irondequoit Bay, and of *Toronto* as the name of Toronto Bay and Lake Simcoe. Each in its place was a gateway of the country."

General Clark explains that the Mohawk term for Lake Champlain meant "lake opening or door," i.e. that Lake Champlain was the door (like the door of one of the Mohawk long houses) leading into their country; that the Senecas, in the same way, applied a similar term to the lake entrance into their country, and that Toronto really means the gate or entry to the Huron country, which, of course, it really was. He quotes from a letter from Jean

1 JONES, *Huronia*, p. 202.

de Lamberville to M. de la Barre, October, 1684: "Had I the honour to confer with you somewhat longer than your leisure allowed me I should have convinced you that you could not have advanced to *Kania-Toronto-Gouat* without being utterly defeated in the then state of your army, which was rather a hospital than a camp."[1] He gives also the following instances of similar spelling of the word: *Gannia-Tareonto-Quat* and *Gannia-Toronto-Gouat*, the Franquelin map of 1684; *Andia-Taronta-Ouat*, the Jesuit map of 1665; *Gannia-Taronta-Gouat*, Denonville's account of his expedition in 1687; and the statement by Spafford in 1813 that *Teoronto* was the proper name of Irondequoit Bay, meaning, in Onondaga, "almost a lake," to which may be added *Teeorondoquo*, in Wraxall, *New York Indian Records*,[2] *Trirontoquot*, in Jefferys' map of 1761, and *Cannonarontagouat* of de Fonuille's map of 1699. Clark on the authority of Dr. O'Callaghan derives the word Irondequoit from *Kaniatare*—a lake, and *Hotontogouan*—to open, the first losing its final "e" in composition and the second its first syllable,[3] the result being *Kaniatarontogouan* or *Ganiatarontagouan*. Apparently it was the central part of this word which survived in *Teeorondoquo*, and a *toronto* would be the entrance to a country. This explanation, of course, fits Toronto Bay quite as well as Irondequoit Bay, and further support is given to the theory by the fact that Teiaiagon and Ganatsekwyagon were Seneca villages and that the Senecas when they came across the lake to Toronto would come from Irondequoit Bay. It is known that the Senecas established themselves at the mouth of the Humber after the expulsion of the Hurons, and that from the Humber they pushed up to Lake Simcoe, which Tonti describes as "right in the Iroquois country"; the word Toronto would then go north with them; it is certain at any rate that it is about this time that the word appears for the first time on the maps.

Admitting that it is impossible to dogmatize about the etymology of the word "Toronto" and that all of these theories may be equally valid and that the name may have originated in several ways, and that the final word will not be said until new matter comes to light, one more theory may be suggested which seems plausible enough. The name *Lac aux Claies* came, as we have seen, from the fish weirs at the Narrows. Now the Huron name for a strait or pass such as there was at Detroit or between the Christian Island and the mainland was *Karontaen*[4] or *Tarontaen;* if the Hurons knew the Narrows at Orillia as *Tarontaen*, the step to *Lac Toronto* is a short one. Jones suggests[5] that there was another word, *karontaen*, derived from *garonta*, a tree, hence the explanation, "trees in the water," would arise from a wrong interpretation of the original name, which might in the same way be confused with *otoronton*. As Lahontan places his Torontogueronons at the Narrows, additional weight seems given to the theory that the name originated at that place. Philologists will be struck by the similarity between *Karontaen*, (Detroit) *Toncharontio* (Lake Erie), *Karontagouat* (Irondequoit Bay-Galinée) and *Taronto*.

1 *New York Colonial Documents*, Vol. IX, p. 261.

2 Wraxall, *New York Indian Records*, McIlwain, p. 131.

3 See Potier, *Elementa Grammaticae Huronicae*, p. 66.

4 *Khahrontha*, modern Mohawk *kharonte, kharonten*, means "an opening, a door or gateway" (Cuoq, 24). *Kahrontha*, meaning to "make an opening" (Cuoq, 93), comes very near to the Lac Tarontha of the Raffeix map of 1688. Consult also Potier, *Radices Huronicae*, pp. 259 and 349; and note that Detroit at the entrance of Lake St. Clair was called *Karontaen* by the Hurons. Potier, pp. 155 and 156; Jones' *Huronia*, pp. 52 and 53. Is Toronto a remnant of Carantoua, the great town of the Hurons?

5 *Huronia*, p. 54.

II

CARTOGRAPHY OF THE TORONTO REGION FROM 1600-1816

Date	Map	Teiaiagon	Ganataekwyagon	Lake Toronto (Lake Simcoe)	Remarks
1600	Anonymous map in Hakluyt's Voyages.				Lake Ontario is "The Lake of Tadenac the bounds whereof are unknown."
1612	Champlain—Paris				Lake Ontario is "Lac Contenant 15 journées des canaux des sauvages." Three villages are shown along the north shore of Lake Ontario.
1613	Champlain—Paris				Lake Ontario appears for the first time as Lac St. Louis.
1632	Champlain—Paris				Gives the Humber. Shows Brûlé's trail to the Andastes beginning south of Lake Erie.
1636	Janson—Amsterdam				Hills shown north of Toronto.
1650	Sanson—Paris				Shows the Quinte and Toronto routes.
1656	Sanson—Paris				Gives the Humber and the Credit rivers. *Pages*
1660	Du Creux—Paris			Oentaron *Lacus Ouentaronius*	Gives the Holland and Humber rivers. *Ouentaron* *Ondaioiss* north of Toronto.
1680	Visscher				Repeats, with additions, Champlain's map of 1612.
1670	Dollier—Galinée				Trail to Matchedash Bay. Mentions Péré.
1673?	Anonymous Mss. map 4044 B. No. 43 Paris. Copy in Public Archives, Ottawa.	Teyoyagon	Ganatsekiagouns Ganatchekiagon	Lac de Toronto	Trail from Ganatchekiagon to Lac de Toronto. This is the first map to contain the name Taronto, and the first to show Toronto Island.
1673?	4044 B. No. 44, similar to above.				Does not show Toronto Island.
1674	Joliet Mss. map, copy in Public Archives.		Ganachieskiagen		Shows trail from Teiaiagon to Lake Simcoe.
1674	Joliet Mss. map in the John Carter Brown Library.				Shows the Toronto Carrying-Place.
1678	Du Val—Paris				Repeats Sanson's indication of the Quinte route.
1683	Hennepin—Paris				Shows a communication between Lake Ontario and Lake Simcoe. Places the Missisaugas where Lahontan places the Torontogueronons.
1684	William Hack—British Museum. Copy in Public Archives.			Oentarona	

Date	Map	Teiaiagon	Ganatchestiagon	Lac Taronto	Remarks
1681	Franquelin Mss. 4040 B. No. 11, T. 150. Paris. Copy in Public Archives.	Teiaiagon (At the end of the lake.)	Ganatchestiagon		
1681	Mss. 4040 B. No. 2. Paris. Copy in Public Archives.			Ouentaronc	
1684	Franquelin. Copy in Public Archives.	Teloiagon (At the end of the lake.)	Ganatchitiagon		
?	Franquelin Mss. 4044 B. No. 40. Copy in Public Archives	Teiaiagon (At end of the lake)			Portage from Teloiagon to unnamed lake.
1688	Coronelli—Paris	Toloiagon (Far to the east.)	Ganaschestiagon (to the east of proper sites.)	Lac Taronto	Shows the Humber and the Holland and the portage. Places the Missisaugas at southern end of Georgian Bay which is called Bay Sakinam.
1688	Raffeix. Copy in Public Archives.	Teyagon	Ganistiquiagon	Lac Taronthe	Gives both portages and the distance. The first map to show the Don.
1688	Franquelin—Paris.	Teiaiagon			Portage to the west branch of the Holland.
1689	Coronelli.	Toloiagon	Ganatchekiagon (far to the east.)	L. Taronto	The portage is given. Under L. Taronto, *Les Piquets* is written.
1695	Coronelli—Venice	Toloiagon. (Too far to the east.)	Ganathe-Kiagon	L. Toronto	Portage shown.
1699	de Fonuille Mss. 4040 B. No. 9. Paris. Copy in Public Archives.	Teiaiagon	Gandaistiagon	Lac Taronto	Shows both portages, with the eastern portage ending at Holland Landing. Péré's name attached to the Moose River.
1700	Delisle—Paris	Teiaiagon. (At the end of the lake.)			Lake Ontario is depicted with a square end. Teiaiagon would thus be "*au fond du lac.*"
1703	Delisle—Paris	Teiaiagon. (At the end of the lake.)	Gandastiagon	L. Taronto	Lake Ontario is depicted with a square end. Teiaiagon would thus be "*au fond du lac.*"
After 1700	Carte de la Nouvelle France. F. 7, Public Archives.	Teiaiagon. (At end of lake.)		Lac Taronto	Shows the portage, and also *Gandavesque-portage.*
1703	Lahontan—Hague				Portage marked. Torontogueronons north-east of Lake Simcoe. Matchedash Bay is called Baye de Toronto. The Humber Bay is *Baye de Tanaouate.* This is a very obvious mistake; the *Baye de Tanaouate* is the bay of Quinte, as will be apparent by a reference to Frontenac's letter to Colbert, November 13, 1673. *Rapport de l'Archiviste de la Province de Quebec pour 1926 et 1927,* p. 37. The engraver of the map misread his manuscript.
1705	Nicolas de Fer—Paris	Teiaiagon	Gandastiagon		
1710	Senex—London				
1710	Mortier—Amsterdam			L. Taronto (misplaced)	Konaevatona(?) on site of Teiaiagon.

Date	Map	Teiaiagon	Ganateekwyagon	Lake Toronto (Lake Simcoe)	Remarks
Before 1711	S. H. Portfeuille. 124. Don. I. No. 2. Public Archives.	Tiaiagon	Gandastiagon		Humber with its two branches shown at the end of the lake.
1718	Delisle—Paris	Teiaiagon			
1719	Atlas Historique, Tome VI, No. 22, P. 82, Public Archives.	Teiaiagon, (At the end of the lake)	Gandatsekiagon		Two branches of the Holland clearly shown.
1720	Covens and Mortier—Amsterdam	Teiaiagon. (At end of lake.)			Georgian Bay marked *Bay de Toronto*. On Lahontan's map the Legend *Bay de Toronto* runs between Christian Island and the mainland.
1720	Atlas Historique, Tome VI, No. 21, p. 90, Public Archives.				This map, a variant of Lahontan's map of 1703, has the *fort supposé* on the site of Ste. Marie II.
1720	Moll—London			Lake of Toronto	Georgian Bay is Toronto Bay; Humber Bay is Bay of Tanaouate.
1733	Henry Popple—London	Tejajon		Lac Toronto	Georgian Bay is Toronto Bay; Humber Bay is Bay of Tanaouate. Lake Ontario much distorted.
1744	Charlevoix-Bellin—Paris. In *History and General Description of New France.*				Shows the Humber and the two branches of the Holland. Sites of Teiaiagon and Gandatsekiagon given.
1744	Charlevoix-Bellin—Paris. *Journal d'un Voyage.*	Tejajagon	Gandat Siagon	Lac Taronto	Has the two trails and the two branches of the Holland clearly marked.
1745	Bellin—Paris			Lac Taronto	Issued as a separate.
1746	Danville—Paris	Teiaiagon	Gandatsiagon Gandatskagon (Too far east.)	Oentaronk L	The map-maker having restored the name Oentaronk finds a place for lac Taronto and the Taronto river further east. This map is the origin of the mistaken statement that the Trent Valley system was known as the Toronto River.
1753?	Vaugondy—Paris	Tejajagon	Gandes Siagon	Lac Toronto	Shows both trails.
1755	Vaugondy—Paris	Tejajagon	Gandas Siagon	Lac Toronto	Places Fort Toronto west of Tejajagon at the western end of the lake.
1755	*Universal Magazine*, F. 49, Public Archives.				Places Fort Toronto at the end of the lake and shows a post on Toronto Lake.
1755	Bellin—Paris				Shows Toronto Bay well but still makes the end of the lake square.
1755	Huske—London		Gandatskiagon	Oentaronck L.	Places L. Taranto east of Oentaronck and show a French fort inland between L. Taranto and Gandatskiagon.
1755	Palairet—London	Tegaogen			Places Toronto Fort near the end of the lake.

Year	Source	Teyagon	Gandataskiagon	Oentaronk / Taronto	Remarks
1755	Evans—Philadelphia				
1755	Danville—Paris	Teyagon (At the western end of the lake near a river called Onontront, probably the Credit.)	Gandataskiagon	Oentaronk	Toronto appears as Tronto. L. Taronto east of Oentaronk; the R de Taronto connects it with the Severn. This map places Ste. Marie des Hurons correctly.
1756	Homann-Danville— Nuremberg		Gandataskiagon	Oentaronck	Follows the Danville map of 1755. *Ganadoke* given at the end of the lake.
1757	Labroquerie Mss. map. Copy in Public Archives.				Gives Toronto, *R. de Toronto* and *presqu'île de Toronto.*
?	Mss. map, undated, N.D. T. 88. Copy in Public Archives.				With inset map of *Fort de Toronto, R. de Toronto* and *Presqu'île de Toronto.*
1761	Jefferys—London	Teyagon		Oentaronk	Teyagon placed near the mouth of Onoront river. L. Taronto placed east of Oentaronk.
1761	Jefferys—London		Gandaskiagon	Oentaronck L.	Taronto R. As in the Danville map of 1746. Gives Fort Toronto at mouth of Credit River Gives Ganadoke.
1764	Bellin—Paris				
1764	Bellin—Paris			Lac Taronto.	Gives the Quinté route.
1771	Johnson—Albany, Mss. original destroyed.				F. Toronto. Shows the Mississaugas and Toronto.
1777	Imbert—Paris				
1777	Faden—London				
1778	Carver		Gandeskiagon	Oentaronck L.	Follows Danville of 1746. Gives *Ganadoke.* Toronto at end of lake.
1783	Bonne—Paris				
1784	Guessefield—Nuremberg				
1784	McMurray— Philadelphia			Toronto L.	Fort Toronto. Toronto Fort at end of lake and Toronto See, two lakes in the Peterborough region. Shows the Quinte route.
1785	Delamarche—Paris	Tegoagen		Oentaronck	Fort Toronto.
1790 ?	Delamarche—Paris				
1794	Kitchin—London			Lake Toronto	Toronto Presquiale (*sic*). Shows the Quinte route.
1794	Kitchin—London	Teyagon		L. Taronto	This plate, prepared in 1773, continued in use till the beginning of the nineteenth century. It is of interest as showing that the village of Teiaiagon continued to be shown on the maps more than a hundred years after it had disappeared.
1796	Arrowsmith—London			Clie Lake	Gives Trent R. and Rice Lake and the Quinte route. Toronto now York.
1796	Anderson—New York				York. Marks Nottawasaga Bay, Iroquoise Bay.
1816	Carey and Warner— Philadelphia				Toronto given as Otranto.

230   APPENDIX

(a) A Plan of the District of Nassau in the Province of Quebec, Compiled in the Surveyor-General's Office Pursuant to an Order in Council of the 22nd day of February, 1790, and dated Quebec this 1st day of October, 1790, and signed by Samuel Holland, Surveyor-General, and John Collins, Deputy Surveyor-General. Of this important map there seem to be three slightly varying copies in existence; one in the Ontario Archives reproduced on page c. of the 1905 Report; one in the Dominion Archives entitled "A Map of Part of Canada for the use of His Majesty's Secretary of State"; and a third in the Surveys Department, tagged Pigeonhole 379. Since the map in the Surveys Department contains details and manuscript notes omitted in the other two, it would seem to be the original manuscript. This map indicates minutely the course of the Toronto Carrying-Place, showing the streams and hills which it crossed. In the same way the carrying-places between the Bay of Quinte and Lake Simcoe are carefully charted in detail as well as the portage from the mouth of the Ganaraska River (Port Hope) to Rice Lake, and from Orillia to Matchedash Bay (the Coldwater Road). This map embodies the information which Collins was instructed by Hamilton to obtain in 1785 (*Ontario Archives Report*, p. 371.) relative to the value of the communication between the Bay of Quinte and Lake Huron by Lac aux Claies, and proves that careful surveys were made of the carrying-places along that route as well as between Toronto and Lake Simcoe, the object being to determine the most convenient communication with the North-West territories. The result of these surveys was a decision in favour of the Toronto Carrying-Place, and little more is heard of the Trent Valley route till the construction of the Trent Valley Canal as a waterway between the Georgian Bay and Lake Ontario; a costly project which has not proved its utility. Champlain and his Huron allies in following this route in 1615 made the communication known at a very early date, but there is no evidence that it was at any time the usual route between the lakes except where war parties wished to avoid observation.

(b) Map showing the cessions from the Indians in 1784, 1787 and 1788, reproduced on p. cxviii of the *Ontario Archives Report* for 1905. This map shows the Toronto Carrying-Place, marking it with the words, "Old Indian Path." A general conference took place with the Indians, both Iroquois and Missisauga, at Carleton Island in 1784, when the lands along the north shore of Lake Ontario were ceded to the Crown; these cessions were confirmed by special treaties in 1787 and 1788. It has been suggested that the first Toronto Purchase confirmed at the Bay of Quinte in 1787 proved defective owing to the amount of liquor consumed; the bargain had to be ratified again in 1805 at the River Credit.

(c) Map reproduced opposite p. 43 of Miss K. M. Lizars' *The Valley of the Humber* with the caption "From a Plan of the New Settlements, 1789." This map shows the trail from the Humber mouth with the legend, "Carrying-Place from Toronto."

(d) Map reproduced opposite p. 38 of Miss K. M. Lizars' *The Valley of the Humber*. This map is by General Gother Mann and bears the date 1791.

(e) Lieutenant Pilkington's map of Governor Simcoe's trip over the Carrying-Place in 1793. A copy in the Ontario Archives. This map gives few details.

(f) A Chewett map of 1793 shows the trail from the Humber mouth to the Holland.

(g) A very rough unsigned map made between the years 1784 and 1790 and reproduced on p. 101 of Miss K. M. Lizars' *The Valley of the Humber*, gives the trail with an Indian village at the mouth of the Humber marked "Toronto formerly an Indian village now abandoned."

CARTOGRAPHY OF THE TORONTO REGION 231

(h) A D. W. Smyth (Faden) map of 1800, reproduced opposite p. 104 of the same book, shows a proposed canal between the East Branch of the Holland and the Nen or Rouge River.

(i) Plan of Tarento (*sic*) Harbour with the proposed Town and Settlement. Gother Mann, Quebec, December 6, 1788. This map shows the location of the buildings in the French Fort.

(j) Descriptive plan of the Toronto Purchase made September 23, 1787, and completed August 1, 1805, by W. Chewett, Senior Surveyor and Draughtsman. This map was published by the Department of Indian Affairs, Ottawa, on October 27, 1890. It bears the totems and signatures of the chiefs and officials who completed the negotiations. There is a map of the Toronto Purchase in the Surveys Department, Toronto, which differs in some slight details.

(k) Map No. Q. 36, Indian Drawer No. 2, Toronto Purchase, 1817. This map is in the Surveys Department in the Ontario Parliament Buildings; it is on the scale of 80 chains to the inch, and gives the survey of the northern boundary of the Toronto Purchase. The survey of the boundaries of the Purchase were made by Augustus Jones in 1817. This is the map which determined the northern terminus of the trail.

(l) Large map by La Force and Kotte of Lake Ontario, 1783 and 1789. Shows the ruins of Fort Toronto, but does not mark the Carrying-Place. Copy in Toronto Public Library. This is the earliest map to show the ruins of the French Fort Toronto.

(m) Three manuscript maps originally in the possession of Governor Simcoe and now in the possession of W. P. Cole, Esq., 116 Highfield Lane, Southampton, England. Copies of these maps are in the Public Archives, Ottawa.

No. 6. Plan of Toronto as surveyed by A. Aitkin in 1788. This map shows the work done in the summer of 1788 as described in the recently discovered letter published in this volume. The Carrying-Place is shown as a straight line running back from the mouth of the Toronto River and is marked, "Carrying place to Lake le Clay about 30 miles." The town plot is shown as laid off by Aitkin, commencing 90 chains west of the Nichingguakokonik River (the Don) and extending to the Garrison Creek. The word "York" has been added by a later hand. This map confirms Aitkin's letter and establishes the fact that Toronto was first laid out in 1788 under that name in accordance with instructions of Lord Dorchester.

No. 7. This map is the survey of Toronto Harbour drawn by Joseph Bouchette, November 15, 1792 (1793?). The map shows Mr. St. John's house (Rousseau) at the mouth of the Toronto River. There is a picture of a two-masted ship riding at anchor which is, no doubt, Bouchette's vessel. The following directions are given for entering the harbour: "Toronto harbour is very safe for the shipping that can enter into it the least water at Entrance being two Fathom and a half. It is sheltered from every wind except the S.W. which blows directly into the Harbour, but it does not occasion much sea the said Harbour being perfectly shut up by the Bar.

"Directions to Enter into the Harbour: 1st. When the Blacksmith's House[1] Bears NW by N and the middle of the Sandy Point Bears E.N.E. you will find 8 Fathom of water, Sandy Bottom. 2nd. When the said House Bears W. by N ½ N you will find three Fathoms of Water. The end of the Sandy Shoal Bearing from the Vessel NE ½ E and then from thence

1 "Father, I forgot to tell you that a blacksmith was promised us when we sold the Toronto land who was to be at the Humber; but you have removed him to York and he is no use to us." Miss K. M. Lizars, *The Valley of the Humber*, p. 108.

a N.E course coming gradually round to NE by E&ENE after being clear of the shoal will bring a vessel safe into Toronto Harbour."

No. 8.   This map is similar to No. 6.   It indicates the place for a fort at the creek later known as Garrison Creek. The Nichingquakokonik is said to be navigable for two or three miles.

No. 9.   Map No. C.2668 T.39.   Map of York by George Williams, November 7, 1813.   In the Public Archives, Ottawa.   This is the best map in existence of the ruins of the French Fort Toronto.

No. 10.   Map entitled "Communication between Lake Ontario and Lake Huron via Lake La Clie in Governor Hamilton's Correspondence, 1785."— *Simcoe Papers*, Vol. I, p. 8.

III

PHILIPPE FRANÇOIS DE RASTEL DE ROCHEBLAVE

By THE HONOURABLE MR. JUSTICE E. FABRE SURVEYER, F.R.S.C.

Among the fifty citizens elected by the people for the first time to represent them at Quebec in 1792, no one, not excepting those who had borne arms
either in 1759 or in 1775, or those who had engaged in the fur trade in the far
west, had had a more stirring and adventurous career than the representative
who came from the quiet village of Varennes to sit in the Assembly, in which
he seems to have been the senior member, Philippe François de Rastel de
Rocheblave.[1]

M. de Rocheblave was of noble birth, as is attested by the following
document:

"1747, April 14th. We Louis Pierre D'Hozier, King-at-Arms for France,
Knight and Sub-Dean of the Order of the King,
Councillor in His Councils, Master-in-Ordinary of
the Department of Accounts, Paris, Genealogist of
the House, Bed-Chamber and Stables of His Majesty,
of the Queen and of the Dauphiness,
hereby certify that Philippe François de Rastel de Rocheblave, one of the
children of Jean-Joseph de Rastel, Seigneur de Rocheblave & de Savournon,
and of Dame Diane Françoise Elizabeth de Dillon, his wife, has submitted
to us the proofs of his ancient military extraction, and that his filiations
have been carefully traced to his ancestor in the tenth degree, the Sieur
Raimond du Rastel, Chevalier, Seigneur of the said land of Rocheblave,
for which he took the oath of fealty the 30th of August in the year one thousand
two hundred and seventy-four; and that accordingly his lineage may be
classed among those for which the most distinguished and the most ancient
proofs are demanded.   Wherefore we have delivered these presents at Paris,
on Friday, the fourteenth day of April, in the year one thousand seven hundred
and forty seven."

There is also his baptismal certificate preserved in the Archives of the
Département des Hautes Alpes:—"In the year one thousand seven hundred and
twenty-seven, the fourth of March, I, the undersigned parish priest of Savour-
non, have solemnly performed the christening of Philippe François de Rastel,
nobleman, natural and legitimate son of Jean Joseph de Rastel de Rocheblave,
Segnor of Savournon, of Le Bersac and of other places, and of Dame Françoise
Elizabeth de Dillon, his wife, born yesterday.   The child's godfather was
Alexandre de Rastel Chevalier de Rocheblave, gentleman, and his godmother
Elizabeth de Gillier his grandmother, lady; in testimony whereof they have
affixed their signatures.   Signed, Gillier Dillon, Rocheblave, le Chevalier de
Rocheblave, Carltrand, Parish Priest."

D'Hozier also records that the father of M. de Rocheblave had been a
captain in the Dauphiné Regiment, that he resided at Savournon near the
city of Gap, that he was lord also of Bersac and Mourmoirière, that he married
in 1720 Mademoiselle Françoise Elizabeth Diane de Dillon, a daughter of
James de Dillon, captain of the grenadiers of the *Régiment de Dillon* and a

1 The County of Surrey, which de Rocheblave represented, corresponds to the present
county of Verchères.

233

scion of the Lords Viscounts de Dillon of Ireland; that of this marriage twenty
children were born, of whom twelve were then living. On his mother's side
M. de Rocheblave was thus of Irish descent and must have been connected
with that spirited Madame de la Tour du Pin, herself also a Dillon, who has
left so sprightly a record of the sufferings of her family during the Revolution.
As the oldest surviving son, M. de Rocheblave, on the death of his father,
would have had the right to assume the title of marquis.

Philippe de Rocheblave appears at first to have been destined to the
Church; but his parents realizing that he had no religious vocation, selected
a military career. In the announcement which appeared in the Quebec
Gazette October 7, 1840, of the death of his son, Pierre, mention is made of the
fact that Philippe de Rocheblave had been an officer in the French army and
had taken part in the battle of Fontenoy, May 11, 1745, when he was only
eighteen years of age. He was, it seems, put on half-pay in 1748, and went
off to the French Antilles under the command of François Raynaud, count de
Villeverd, at that time Lieutenant-Governor-General of the French Islands
of America. Raynaud was the maternal uncle of Marianne de Rivole, wife of
Gabriel de Rastel de Rocheblave, and even before the marriage of the latter
with his niece, was closely connected with the families of de Rivole and de
Rocheblave.

Of his career up to 1755 we can give no further account, nor is it known
when he came to America. He must have acquired experience, however, in
encounters with the Indians, for he was one of the officers who in 1755 served
under Charles de Langlade when the latter led his bands of savages from Lake
Michigan to Fort Duquesne on the banks of the Ohio.

At the battle of Monongahela, July 9, 1755, de Rocheblave distinguished
himself and won the praise of his chief. But after the remnant of Braddock's
army had been put to flight, the French and Indians began rifling the bodies
of the dead along the banks of the Monongahela. La Choisie, a young soldier
of great promise, discovered the body of a richly-dressed English officer.
Almost at the same instant de Rocheblave claimed that he had found it. La
Choisie seized the dead officer's well-filled purse; de Rocheblave demanded a
share of it; his companion refused and they parted in no friendly manner. The
following morning La Choisie was found assassinated, and the purse of gold was
missing. There was no direct evidence of de Rocheblave's guilt, but suspicion
was fastened on him. At least so de Langlade and Augustin Grignon maintained, but their testimony is highly questionable.[1] De Rocheblave appears
to have continued to serve under de Langlade.

In August, 1756, Vaudreuil, Governor of Canada, writing to one of the
French ministers, relates that Sieur de Rocheblave, along with another cadet,
a corporal and twenty Indians, captured a small fort situated beyond Fort
Cumberland, killed four Englishmen, wounded three others and took three
prisoners. The Fort Cumberland in question is not Fort Beauséjour, but a
fort situated in Maryland. That year de Rocheblave seems also to have been
at Fort Duquesne (Pittsburg),[2] where we find him again the following year.

In 1758 he is sent by M. de Ligneris on a scouting expedition in the
neighbourhood of Loyal Hannon (later Fort Ligonier), in the county of
Westmoreland in Pennsylvania. The reports he brought back were not
favourable. A few months later, M. de Ligneris evacuated Fort Duquesne,
which was renamed Fort Pitt on November 25, 1758.

---

1 *Wisconsin Historical Society's Collections*, VII, p. 132; Tassé, *Les Canadiens de l'Ouest*,
I, p. 15.

2 *Wisconsin Historical Society's Collections*, XVIII, p. 214.

In 1759 de Rocheblave was under the command of de Laperrière Marin, who, like de Langlade, played such an important rôle in the history of old Wisconsin. In June, 1759, Marin, with the assistance of Lieutenant de Rocheblave and three Canadians, left Fort Niagara at the head of three hundred Delaware and Shawnee Indians "to insult Fort Pitt," as they said. This fort was in poor condition and might have been captured if a larger number of Frenchmen had taken part in the expedition, the Indians being of very little use. But there was not time to get reinforcements. The Commandant of Fort Niagara suddenly recalled his troops to face General Prideaux and Sir William Johnson, who were marching against Fort Niagara. Marin was on the way to join the reinforcements *en route* and was made prisoner of war under the very walls of Fort Niagara. De Rocheblave had been left with fifty men to guard the canoes on an island above the Niagara portage, where they were joined by the French fugitives and the whole party sought refuge at Detroit.   On May 22, 1763, Major Pierre Neyon de Villiers, commanding in the Illinois, ordered de Rocheblave, then "lieutenant in a company of detached marine troops in that colony," to go from Fort Chartres to Fort Massiac to replace Sieur de Clouet.   The following are among the recommendations made to him:

"We will simply content ourselves with suggesting that, drink being the one thing that can disturb the tranquillity and unity so necessary in that post, we find ourselves unavoidably obliged to order him to keep his hands upon all that may be shipped of every kind except that which the King is accustomed to send for the relief of the sick and wounded that may be in the garrison.

". . . As to that which every good Christian owes to God his creator, we know too well the sentiments of le Sieur de Rocheblave to think it necessary to recommend to him prayers offered evening and morning and to put a check upon the blasphemy and oaths to which soldiers are only too much addicted."

From this time on, until 1763, we lose sight of de Rocheblave completely. The de Rocheblave who was in Louisiana in the employ of the French government in 1762, after whom a street in New Orleans was named, was a brother, Paul de Rocheblave. He, too, had a somewhat checkered career.

In 1763, at the conquest, Philippe de Rocheblave retired from the army, was placed on the half-pay of a lieutenant, and went to Kaskaskia as a trader. Kaskaskia was founded in 1700 on the banks of the Mississippi, and prospered until 1844, when floods destroyed its trade, which never again revived. Fresh inundations occurred in 1851, and again in 1857; and on January 1, 1902, the name of Kaskaskia was permanently removed from the post office list. It was in the old parish church in Kaskaskia that, on April 11, 1763, de Rocheblave, with the permission of Major Neyon de Villiers,[1] officer in command, married Marie Michel Dufresne, daughter of Jacques Michel Dufresne, an officer in the militia in that parish.

When the Illinois country surrendered to the Revolutionary troops in 1765, de Rocheblave abandoned his property and, preferring Spanish rule to British, took the oath of allegiance to the King of Spain.[2] On May 16, 1766, he was in command at Fort Sainte-Geneviève on the banks of the Mississippi and remained in charge when Sainte-Geneviève came into the possession of the King of Spain, November 22, 1769. De Rocheblave zealously protected the rights of Spain, and in 1767, when Father Meurin presented himself at Sainte-Geneviève with letters from the Bishop of Quebec, de Rocheblave

1 Brother-in-law of Captain Alexandre Douville.
2 Petition to Carleton, April 10, 1777. Canadian Archives.

declared: "I know no English bishop here in a post which I command; I wish no ecclesiastical jurisdiction other than that of the Archbishop of Saint Domingo." He ordered the proscription of Father Meurin and his arrest as a state criminal for having recognized a jurisdiction not admitted by Spain. A friend warned Father Meurin of his danger and the latter crossed the Mississippi into English territory.[1]

This zeal for Spain did not last long. Irregularities were found in the accounts of the Governor of Sainte-Geneviève. De Rocheblave was prosecuted, turned out of office by the Spanish Governor, O'Reilly, and fell into disgrace.[2] De Rocheblave was responsible for the introduction of courts of justice and administration at Sainte-Geneviève; he registered marriages and transacted forced sales of land.

Let me here quote Edward Mason, President of the Historical Society of Chicago:

"By what process this foe of Great Britain, who as a Frenchman had fought against her troops, and as a Spaniard had quarrelled with her officials, was transformed into a subject of George the Third is a mystery. Nor is it known when the marvellous change took place. It was alleged against him that he never took the oath of allegiance and supremacy required of those who held office under the British crown. However this may have been, de Rocheblave returned to Kaskaskia some time between 1770 and 1776[3] and posed as a British subject.

"Captain Hugh Lord was then in command of the Illinois, and in the spring of 1776 he rejoined the English forces after the disasters to royalists when the colonial troops invaded Canada. In the spring of 1776, Captain Lord and his men departed from Kaskaskia to join the British forces by way of Detroit and the lakes. He had received orders to hand over the administration to such a person as he judged proper. He chose de Rocheblave as his successor, and as proof of his confidence, Lord left his family in de Rocheblave's care. Four years later they were still with Madame de Rocheblave.

"Carleton, commander-in-chief in Canada, included under his jurisdiction the country of the Illinois. He wrote to Hamilton, Lieutenant-Governor at Detroit, that the troops had been withdrawn from the Illinois, and that a salary of 200 pounds a year had been granted de Rocheblave to watch over the interests of the King in that country, and to advise the government of whatever might be going on there against them, and that his appointment was deemed to have commenced May 1, 1776.

"De Rocheblave naturally magnified his office, and considered that Captain Lord had appointed him judge and commandant of a vast country, and he lost no time in impressing this upon the people of the Illinois country. The French inhabitants were speedily taught to address him as commandant of all the British part of the Illinois, and with the most humble respect and

1 J. G. SHEA, *Life and Times of Archbishop Carroll*, p. 120. More recently, Bishop J. H. Schlarman, Ph.D., in *From Quebec to New Orleans*, pages 442 and 443, enlarges upon that statement. On the other hand Father Lawrence J. Kenny, S. J., professor of history at St. Louis University, points out, in a private letter, that Shea merely draws his information from a letter of Father Simplicius Bocquet to Bishop Briand of May 17, 1762. He points out that de Rocheblave was godfather in the old Kaskaskia church on not less than fourteen occasions, which does not indicate an anticlerical bias, and considers that, on the whole, de Rocheblave has been much maligned by American historians, a statement which his subsequent conduct in Canada would seem to bear out.

2 O. W. COLLET, secretary of the Historical Society of Missouri, postcard to L. C. Draper of Wisconsin, October 8, 1885; *Chicago Historical Collections*, IV, p. 364.

3 According to other historians this would be in 1773: *Wisconsin Historical Society Collections*, XVIII, p. 214.

submission. The British inhabitants were less docile and complained, by petition to Carleton, that de Rocheblave trampled upon their liberties, despised Englishmen and English laws, acted both as counsel and judge, traded with the savages against his own edicts, and was partial to the French."

De Rocheblave, nevertheless, seems to have been loyal to the government and, in spite of his previous changes of allegiance, he served the British Crown with zeal and persistence during his stay in the Illinois.

Sir Guy Carleton, Governor of Canada, who, in the beginning, had carefully limited de Rocheblave's powers, paid no attention to the complaints against him and gave him authority to call out the militia, which was practically appointing him Commandant. The British government made no objection to his assuming the title, and Haldimand, who succeeded Carleton as Governor of Canada, always treated de Rocheblave as former Commandant of Illinois, after the capture of Fort Gage by Clark, and paid him his salary as such and his expenses in that office until 1783.

De Rocheblave was untiring in his efforts to obtain information concerning the schemes of the Spaniards and the Americans. He was really in charge of a vast province; without troops, without money, without resources, he accomplished a great deal with very limited means. Particularly valuable were his services in connection with the Indians, among whom he had a good deal of influence because of his military experience and his long association with them, and for a long time it was through his efforts solely that the neighbouring tribes were kept quiet and the routes along the Ohio and the Mississippi open.

He was anxious that some troops should be sent to protect the Illinois country, the importance of which he seemed to understand far better than any one else in the British service. He used to insist that if the Illinois were better known, that country would constitute one of the richest colonies of Britain. But Carleton wrote to Lieutenant-Governor Hamilton that it was impossible to send troops to de Rocheblave; his requests for soldiers were unheeded; his accounts for more or less legitimate expenses were disallowed and his drafts on the representatives of the Government at Detroit and in Canada were protested.[1] Hamilton continually urged him to be patient while allowing him to hope for the post of Governor of New Orleans.

A letter written on September 22, 1778, at Detroit, by a Frenchman, M. Montforton, to M. Arès at Kaskaskia, indicates that at this time M. de Rocheblave was exposed to persecution which the former considered most unmerited.[2]

On July 4, 1778, the very day when de Rocheblave had signed a long report to Governor Haldimand[3] and had made a draft of £1,262 on the Treasury of the Province of Quebec, Colonel George Rogers Clark, with fifty-three followers, seized Fort Gage, an old house in Kaskaskia formerly occupied by the Jesuits and confiscated in 1764. De Rocheblave was taken in his bed, made prisoner of war, and sent under escort to Governor Patrick Henry at Williamsburg, capital of Virginia[4] and there released on parole. He was accompanied by a certain Mr. Schifflin, first lieutenant of the volunteers in Detroit. Both of them received a hundred guineas from Sir Henry Clinton to enable them to return to Canada. De Rocheblave afterward claimed it was proposed to him that he should return to Illinois in the name

1 Canadian Archives, *Haldimand Papers*, Series B, Vol. 185, p. 2. *Illinois Historical Collections*, II, pp. xxvi, xxvii.

2 *Michigan Historical Collections*, X, p. 295.

3 Canadian Archives, *Haldimand Papers*, Series B, Vol. 122, p. 91.

4 *Clark's Campaign in the Illinois*, p. 37.

of the Congress as Governor, superintendent of the Indians, and colonel, with the promise that all his losses would be made good. According to his own account, de Rocheblave resisted all temptations and escaped to New York in July, 1780.[1] A certain Chevalier de Saint-Joseph wrote to Major de Peyster that Commandant Willing had put de Rocheblave and a man named Crie in chains for refusing to swear allegiance to the King of Spain, to the King of France and to Congress.[2] In October, de Rocheblave wrote to Haldimand stating his desire to form a regiment of volunteers in order to chase the rebels from the regions of the Mississippi and the Ohio.[3] October 7, 1781, we find him at Quebec, addressing a memoir to Haldimand setting forth the advantages of occupying the country of the Illinois.[4] In February, 1782, he applied for a passport to Detroit and obtained from the Government a warrant for the reimbursement of the expenses incurred by him as Commandant of Illinois.

In March, 1782, he suggests securing the Illinois with the aid of Germans and Acadians from Virginia and Maryland, and failing this he demands a passport and a circular letter to the commandants of posts where he might wish to trade in furs; lastly he demands reimbursement of all his losses. Haldimand permits him to engage in trade, but before setting out on his expedition, de Rocheblave forwards from Quebec, in 1782, a fresh petition for the payment of his salary and the expenses incurred by him during his captivity. The salary of Commandant of Illinois is granted to him.[5] He then sets out, but as soon as he arrives at Mackinac, he draws a draft on the Government which the Government refuses to pay.[6]

In the winter of 1782-1783 de Rocheblave revisited his old home in Kaskaskia. In March, 1783, he was back in Quebec and a new warrant for the payment of his salary as Governor of Illinois was signed. In the fall of 1783, having learned that Parliament had voted a law for indemnifying the Loyalists, de Rocheblave made fresh demands, asking for immediate settlement, because, he said, he was going to find his wife at "Chikagou."[7] He appears to have remained in Quebec, however, for in January, 1784, he was asking for a situation in the Government. In March he applied for a passport, a circular letter to the Commandants of posts, advances of powder and clothing, and a grant of lands on the shore of the Rideau River.[8]

On March 26, 1784, Haldimand sent him a letter of recommendation permitting him to send merchandise up-country, but de Rocheblave still asked for assistance, and his wife supported his petition with a touching letter. Haldimand succumbed and ordered that a thousand acres of land be set aside for him on Grande Ile, near Cataraqui.[9] This concession, however, does not appear to have been consummated.

In 1785 he is still at Quebec, whence he writes to Haldimand in London on January 21st, that he has not, like all the Loyalist refugees, been indemnified for his losses, that he has even been deprived of rations and that this treatment is having a bad effect on the Canadians. About this time, Haldimand, who

1 American writers accuse him of breaking his parole: Burk's *Virginia*, IV, p. 425; *Jefferson's Writings*, I, p. 258; *Mr. Carleton's Papers*, pp. 184, 185.

2 *Michigan Historical Collections*, IX, p. 369.

3 Canadian Archives, *Haldimand Papers*, Series B, Vol. 73, p. 221.

4 Ibid.   B, 122, p. 545; B, 123, p. 141.

5 Ibid.   B, 75-1, pp. 14 *et seq.*; 81, *et seq.*

6 Ibid.   B, 219, p. 80, "Haldimand to de Rocheblave, 2nd November, 1787."

7 *Illinois Historical Collections*, V, p. 353.

8 Canadian Archives, *Haldimand Papers*, Series B, 219, p. 22.

9 Ibid.   B, 75-2, p. 45; B, 75-1, pp. 14-25; 81-83

was in London, received reports from Canada reflecting upon the loyalty of de Rocheblave. Haldimand's secretary, Captain Mathews, made an investigation into the conduct—past and recent—of de Rocheblave, and wrote to Haldimand in London describing what he called the odious character of de Rocheblave.[1]

June 12, 1786, de Rocheblave obtained a permit to engage in trade at Michilimackinac.

On January 16, 1787, de Rocheblave, renewing a petition that he had addressed to Lieutenant-Governor Hamilton in 1785, asked Lord Dorchester to change the route to the Upper Country and to give him the preference for the Toronto portage with a tract of land sufficient for the purpose. May 25, 1787, he returned to the attack and begged the Governor to give him a grant of land of a thousand acres by the Bay of Toronto "beginning at the River which empties into Lake Ontario above the bluffs east by north-east of the said Toronto and extending to the old Settlement at the said Toronto." He further requested "a small island situated between the aforesaid old Settlement and the aforesaid River in the same Bay, in order that he may keep some animals there" and for his wife, his three male children and his daughter he demanded lands in the neighbourhood, of the usual amount. His various requests were referred to a committee of the Council on June 25, 1787. The matter seems to have gone no farther. October 7, 1787, de Rocheblave again writes to Governor Haldimand suggesting an expedition into the Illinois. He concludes by saying: "The English of the Mississippi, in spite of their apparent resignation, would be glad to shake off the Spanish yoke, and would not fail to join us; New Orleans attacked from above could not hold out."

After this we lose sight of M. de Rocheblave until February 22, 1790, when we find him in Montreal where, along with six other citizens, he signed a document nominating Jean Guillaume Delisle, Notary, as master of "The Brothers of Canada" (*Frères du Canada*), a Masonic lodge founded in 1785.[2]

When the first elections to parliament under the Canada Act of 1791 were to be held, M. de Rocheblave published the following statement in the Montreal *Gazette* of May 22, 1792:

"To The Free Voters:

"Should the contingency arise when those persons best fitted to serve their compatriots in the next Assembly by reason of their talent and their means, find that their private affairs prevent them from exercising so sacred a duty, you will find me at such a time ready and waiting to serve the province with all possible zeal."

At this period, he was living at Varennes; we do not know how long he had been living there. Once elected, M. de Rocheblave, in 1792, vigorously opposed the nomination of an Englishman as President of the Assembly. "Why then," said he, "do our British brethren ever cry out against the decision we have come to of retaining our customs, laws and mother tongue, the only means left us with which to protect our property? Is it possible that the barren pride in seeing their language prevail makes them so blind as to rob of force and energy the very laws, usages and customs which form the secure foundation of their own prosperity? Being the uncontested masters of the trade of the country which delivers our produce into their hands entirely,

1 Ibid. B, 64, p. 452; B, 76, pp. 198-223.   All this part of the biography since 1755 is due chiefly to the patient researches of M. Émile Audet, formerly notary in Montreal and now professor in Chicago, to whom we express our thanks.

2 *Bulletin des Recherches Historiques*, Vol. XII, p. 219.   (Article by M. E.-Z. Massicotte.) See *la chanson de l'ordre*, Ibid. XXVI, p. 152.

240 APPENDIX

would they not be the greatest losers if the Colony were upset by the convulsions which their injustice, if continued, will inevitably provoke? And are we not rendering the greatest of services to them as well as to ourselves by opposing them in this matter?"

At the same session, M. de Rocheblave further demanded that the Jesuit estates be used for the education of the young in conformity with the intention of the King of France, who had granted the property for this purpose. At the session of 1795 he also opposed the abolition of seigniorial tenure, on the ground that the advocates of this measure were not acting from motives of true and sane reform.

One of the first acts of M. de Rocheblave as deputy was to bring before the House on March 2, 1793, a petition from two hundred residents, urban and rural, of the county of Quebec, concluding as follows:

"The petitioners conclude by calling attention to the fact that since the abolition of the Jesuit Order, the members of that order resident in Canada have generously offered to turn over to this Province all the property of this College for the benefit of the public to whom it belongs, and they ask for nothing more than food and clothing for themselves. This transfer has been retarded and impeded by numberless difficulties. That the nature of the titles and the foundation of this College had been disguised in Europe and that by this means this Province has been deprived of public education since the conquest, although everywhere else in the British Empire public education is encouraged.

"That this misfortune is due solely to the efforts of some persons prior to the sanctioning of the New Constitution, who have urgently solicited from His Majesty, under various pretexts, the gift or the concession of these properties, but fortunately without effect. The petitioners are assured that His Most Gracious Majesty, in his royal edicts and instructions, has always endeavoured to be well informed and to reserve from all this property sufficient for the purpose of public instruction in this country, without infringing in any manner upon the objects and aims of this foundation.

"To this end the petitioners, in the hope and confidence that this Honourable Chamber will consider that this property has been acquired only through the labour, the courage and the sweat of the inhabitants of this country in the hope of securing an education for their children, and that this property although adequate does not exceed in revenue the minimum required for public education on a liberal basis for which purpose this property has been granted, request and claim these revenues as their just right with all the respect due to this Chamber, and your petitioners will ever pray."

The stand which de Rocheblave took on this question won him the congratulations of the Constitutional Club, in terms similar to those which the club used on this very occasion to congratulate Papineau.

M. de Rocheblave was re-elected in 1796 and in 1800. A speech made by Judge de Bonne indicates that he had succeeded in having his constituents pay his election expenses.

He was appointed registrar of the Land-Deeds, but he soon realized that there was no registry office, and asked the Governor to open one. His request was referred to the executive. On May 13, 1801, M. de Rocheblave and his colleagues, Messrs. Joseph Planté and Felix Tétu, were commissioned to organize a Land Registry. On July 16, 1801, they signed a report—quite a non-committal document—raising the question as to whether or not the King's franchise holders paid their declarations to the court-rolls.

April 27, 1798, M. de Rocheblave asked permission to take the oath of loyalty and service for the Fief of Saint-Michel (Varennes). This request does not seem to have been granted.

M. de Rocheblave died on April 3, 1802, at Quebec, during the session of Parliament. He was buried on April 5 in the smallpox cemetery (on Couillard Street), in the presence of Messrs. Robert Lester, A. J. Raby, Louis Marchand, François Levesque and the officiating clergyman, Abbé Desjardins.

The Quebec *Gazette* prints the following eulogium in its supplement of April 22, 1802:

"Died in this city, Saturday evening, the 3rd instant, Philip de Rocheblave, Gentleman, Member of the Provincial Parliament, representing the county of Surrey, and Registrar of the Crown. M. de Rocheblave was during his lifetime a loyal subject of the King whom he has served with honour and devotion on many occasions. He takes with him the regrets of his friends, especially of those who knew his patriotic and social qualities."

This is what M. Sulte says of him: "A good orator, a scholar, of pleasing manner, a tried patriot, he died in the midst of the session of 1802, deeply regretted by the Canadians."[1]

The words "loyal subject of the King," "scholar," "tried patriot," set one musing.

In one of his many petitions M. de Rocheblave stated that he had six children. On May 25, 1787, he stated that he had three sons and on daughter living. His daughter Rosalie died in Montreal, February 19, 1844, aged 71. As for his sons, one of them, Pierre, traded in furs with the North-West Company. In 1817, he sold his interests in the trade of the West and the North-West to the American Fur Company, of which John Jacob Astor was the head. He was a member of the Special Council and of the Executive Council. He was elected to the Legislature on January 9, 1832. On February 9, 1819, he married Anne Elmire Bouthillier, daughter of Jean Bouthillier, justice of the peace and lieutenant-colonel, and of the late Madame Louis Perthuis. He died October 5, 1840, at Côte Saint Louis after a long and cruel illness. The Quebec *Gazette* of October 7, 1840, and the Montreal *Transcript* of October 10, 1840, pay him a high tribute. He was survived by his widow. They had several children, among them Madame Willoughby, of whom we shall hear later, and another daughter, Elmire, who died a nonagenarian at the beginning of the present century.[2]

Another son, Noel, was representative for the county of Surrey from August 6, 1804, to December 10, 1805, the date of his death. M. de Rocheblave had left Detroit accompanied by a Mr. Gillespie and was going to Philadelphia there to confer with the American authorities on the question of trade on the Missouri. A storm arose on Lake Champlain, the boat upset and M. de Rocheblave was seriously injured. The two travellers returned to Montreal; they arrived on December 6th. Gangrene in the wound received in the wreck caused the death of M. de Rocheblave.

There appears to have been a third son, Philippe, who is believed to have lived at Kaskaskia, where he seems to have executed a document on July 28, 1801,[3] at a time when his father was in Canada. In a report from the land commissioners of the District of Kaskaskia dated December 31, 1809, they reject a claim from one Philip de Rocheblave (seven and a half years after the death of our deputy). Mr. Collet, secretary of the Historical Society of

1 *History of French-Canadians*, VIII, p. 17.

2 *Bulletin des Recherches Historiques*, Vol. IV, p. 357. (Article by the Hon. Désiré Girouard.)

3 *Chicago Historical Society's Autograph Letters*, Vol. 61, p. 399.

Missouri, claims that there were several Philip de Rocheblaves, which leads one to believe that there was a son by this name.

How could our historians—usually so clever in tracing kinship—how could they have thought Pierre and Noel de Rocheblave merely nephews of the first deputy of Surrey? No doubt the reason for this error is that a younger brother of Philippe de Rocheblave, Pierre Louis, born at Savournon, France, in 1729, and officer of the marines, was married at Montreal on September 30, 1760, to Marie Joseph Duplessis. He became Governor of Goree in Africa.[1]

We know nothing of Madame de Rocheblave except that she wrote several letters to Haldimand which have been preserved, and that in 1778 Patrick Henry gave express instructions to John Todd and to Clark that she be well treated and that her property be restored to her, which is ground for the supposition that she was at Kaskaskia at the time. To what extent could she have shared the expeditions of her husband? We have no information. M. de Rocheblave seems to have stayed in Varennes very little during the last ten years of his life. It was there that Madame de Rocheblave died on February 21, 1813, at the age of seventy-six. She was buried there two days later, in the presence of a large number of parishioners, among whom no relative is noticed.

W. F. Poole, librarian of the Public Library of Chicago, wrote in 1886 à propos of de Rocheblave: "He was an able man and a very interesting character. . . . He ought to be written up." Mr. Mason of Chicago has told the story of the first part of his life. Unfortunately, all the family documents have been sent to France in the interest of a descendant named Willoughby, to be produced in connection with a lawsuit, and they have not been returned. Copies of some of these documents appear to be available at the presbytery of Notre Dame, Montreal, and a copy of the judgment is in my possession. Part of the land in dispute was awarded to the Canadian branch of the de Rocheblave family. The Louisiana branch does not seem to have heard of the litigation. Descendants of Paul de Rocheblave, Philippe's brother, still exist; one of them, a captain Benito de Rocheblave, of Pensacola, Florida, was still living in October, 1928.[2]

---

1 *Bulletin des Recherches Historiques*, XXIII. (Article by M. P.-G. Roy.)

2 I cannot conclude these notes without calling attention to the kindness of Monsieur Charles Bouthillier, of the manor of Sainte-Thérèse de Blainville, nephew of Mademoiselle de Rocheblave, who has furnished me not only with the documents which he had copied, but also with some private notes. Some weeks before his death Monsieur Bouthillier placed several interesting papers at my disposal, including a list of de Rocheblave's children. They were the following: Marie Adelaide, born January 7th, 1764; Philippe François; Noel, born in 1766; Pierre; Rosalie, born in 1773, died at Montreal in February, 1844, and Marie Thérèse, born May 26th, 1777, at Kaskaskia.

Willoughby just mentioned was Captain William L. P. de Lemos Willoughby, of the 23rd Royal Welsh Fusiliers. On May 20th, 1845, he married Louise Hermine de Rastel de Rocheblave, Pierre's younger daughter. She died of child-birth in Montreal on May 1st, 1846, age 23. Her child, Louise, survived her 23 days. As heir, Willoughby claimed the diamonds bequeathed to his wife by her grand-aunt when she married Antoine d'Albert, marquis de Saint Hippolyte, as well as a share in the real estate in France.

I am indebted to Mr. John N. d'Arcy, of Montreal, for the translation of this article, and to Mr. Percy J. Robinson for the revision thereof.

IV

Iroquois Place-Names on the North Shore of Lake Ontario

By J. N. B. Hewitt
Smithsonian Institute, Washington

Mr. J. N. B. Hewitt, of the Bureau of American Ethnology, Washington, has furnished me, in answer to inquiry, with the following explanations of Indian place-names along the north shore of Lake Ontario:

"The probable meaning of the name *Teiaiagon* (for Teyoya' hiă" goⁿ') is 'It crosses the stream.' The antecedent of the pronoun 'it' is understood from the context or situation, so it could have been 'path,' 'log,' or 'bridge,' but it does not mean 'place where trails meet.'

"The other term submitted for explanation, *Gandatsekiagon* (for Ganatse'[1] kwyăgoñ') has nothing in common with Teyoya' hiă" goₙ'. Ganatse" kwyăgoñ' signifies 'Among the birches,' i.e. 'Among birch trees.'

"The name Toronto, probable *Tiyoroñ'to*', is a name which is applicable to an indefinite number of places. It is a neuter plural form, meaning 'There, yonder, are trees under water,' referring, it is said, to trees growing so near the water's edge that they appear to be in the water; that is, reflected in the water where the water is clear.

"The name *Lac Oentaronck*, appearing on Du Creux's and other early French maps as the name of Lake Simcoe, appears to be merely a form of the well-known mutual name of *Attiwendaronk*, employed by the Hurons and the Neutrals as designations for each other, so that *Lac Attiwendaronk* was probably meant.

"Father Jones gave *Ondechiatiri*[1] as the Huron name of Toronto, but I do not know his authority for the statement. The term means 'the supported or solid earth or ground.' The final verb '*-tiri*,' could be used to mean 'firm,' as a firm snowbank, i.e. one that could support great weight.

"Without available historical data indicating reasons for the use of the Iroquois village names along the northern coast of Lake Ontario, the following suggested meanings are, of course, based on inferences from poorly-written originals, important parts of which do not appear in these records.

"Ganaraske probably means 'at the spawning-place,' as this locality was reputed to 'abound' in salmon. Kenté signifies a prairie or meadow. Kentsio (Rice Lake) probably means 'abounding in fish'; and Ganneious is evidently a misprint for the French Gannejout(s), meaning Oneida, referring probably to a village of these people."

Mr. Hewitt's reply to my inquiries was received after I had written my chapter on the meaning of the word "Toronto." Mr. Hewitt is the most eminent living authority on the Iroquois language.

[1] JONES, *Huronia*, p. 265.

243

APPENDIX TO SECOND EDITION

THE TORONTO PURCHASE

[From the *Evening Telegram*, Toronto, August 27 1938]

Driving up from Kingston the other day, Lake Ontario, seen in glimpses as the car slid over the hills, was a lovely sight; lovely indeed but lonely, remote and desolate; none of the white gleaming sails of long ago, and, as it happened, no trailing smoke of laboring freighters; just a deep azure expanse hung with faint rosy fragments of cloud. Old, old as time, this banded blue and green and purple looked young as yesterday. From such a waste of water, history is washed out over night. And yet for two centuries the story of exploration and settlement is the story of the great lakes and rivers of the continent.

On August 1, 1788, a century and a half ago, a strange looking craft might have been seen entering the land-locked bay at Toronto, whose shores were still clad in unbroken forest. His Majesty's ship "Seneca" was a square-sailed vessel of one hundred and thirty tons, of a rig now obsolete, and one of the larger vessels in the small but efficient navy protecting the British flag on the lake at that time. The "Seneca" carried a crew of thirty-five men and mounted eighteen guns. In her hold, packed in 149 barrels, was a cargo of presents and provisions for the Mississauga Indians about to assemble at Toronto. A surveyor and his party of assistants were the passengers. A few days later another vessel arrived from Niagara bringing Lord Dorchester, Governor-General of Canada; Sir John Johnson, Superintendent of Indian Affairs; and Colonel Butler, veteran commander of Butler's Rangers.

Dorchester intended to go as far as Detroit, but on his arrival at Fort Erie there was no ship available and he had to abandon his intention of visiting that outpost.

On the 24th October, 1788, R. Matthews, who had accompanied Lord Dorchester, wrote: "I am but a short time returned from attending Lord Dorchester on a tour of the Upper Posts

247

and new settlements. He went as far as Fort Erie, but no vessel being there, and the season too far advanced to wait he was obliged to abandon Detroit, visitted Toronto and Oswego, and every part of the Bay of Kinte. The progress of the new settlements would astonish and delight you from Lake St. Francis to the Bay 50 miles above Cateraqui, and from 20 miles on the Toronto side of Niagara to 30 miles above Fort Erie is thickly settled, finely cleared, and many excellent houses built   some of the farmers have sold 500 bushels of wheat this season, tho the Crop was indifferent. The settlement I began last year at Detroit has extended 30 miles from the mouth of the River, and will in very few years meet that from Niagara." (Original spelling and punctuation.)

Hitherto historians have known nothing about this visit of Dorchester. Toronto has been strangely indifferent about its past.

The occasion of this gathering of important persons was the completion of the Toronto Purchase; the Mississaugas were to be paid for the five hundred square miles of territory surrendered to the Crown three years before at Quinte; a new purchase was to be arranged extending eastward to the Ganaraske River (Port Hope); a survey was to be made at Toronto and a town and township laid off for settlement.

Of these distant events Toronto remembers little; growing cities forget their past. Yet there is romance and inspiration in the first contact of an old race and a new land; the vigor of such an origin is far from exhausted. The story of what happened in August, 1788, now for the first time published, has only recently been pieced together from the fragmentary records which survive.

Though there were as yet no permanent settlers the region, Toronto, was not entirely uninhabited. About the ruins of the French Fort there were some three hundred acres of cleared ground abandoned since the evacuation of the post in 1759. On the banks of the Humber J. B. Rousseau (afterwards Colonel J. B. Rousseau of Ancaster) had been established for some years engaged in trade with the Indians. Richard Beasley, U.E.L. trader at the head of the lake, also had a house at Toronto and was present at the gathering.

News of the arrival of the "Seneca" spread rapidly and the shore soon assumed the appearance of an encampment. The Mississaugas from the Thames and the Credit on the west, and from Lake Scugog and Rice Lake on the east set up their wigwams. The Indians from Lake Simcoe (Lac aux Claies) and Matchedash, came late and failed to secure their share of the presents. Gatherings of this kind always attracted Indian traders and it is probable that many of these enterprising persons were present anxious to barter their wares for the new wealth of the savages.

We can best follow the course of events from the report submitted by Alexander Aitkin the surveyor. The records of the new purchase to the east of Toronto and of the conference of Lord Dorchester and Sir John Johnson with the Indians are extremely fragmentary.

It was on July 7, 1788, that Deputy Surveyor-General John Collins had written from Quebec instructing Aitkin to proceed with the survey. Communication was difficult in those days and Aitkin did not receive the letter in Kingston till the twenty-fifth. Collecting his party he embarked without delay on the "Seneca" taking with him Nathaniel Lines as interpreter; the latter had been present the year before at the Bay of Quinte. A memorandum dated Montreal, July 9, 1788, supplies us with accurate information as to the supplies which accompanied the expedition. The memorandum reads: "Calculation of Provisions that will be required for the approaching meeting of the Messesagey Indians on the north side of Lake Ontario and the transport necessary for the provisions and the present of Indian stores to be given to them as a compensation for the Cession of Lands made to the Crown.

"1,000 Rations in all species for the Surveyors & the Party who will attend them.

"10,000 Wt. Flour; 24 Barrels Pork, For the Indians.

"The Present for the Indians is supposed to be about 67 Barrels Bulk; The Provisions & Present making together 149 Barrels Bulk allowing 200 Wt. to each Barrel Flour."

Another memorandum which has recently come to light gives accurate information as to the amount of Indian stores paid to the Mississaugas at Toronto in 1788 as the price of the Toronto Purchase. (Previous descriptions of this transaction are inaccurate and have been confused with the bargain made at the Credit in 1805. It is necessary to rewrite the account published in Robertson's *Landmarks*, Vol. V, p. 150.) The memorandum reads as follows: "Return of Indian Stores given to the Missesagey Nation of Indians as a payment for the Lands at Toronto & the Communication to Lake Huron . . .; 72 Pieces Strouds (coarse blankets); 55 do . . . Molton (Linen cloth) 131 do . . . Linen; 10 do . . . Embossed Serge; 30 do . . . Ribbon; 10 do . . . Callicoe; 154½ Grose Gartering; 64 yards scarlet Cloth; 287 Blankets of 3 points; 331 do . . .; 2½ do . . .; 200 do . . .; 2 do . . .; 200 do . . .; 1½ do . . . ; 50 lbs. White Thread; 10 Dozen looking glasses; 80 lbs. Vermilion; 3 grose Knives; 3 grose Fishocks; 2 grose lines; 100 Bunches Beads; 500 lbs. Gun powder; 1,500 lbs. Shott & Ball; 24 Silver Gorgets; 24 Medals; 36 pair Arm Bands; 1,000 Broaches; 1,000 pair Earbobs; 500 lbs. Tobacco; 200 Half Axes . . . 300 Hoes; 100 Fish Spears; 5 dozen plain Hatts . . . 2 Doz. Laced Hatts; 3,000 Gunflints . . . 150 Guns."

This document is endorsed: "Return of Indian stores given to the Missesagey Nation of Indians as a payment for the Lands at Toronto & the communication to Lake Huron relinquished by them to the Crown. This calculation is made for a Double Equipment of cloathing for that Nation consisting of 287 Men, 331 Women, 399 Children. (Signed) P. Langan."

Nathaniel Lines' invoice of these goods as delivered to Colonel Butler differs in some particulars. No mention of the medals and jewelry is made and an item of 96 gallons of rum is appended. There is no reason to suppose that there was any actual discrepancy. Lines' invoice reads: "Memorandum of Bales and Boxes brought from Cataraque by Mr. Lines to Toronto and delivered to Col. Butler—6 Bales Strouds 5 pieces each 30 Pieces; 4 Bales Moltons Each 10 pieces 40 Pieces; 4 Kegs hoes 49 each 196; 8 Half Barrels Powder; 5 Boxes Guns; 3 Cases Shott; 24 Brass Kettles; 10 Kegs of Ball; 200 lbs. Tobacco 47 Carrots; 1 Cask containing 3 Gro. Knives; 10 Doz. Looking Glasses; 4 Trunks of Linen; 1 Hogshead containing 18 pieces Gartering; 24 Laced Hats; 30 Pieces Ribbon; 3 Gro. Fish Hooks; 2,000 Gun Flints; 1 Box 60 Hats; 1 Bale flowered Flannel 10 pieces; 5 Bales 3 point Blankets 16 pair each; 1 Bale Broad Cloth 4 pieces; 5 pieces embossed Serge; 1 Case Barley Corn Beads; 96 Gallons of Rum."

There remains to be added in calculating the price paid for the Toronto Purchase the value of the distribution of arms, ammunition and tobacco made to the Mississaugas assembled at the Bay of Quinte, at Toronto and at the River French (Thames) in September, 1787, when the preliminary negotiations were completed. This amounted to: "$9\frac{1}{4}$ half barrels of gunpowder and 241 lbs.; $8\frac{1}{2}$ cases of shot and 361 lbs.; $25\frac{1}{2}$ kegs of ball and 361 lbs.; 171 guns; 69 carrots of tobacco." The total number of Indians, men, women and children who had an interest in the transaction is given as 1,017.

Just where the "Seneca" came to anchor at Toronto on August 1, 1788, and landed her passengers and stores is a matter of conjecture. It would seem likely that the conference with the Indians took place in the neighborhood of the ruins of the French fort where trails converged and there was cleared land. This is by no means certain, however, as the best anchorage was at the eastern end of the bay where there was an easy shore and a landing place much frequented later on by the Indians when they came to Little York.

Aitkin's first duty was to erect a store-house to shelter the 149 barrels of provisions and presents against the weather. This task occupied two or three days. The weather was of the finest and he was anxious to proceed at once with his survey. He was hindered, however, by the Indians, and especially by their chief, Wabukanyne, who exercised a kind of sway over the whole nation. The Indians maintained that they had sold to the Crown only that land which lay between the Nechenquakekong (Don) River and the Toronto (Humber) River. It was not till the 11th of August when other chiefs had assembled that Interpreter Lines was able to secure permission for Aitkin to begin his survey at the western end of the High Lands (Scarborough Bluffs). Running his line westward to the mouth of the Humber, Aitkin again encountered opposition. Fortunately by this time Colonel Butler, who was well known to the Indians, had arrived and Aitkin was permitted to advance to the River "Tobicoak." Beyond this point he was unable to advance nor did he venture to run the western boundary of the tract in a northerly direction further than 2¾ miles. He was now alone and had no one to support him in the event of a struggle with the Indians who wished the Etobicoke to remain as the boundary; a surveyor's line they maintained would become obliterated in time.

Aitkin's map shows the town plot. The plan which had been prepared in Quebec did not reach him till he was on his way back to Kingston. The town plot was to be a block of land a mile square fronting on the bay and surrounded on three sides by a tract half a mile wide; the southwest corner of the whole enclosure rested on the mouth of what was afterwards known as Garrison Creek. Five years later Aitkin's plan and the more elaborate plan shown in Gother Mann's map of 1788 were both rejected when Simcoe placed his town of York at the mouth of the Don.

When the presents had been distributed, Lord Dorchester and Sir John Johnson took their departure. The Indians then prepared to disperse. Colonel Butler as Indian Agent had been instructed to arrange for the purchase of additional territory to the east, and since the Indians from the Lake aux Claies (Lake Simcoe) and from Pawastink (Port Hope) had not yet arrived Butler induced the chiefs to send their young braves home with the women and children and to remain on the ground till the arrival of late comers. After two or three meetings the desired transfer was arranged. The sum of twenty-five guineas induced

Wabukanyne and Pakquan to permit the western boundary of
the 1787 purchase to be run back 15 or 16 miles as that was
supposed to be the width of the land purchased. Butler then
returned to Niagara leaving Aitkin alone to complete his survey.
Further opposition from the Indians, however, prevented him
from completing the western boundary and since the land eastward from Toronto now belonged to the Crown he did not consider it necessary to survey the eastern limit of the original
purchase.

On August 28, those Indians who had returned to Pome-
tashcooting Landing (Port Hope), sent a rather pathetic letter
through Lines the interpreter to Sir John Johnson:

"Shawanecupaway with two other chiefs of the Rice Lake
in Council assembled says that they have not forgot what was
told them at Toronto, but have been thinking of it ever since
and now they are all met at the great Fire. Mr. Lines was so
good as to make for that purpose to nourish them with a little
of their Great Father's Milk; they have considered amongst
themselves and have agreed to let their Great Father have the
Lands according to his own proposals, which they understand
is from the purchase made by Captain Crawford, 1784, to the
east bank of the Ganaraske, to that made by their Great Father
at Toronto. They likewise understand that the lands are not to
run further back from the shore of Lake Ontario than ten miles.
They say they have taken the liberty of pointing out two stakes,
which they have put up, a small piece of land for their great
Friend the Trader at Pemetashcootiang, who has always been
very good to them, they hope, therefore, their Father will take
it into consideration and let him keep that small present which
they have given him for his kindness to them. But if their great
Father should not approve of the liberty they have taken they
leave it to himself to use his pleasure, they say now they have
given their lands, which their Great Father requested, they hope
he will take pity on them as they are very poor and assist them
a little in sending them a few kettles, tomahawks, spears, etc.,
etc., and as it is coming on cold winter, they hope their Father

will try and press his breasts sufficiently to give his children a good suck."

A year later at Quinte, the Rice Lake Indians received the price of the additional lands surrendered by them at Toronto in 1788. The price was paid in Indian stores and a considerable quantity of rum. A payment in money was not made in any of the earlier purchases.

A month later on the 23rd of September, Butler again wrote to Sir John Johnson: "Mr. Beasly has wrote to me from Toronto that about a hundred Indians have arrived there who say they have not been clothed and were not there when the goods were distributed for the lands. I have sent word to them to go to Cataraque and will write to the Mr. Lines to cloathe those that he knows have not received any before."

From other documentary sources it would seem that these were the Indians from Matchedash, who afterwards made the claim that they had not been paid for their part of the Toronto transfer; men, women and children, they amounted to about four hundred.

The council of 1788 at Toronto was not the last of similar gatherings, but it was in ways the most important. It marks in a very real sense the beginning of the city of Toronto and the County of York.

THE NAME TORONTO

[From *Transactions* of the Royal Society of Canada, 1944, Section II]

I should like now to add some fresh information in regard to the antiquity of the name Toronto. Further study of the various passages cited in *Toronto during the French Régime* has convinced me that wherever the name Toronto is found in documents of the seventeenth century the reference is to the Huron country on the Georgian Bay from which the Hurons were expelled in 1650 by the Iroquois.

Perrot (1620–97), who was acquainted with the lake region immediately after this expulsion, applies the name Toronto to what was formerly the Huron country.[1] In one of the Margry documents bearing the date 1703, the Huron chief Mitchipitchi when addressing his countrymen at Mackinac and urging them to remove with him to the newly founded Detroit, alludes to the country from which the Hurons were expelled in 1650 as Toronto.[2] In the *Relatio du Detroit* which has been conjecturally ascribed to Cadillac, the writer explains that the new post at Detroit is conveniently situated with reference to the Mississippi, Mackinac, and Toronto. Toronto he defines as the region lying between the foot of Lake Huron (i.e., Georgian Bay) and the foot of Lake Ontario.[3] In the second Galinée map, a copy of which came to light shortly before the present war. Lake Simcoe appears for the first time (1670) as Lac de Tar8nteau. Finally Frontenac himself gives the name of the Onondaga chief with whom he conferred at Cataraqui in 1673 as TARONTISHATY, which means, "he struck Toronto," a name no doubt assumed in

[1]Nicolas Perrot, *Mémoire sur les moeurs, coustumes et religion des sauvages de l'Amérique septentrionale* (1864), p. 9.
[2]Pierre Margry, *Découvertes et établissements des Français dans l'ouest et dans le sud de l'Amérique septentrionale* (Paris, 1879–88), vol. V, p. 292.
[3]This document is in the Library of Congress; there is a photostat in the Public Archives of Canada.

honour of the expulsion.[4] In the light of this new matter which has not previously been studied, and of passages already familiar in the writings of La Salle, Dennonville, Lahontan, and others of the seventeenth century it may be considered as established by documentary evidence of unimpeachable authority that the Huron country after their expulsion was known as Toronto. The assumption is natural that the name was also employed by the Hurons themselves prior to 1650.

There is one passage in Sagard's *Histoire du Canada*[5] which seems to support this assumption. Sagard publishes "a copy or summary" of a letter written in 1627 by Father Daillon from the Huron country to a friend in France describing a recent visit to the Neutrals to the north of Lake Erie. In this letter Daillon mentions the excellent oil made by the Neutrals and after the word "huile" he adds "qu'ils appellent à Touronton"; these words are unintelligible and bear an asterisk in the Tross edition. The same passage occurs verbatim in the original edition but without the asterisk. It would seem that the copyist from whom Sagard received the manuscript omitted a word. Inserting the Huron word for oil "gayé" which is to be found in Sagard's dictionary the passage would read "qu'ils appellent 'gayé' à Touronton." This would make sense and carries the name Toronto back to the beginning of the seventeenth century.

[4]Roy, *Rapport de l'archiviste de la Province de Québec pour 1926-27*, pp. 38 and 40.
[5]Gabriel Sagard, *Histoire du Canada* (Paris, 1636), vol. III, p. 806.

MORE ABOUT TORONTO

[From *Ontario History*, vol. XLV, 1953, no. 3]

In 1873 Dr. Henry Scadding in his *Toronto of Old* expressed the opinion that the name Toronto was a Huron word and "the name of the headquarters or rendezvous of the Wyandots or Hurons." "It was in short the place of meeting, the place of concourse, the populous region indicated by the Huron term Toronto. In the form *Toronton* the word Toronto is given by Gabriel Sagard in his *Dictionnaire de La Langue Huronne,* published in Paris in 1636 [1632 actually]" [*Toronto of Old*, p. 74].

In Sagard the meaning of the word Toronton is *Il y en a beaucoup* (p. 99), and several examples of its use are given. There is nothing at all about "place of meeting, rendezvous, or populous region."

In formulating this theory Scadding relied upon tradition and conjecture; he was indeed compelled to do so for material now readily available was then unknown. With the aid of maps, despatches and other documents it is now possible to restate the problem.

The word Toronto does not occur anywhere in maps or documents during the first half of the seventeenth century—the period of the Recollet and Jesuit missions which ended in 1650 in tragedy.

In the second half of the seventeenth century the name Toronto occurs frequently within a given area as the name of the Georgian Bay, the former Huron country between Lake Simcoe and Lake Huron, the Severn River, Lake Simcoe, the trail from Orillia to Matchedash, but nowhere as the name of any town.

In the eighteenth century the name Toronto appeared south of Lake Simcoe as the name of the Humber and of various posts and forts on Lake Ontario.

The promiscuous use of the name is proof that whatever its

original meaning it was no longer a descriptive name as were all Indian names, applicable to one spot and not transferable. The word was passed on from north to south by French explorers and *coureurs de bois.*

That the name Toronto was originally employed to indicate the Huron country after its evacuation is a matter of fact, and the assertion of Carver that the Missisaugas had a large town called Toronto is not correct. Having no "r" in their language they could not even pronounce the word. In the eighteenth century Algonquins occupied the area between Matchedash and Lake Ontario. The name Toronto was preserved by the French.

The word "Huron" was a French word meaning "a rough fellow." The Hurons called themselves *Houandate*—"Islanders," either because their country was virtually an island, being almost entirely surrounded by water, or because at their front-door lay the Thirty Thousand Islands of the Georgian Bay. The name *Houandate* persisted in the form "Wyandots" after their exiled wanderings.

The old Huron country, as Champlain found it, was populous and fertile, and the name Toronto, if it is a form of Sagard's Toronton ("much or many") is an appropriate name both for the many islands through which every Frenchman had to pass on his way to or from Huronia in the early years, and for the populous land with its abundant and varied supply of food, corn, fish, game, and wild fruits.

I now intend to discuss certain new uses of the word "Toronto" which seem to throw considerable light upon the use and meaning of the word.

In Dollier de Casson's account of the building of Fort Frontenac in 1673 there is mention of a certain Onondaga chief called "Torontishati," to whom Frontenac felt impelled to pay considerable attention. This man is described as follows: "Torontishati, one of their orators, and the cleverest and most intelligent and most respected among them, who had been dour and thoughtful before, now assumed an air of unusual gaiety. Torontishati had always been hostile to the French and very much in the interest of the Dutch. This obliged Frontenac to pay him special attention: he invited him to dine with him." (See Margry.)

The cause of Torontishati's cheerfulness was that Frontenac had held out some hope of assistance against the Andastes, old allies of the Hurons and inveterate enemies of the Iroquois, in the time of Champlain.

Frontenac himself in his letter of November 11, 1673, mentions this man and adds some additional comments. He was evidently a man of over sixty and had the rank of "sachem," but no longer went to war.

It has occurred to me that Torontishati may have been a leader in the raid against the Hurons in 1649 and that his name which seems to mean "he struck Toronto" may have been assumed in honour of that exploit.

If I am right in translating the name thus, here is another proof of the theory that the name "Toronto" was applied to the Huron country at an early date.

Torontishati is a compound of the name Toronto and the radical *isati* which means according to Potier: (1) *heurter*, to strike; (2) *être enfossé*, to be broken into. Torontishati means then either "he struck Toronto," or "Toronto in ruins."

In Dollier de Casson's account, Torontishati is represented as deeply interested in an attack on the Andastes. Frontenac in his letter of the 16th of February 1674 remarks, "Tout ce que j'ai sceu par les lettres des Pères Jesuits qui sont dans les missions Iroquoises, c'est que les Hollandais font tous leurs efforts pour obliger les Iroquois à rompre avec nous, mais maintenant jusques icy parce qu'ils leur ont toujours repondus qu'ils no vouloient non plus se mesler de leur guerre avec les Européans, qu'ils se mesloient de celle qu'ils ont avec les Andostoquez et autres Nations Sauvages qu'ils avoient lieu de se louer de moy, que j'estois leur Père est qu'ils éstoient mes enfants."

There is a sinister note in these lines. Somewhat later La Hontan remarks on the fact that the Iroquois had destroyed both the Torontogueronons and the Andastogueronons, i.e., the Hurons and the Andastes, allies since the days of Champlain. (See

Quebec Archives, *Rapport*, 1926–27, p. 52.) Evidently the wily Torontishati won a diplomatic success at Cataraqui.

We are concerned, however, only with the fact that the name Torontishati carries back the place name Toronto at least to 1649 and possibly even earlier.

The Baron de La Hontan arrived in Canada in 1683, ten years after the building of Fort Frontenac, and in the next fourteen years he was active in the lake region, explored Wisconsin, made the acquaintance of the exiled Hurons at Michilimackinac, studied their language and customs, and gathered materials for the book which he was to publish in 1703 at the Hague. This book was enormously popular, passed through fourteen editions in the next fifty years, and was translated into English, German, Danish, and Dutch. La Hontan's map (Plate VIII Karpinsky) is to be found in the 1703 editions, with variants in later volumes. This map, though crude and eccentric, is of great interest, and is unique in locating the Torontogueronons in the homeland of the Hurons. Though bearing the date 1703, it must be dated approximately 1685. Having put La Hontan's map in its proper chronological sequence in the later seventeenth century, I need not further evaluate the information which it contains. La Hontan is the sole authority for the name Torontogueronons. The form of the word is in accord with the laws laid down by Potier.

In the Library of Congress, Washington, in the Division of Manuscripts, there is a document entitled "Relatio du Detroit, extraits d'une lettre écrite a M. de P." This manuscript is in the hand of a copyist, and appears to be a contemporary extract of a larger document. It came to the Library of Congress in 1867, in the collection of books, manuscripts and transcripts assembled by Mr. Peter Force and purchased by the Library. Mr. Quaife is of the opinion that this communication is to be ascribed to Cadillac. It was printed in translation in the *Collections* of the State Historical Society of Wisconsin, vol. XVI, pp. 127–30, and ascribed there to Du Luth, *circa* 1686, addressed to Ponchartrain. It is a fair inference that the writer was Enjelran, who in Margry's opinion was the deviser of the plan to construct a chain of posts for the protection of the country.

A sentence in this document explains the original application of the name Toronto, and gives strong support to the opinion that Toronto was the name given to the Huron country after the expulsion of the Hurons in 1649–50, and perhaps before. After making it plain that the proposed post at Detroit would have the great advantage of being closer to the Mississippi and closer to Toronto, as the two roads north to Hudson Bay and the fur trade and south to the Gulf of Mexico, the writer states that "Toronto is the mainland between the southern end of Lake Huron [i.e. the Georgian Bay] and the west end of Lake Ontario."

This explains and justifies La Hontan's giving the name Toronto-gueronons to the inhabitants of the country.

A further confirmation of this use of the name comes from the report of a council held with the miserable remnant of the wandering Hurons at Mackinac, when an effort was being made in 1703 to induce them to settle at the new post at Detroit. This runs as follows (Margry, vol. V, p. 292, Archives du Ministère de la Marine):

Quarante-se Sols, autrement Micipichi parle....
Par un collier J'envite Sastaretsy à quitter son feu à Missilimakinak et à le porter au Detroit, afin que toute notre nation soit réunie ensemble—Onontio le désire ainsi—Il a les yeux bons; il a vu que la terre de Missili-mackinak est une mechante terre. Autrefois, il est vray, nous avons été tués à Taronto, mais la raison en est qu'il n'y avoit point de François avec nous. Il y en a au Detroit, un grand village. Çela nous a mis en securité. Celuy qui y commande a de l'esprit; il veille venit et joint, il prend gard à tout....
Conseil tenu par les Hurons dans lequel se trouvoient les Outeonans —12 juin 1703.

This may be translated thus:

The speaker is the Huron chief known as Quarante-Sols or Michipichy ....
I invite Sastaretsy [another Huron chief] to leave his camp-fire at Michilimackinac and to carry it to Detroit so that all our nation may be united together. Onontio too wishes this—he has good eyes, he has seen

that the land of Michilimackinac is a bad land. *In other days, it is true, we were killed at Toronto,* but the reason was that there were no Frenchmen there. There are French at Detroit which is a large village. That will make us safe. He who commands there has spirit; he watches night and day; he oversees everything.

Council of the Hurons in which Ottawas participated, 12th June 1703.

In 1787–1788, when Lord Dorchester arranged the Toronto Purchase with the Missisaugas, he used the old Huron name in the sense in which it was employed in the "Relatio du Detroit" —he bought the land between Matchedash and Lake Ontario, the northern part of which was the Huron home land. He intended the name Toronto to continue, and visited the site of the city in 1788.

Five years later in 1793 Toronto became York. The original map, on which the name Toronto was erased and the name York substituted, is still extant. The name Toronto disappeared for forty years, and all interest in the problem of origin and meaning expired. In 1873 Dr. Scadding wrote his book.

No one seems to have interrogated the Wyandots at Detroit who still spoke the Huron language. They emigrated to Oklahoma and were forgotten. The Huron language is dead both at Oklahoma and at Lorette.

Mr. W. E. Connelly, however, in the *Ontario Archaeological Report* for 1899 states that the Wyandots of Oklahoma once had a settlement at Toronto, from which they had been forced to flee, that they called this settlement Tahroontahuk, which meant in their language "plenty," and that they used this word because food was to be found there in abundance: Toronto was a land of plenty. This information Mr. Connelly professed to have obtained from the Wyandots themselves.

LATER NOTES TO THE ORIGINAL TEXT

[Asterisked in Second Edition]

Page 34, line 13. The "original owner" was John Lawrence. See the *Annual Report* of the York Pioneer and Historical Society 1949, p. 9.

Page 76, opposite. The caption for the Danville map had been marked by the author for revision. The reader is referred to Mr. Robinson's note in the *Canadian Historical Review*, September, 1939, p. 293.

Page 165. The author left a marginal note: "For the correct account of the Toronto Purchase as recorded in documents discovered later, see my article in the Toronto *Evening Telegram*." This article is reprinted in the present edition. The reader should also consult Mr. Robinson's article in the *Transactions* of the Royal Society of Canada, 1937, Section II, "The Chevalier de Rocheblave and the Toronto Purchase."

Page 166. In line 10, *read* Louis Kotte.

Page 186, footnote. *For* Dummer Powell *read* Osgoode.

INDEX

265

Fort Frontenac, curbs the Iroquois, 14; Le passage de Toronto a link between Fort Frontenac and Michilimackinac, 15; Talon's proposed post at, 22; trade at Ganatsekwyagon foiled by, 23; inhabitants of Teiaiagon not present in 1673 at, 24; La Salle describes effect of, 25; Father Hennepin at, 26; Teiaiagon seventy leagues from, 27, 118; Hennepin's residence at, 29; traders at Teiaiagon from, 31; La Salle in 1680 and 1681 at, 36; Denonville's plans for, 45; Durant returns to, 76; trade at, 82, 83, 84; not sufficient for needs of savages, 97; Toronto seventy-five leagues from, 98; Portneuf sets out from, 99; returns to, 100; lumber shipped from, 102; Dufaux sets out from, 106; Abbé Picquet at, 118; Stephen Coffin at, 126; *bateau Victor* from Toronto arrives at; Malartic and Béarn at, 133; Five Nations beg Ononthio to stock, 135; trader Knaggs at, 149; La Force in 1783 employed at, 180; J. B. Rousseau living at, 212-213, 215; daughters of Molly Brant at, 215; Margaret Clyne at, 215.

Fort Lévis, 179.
Fort Miami, 40.
Fort Niagara (see also Niagara), 81, 82, 83, 89, 97, 99, 124.
Fort Orange, 16, 22, 44.
Fort Pitt, 145.
Fort Pontchartrain, 58.
Fort Rouillé, or Fort Toronto, generally called Fort Toronto, 84; Alexandre Douville burns, 86; inscription marking site of, 93; an offset to Oswego, 94; part of Galissonnière's ambitious plans, 96, 97; named after M. Rouillé, 97; Pierre de Portneuf founder of, 99; trade at, 113; a sawmill at, 114; plan of, 115; Pouchot describes, 116; Abbé Picquet at, 118; sometimes called Saint-Victor, 120-121; Basile Gagnier, blacksmith at, 127; letters from, 117, 122, 124, 125, 126, 128, 129, 130; M. de Noyelle assigned to, 128; Chabot at, 130; Montcalm mentions, 131; Menominees at, 132; Béarn at, 132; Malartic at, 133, 134 and note; Missisaugas threaten, 135;

Pouchot sends aid to, 136; Augé engaged by Cadet as clerk at, 136; de Montigny at, 138; commandants at, 139; trails to, 140.
Fort Ste. Marie I, 1.
Fort Ste. Marie II, 13, 52, 53, 58 note.
Fort Supposé, 51.
Fort William Augustus, 148.
Fort William Henry, 2, 179.
Francis, Lieut., 139.
Frobisher, Benjamin, 34, 160, 165, 210.
Frontenac, Louis de Buade, Comte de, 15, 18, 22, 41.
French Company of the Indies, 90.
Frenchman's Bay, 17.

G

Gage, General, 145, 146, 147, 148, 149, 152.
Gagnier, Basile, 127 note.
Galinée, René de Brehant de, 18.
Gallop Islands (near Sackett's Harbour), 134.
Ganaraske, 15, 16 note, 24, 172 note, 243.
Ganastogué Sonontoua Outinaouatoua, 64 note.
Ganatsekwyagon, at the mouth of the Rouge, 16; Fénelon and d'Urfé at, 17; derivation of, 17 note; Péré and Joliet at, 18, 20; Frontenac mentions trade at, 23; deputies sent from, 24; trail from, 25; Teiaiagon preferred to, 26; salmon fishing at, 29; on Raffeix's map, 32; Denonville instructs Durantaye to enter Lake Ontario at, 51; no good maps of trail from, 53; Denonville at, 57; reoccupied by the Dowaganhaes, 59; trail from Holland Landing to, 195; etymology of, 243.
Ganneious, 15, 24, 56, 57, 243.
Garrison Creek, 144.
Gascouchagon (Genessee River), 125.
Gaustassy, 49.
Genessee River, 125 note.
Georgian Bay, 15, 18, 149, 150.
Givins, Lieut. James, 189, 190, 192, 194.
Globes, bronze, showing Toronto region, 73 note.
Gore, Sir Francis, Governor, 217.
Gorgendière, Joseph de Fleury, de la, 67.